SUBVERTING *the* LEVIATHAN

Non est potestas Super terram quæ Comparetur ei   a Iob 41 24

SUBVERTING *the* LEVIATHAN

READING THOMAS HOBBES AS A RADICAL DEMOCRAT

James R. Martel

COLUMBIA UNIVERSITY PRESS   NEW YORK

COLUMBIA UNIVERSITY PRESS
Publishers Since 1893

New York   Chichester, West Sussex
Copyright © 2007 Columbia University Press
All rights reserved

Library of Congress Cataloging-in-Publication Data

Martel, James R.
    Subverting the Leviathan : reading Thomas Hobbes as a radical democrat /
James R. Martel
        p. cm.
    Includes bibliographical references and index.
    ISBN 978-0-231-13984-7 (cloth : alk. paper) —
    ISBN 978-0-231-51148-3 (ebook : alk. paper)
    1. Hobbes, Thomas, 1588–1679. Leviathan. 2. Political science—Philosophy.
    1. Title.

JC153.H659M35 2007
320.1—DC22

                                                    2007009049

Casebound editions of Columbia University Press books are printed on permanent and
durable acid-free paper.

Printed in the United States of America

c 10 9 8 7 6 5 4 3 2 1

DESIGNED BY VIN DANG

CONTENTS

Acknowledgments

THIS BOOK BEGAN while I taught in the Rhetoric Department at the University of California, Berkeley. I am particularly indebted to Karen Feldman, who helped make the joys of rhetorical analysis more clear to me, and to Judith Butler, who, besides being an inspiration through her writing, was the chair of rhetoric at that time and instrumental in my coming to Berkeley. Karen has been one of my most faithful readers, and her precise, careful way of thinking and writing remains an admirable example. Victoria Kahn, who had left the Rhetoric Department by the time I arrived, was extremely gracious and helpful, both as a superb writer in her own right and as a source of encouragement, advice, and support. I also learned a great deal from Felipe Guterriez, Michael Mascuch, Nancy Weston, Pheng Cheah, Caroline Humfress, Ramona Naddaff, Fred Dolan, and David Bates.

At San Francisco State University, I have been privileged to know Gerard Heather and Matthew Stolz (now deceased), both political theorists who took me under their wings when I got there and who have been steadfast friends ever since. Sandra Luft familiarized me with the work of Aryeh Botwinick and has been a great colleague. I also appreciate the support and friendship of Anatole Anton and Roberto Rivera, as well as my dean and fellow political theorist, Joel Kassiola. Above all, I am grateful to Deb Cohler, Amy Sueyoshi, and Angelika von Wahl. All three worked in a reading group with me. Their support and encouragement helped bring the book along and untangled some of the denser sections. Deb has been my main reader from beginning to end and her guidance and friendship were indispensable. Angelika has been a wonderful office mate and friend as well as insightful reader. Thanks to Tiffany Willoughby-Herard, an exciting new colleague and friend. The presidential leave award I received for the fall of 2006 was very helpful in allowing me to finish this book.

I also want to thank my students at both Berkeley and SFSU, particularly those in my recent graduate seminar on Walter Benjamin. Teaching these works (including *Leviathan* many, many times) and trying out ideas by discussing them with students has been a vital part of how I have studied and read these texts. Among students who stand out in this regard are Dieyana Ruzgani, Matt Freeman, Colin Dingler, Rebecca Goldman, Anatoli Ignatov, J. P. Cauvin, John Wesley Vavricka, Adam White, Noa Bar, Randall Cohn, and Rebecca Stillman.

Other friends and colleagues whose help has been essential include above all my dear friend Nasser Hussain, just for being who he is and for helping me think beyond the narrowest confines of political theory. Mark Andrejevic has inspired me with his insights and approach to philosophy. Tom Dumm and Austin Sarat have both been unfailingly encouraging, tracking the progress of this book from conference to conference. Jodi Dean and Paul Passavant actually helped me enjoy going to American Political Science Association meetings. Wendy Brown remains one of my greatest influences, a model for how to write and think and also how to support one's students and their work. Peter Fitzpatrick and I have from an early stage shared our mutual interest in Hobbes, and he has helped me to think to a greater and deeper extent about *Leviathan*. Peter Goodrich has likewise challenged me to think more deeply about texts and interpretation in general. Samantha Frost has written a great (forthcoming) book on Hobbes and I enjoyed following its development. I also want to thank many teachers and colleagues, beginning with the tragically departed Michael Rogin, whom I was lucky to have as dissertation chair and mentor. I also want to thank Hanna Pitkin, Shannon Stimson, Bev Crawford, Bill Chaloupka, Thomas Laqueur, Norman Jacobson, Jane Bennett, Bonnie Honig, Jackie Stevens, Samera Esmeir, Aaron Belkin, Thomas Burke, Javier Corrales, Pavel Machala, Nicole Watts, Francis Neely, and many others. Although I don't know him personally, I also feel very inspired by Richard Flathman; a great deal of this book is an engagement with his work.

Wendy Lochner at Columbia has been an ideal editor; she understood my project from the start and worked with me to bring it to fruition. Christine Mortlock and Susan Pensak have been very helpful, as has my copyeditor, Tom Pitoniak. I also wanted to acknowledge the help and encouragement of Carrie Mullen, Courtney Berger, Jason Frank, Colin Perrin, and Toby Wahl.

I have a large and wonderful family to thank: my parents, Huguette and Ralph Martel; my brother Django and sister-in-law Shalini Arora; my wonderful friends Lisa Guerin, Chris Clay, and Lisa Clampitt; and my "nuclear family"—my partner, Carlos; my children, Jacques and Rocio; and my coparents, Nina and Kathryn, and Elic and Mark. I feel lucky to have them all in my life.

Earlier versions of some of the arguments I make in this book appeared (or will appear) in the following journal articles: Earlier versions of parts of chapter 2 (as well as small parts from various other chapters) appeared in "Strong Sovereign, Weak Messiah: Hobbes and the Rhetoric of the Christian Commonwealth," *Theory and Event* 7, no. 4 (2004); earlier versions of parts of chapter 4 appeared in "The Spectacle of the Leviathan: Thomas Hobbes, Guy Debord, and Walter Benjamin on Representation and Its Misuses," *Law, Culture, and the Humanities* 2 (2006): 67–90. Some parts of my interrogation of Hannah Arendt in this book (especially in chapter 5) will appear in "'*Amo: Volo ut sis*': Love, Willing, and Arendt's Reluctant Embrace of Sovereignty," *Philosophy and Social Criticism* (forthcoming).

SUBVERTING *the* LEVIATHAN

Hobbes's Conspiracy Against Sovereignty

WHAT HAPPENS WHEN we read a book (especially a good one)? What internal states does the book evoke, shape, or produce in us? How do these internal states translate or become externalized, articulated as interpretation and/or meaning? How much do we as readers experience those states as being "our own" as opposed to those of the author? Finally, what are the politics of reading? What limits can we make on claims that this seemingly very private action is a basis for larger public discourse and action, even when each act of reading remains isolated and seemingly unrelated to other readings? What does it mean to speak of a book having an effect not only on a particular act of reading but on a community, ideology, and notions of politics, authority, and truth?

Subverting the Leviathan concerns itself with one particular book, Thomas Hobbes's *Leviathan* and how it addresses such questions. Among its many great attributes, *Leviathan* is distinguished by its particular attention to the question of reading and the relationship of reading to authority (of both the literary and political sorts). As a text, *Leviathan* invites us to consider reading as a kind of extended metaphor for what politics is, for how politics works and how authority—which for Hobbes is itself a commentary about and production of reading and "authors"—is both brought into being and challenged by particular acts of reading (as well as writing). As we will see, in Hobbes's lifetime reading was not seen as simply the act of an isolated individual gazing at pages of text. Puritan and Anglican thinkers of that period saw reading (particularly of religious texts) as the primary and perhaps only way to acquire certainty.[1] While Hobbes is far more skeptical than many of his contemporaries, he too sees "reading" as the operative metaphor for knowing; we read not only books but also, as Hobbes tells us, ourselves,

other people and the world around us. Indeed, I will argue that for Hobbes
the metaphor of reading achieves a centrality that we do not find in his contemporaries: it becomes not just an epistemological tool but the model for
how we know and decide things, the basis for politics itself.

As I will try to show, throughout *Leviathan* Hobbes offers an extended
analogy between reading and politics, between our position as readers of his
text and subjects of the nation, and between his own authority in the text
and the sovereign's political authority. Accordingly, the question of how we
read *Leviathan* becomes crucial, having implications that go far beyond the
reputation or "meaning" of this book. When we take this analogy seriously,
we can apply Hobbes's notions of reading to his politics, rereading the political passages of *Leviathan* in light of this new understanding. As we will
see further, for Hobbes the meaning of a text does not reside in the "bare
Words" of the author, that is, in the overt claims that an author makes at
any given point in a text.[2] Instead "meaning" must be found in what Hobbes
calls the "Designe" of the text, its overall rhetorical structure.[3] In this way,
Hobbes is indicating that the "authority" of the text does not come necessarily from the author per se (at least insofar as she or he is figured in the
text) but rather from our respective interpretations of the text based on its
overall construction. I will argue that instead of looking for a definitive,
single "meaning" for a text, Hobbes, in all of his nominalism and radical
skepticism, sees instead a kind of deliberative and fluid consensus about
how a text is to be interpreted, an approach that decenters the traditional
relationship between author and reader.

This notion of reading and interpretation, as we will see, offers an alternative to the political models that *Leviathan* is usually read as advocating.
Rather than have the author/sovereign tell us what the book means and we
the readers/subjects passively accept that meaning, I will argue, Hobbes invites us to subvert his own textual authority and, by extension, the authority
of the national sovereign. When we learn not to take the author's word for
the meaning of a text, but instead to engage with the text in all its complexity, we readers take back the interpretive power that Hobbes insists belongs
to us all along. Similarly, when we as citizens or subjects of the Leviathan
state take back our interpretive authority from the sovereign, we resume
our own role as political "authors" (a status that Hobbes explicitly confers

on his readers) and challenge and subvert the sovereign's power over meaning, authority, and truth. Moreover, this act of interpretive subversion does
not occur randomly or arbitrarily for Hobbes but succeeds only when we
learn to read a text according to the methods that he painstakingly lays out
throughout the course of *Leviathan,* and particularly in its second half.

To make this argument I will explore what I consider to be *Leviathan*'s
self-reflexive quality: the way in which this text invites us and instructs us
on how to examine and participate in our own act of reading it. The point
is not simply to show that *Leviathan* can be deconstructed; one could make
this claim of any text. Rather, we will see that *Leviathan* is a text that points
to and facilitates its own deconstruction, its own act of being read.

In telling us not only how sovereignty operates but also (by analogy to
his book) how to resist that power, Hobbes can be seen as potentially fomenting a conspiracy of readers not unlike those evoked by Machiavelli in
the previous century. Hobbes models an act of textual (and political) disobedience, one that enables a conspiracy against sovereignty that can be
enacted whenever we read *Leviathan* according to his own instructions and
preferences. In the guise of supporting sovereignty, Hobbes allows us to see
it for what it really is: not the *sine qua non* of politics, but a usurpation and
monopolization of political power and authority at the expense of the very
people in whose name it is wielded. Thinkers after Hobbes, ranging from
Locke to Rousseau, succeeded in making sovereignty and politics nearly
coterminous concepts, a state of affairs that continues in our own time. Returning to the dawn of modernism by revisiting and rereading Hobbes's
Leviathan helps us to conceive of what seems almost unimaginable today: a
politics without sovereignty, a radical democratic practice that depends on
nothing but its own ongoing moments of self-structuring.

A SUBVERSIVE BOOK? *THE PRINCE* VS. *LEVIATHAN*

Because *Leviathan* concerns itself a great deal with questions of reading,
and with being read, it is worth considering how the book was itself read
and interpreted when it came out in 1651. From the moment it was first
circulated (in two separate editions, one for the king in "a copy engraved in
vellum, in a marvellous fair hand"—which the new king apparently never

bothered to read—and one for everyone else), *Leviathan* generated a storm of controversy.[4] Many Anglican bishops who had previously seen Hobbes as a stalwart defender of orthodoxy now saw him as defiling the very church he once promoted. After the restoration of the Stuarts to power in England, parliament came very close to banning the book and Hobbes had to defend his reputation against charges of atheism and treason into old age. Even Hobbes's death did nothing to stop this ongoing controversy of interpretation. Concerning Hobbes's reputation at the hands of his contemporaries, Miriam Reik writes that "the irony which often plagued Hobbes in his life—that supporters of the king could find this monarchist an enemy as dangerous as the Presbyterians—continued after his death."[5]

It is a peculiarity of *Leviathan* that Hobbes's contemporaries tended to read him as being far more radical and subversive than he is viewed as today. It is also peculiar that his erstwhile allies in particular should have spotted in Hobbes a renegade spirit—even an anarchist one—an opinion about Hobbes that history seems to have subsequently largely erased.

In their interpretations of *Leviathan,* these critics shared a skeptical attitude toward Hobbes's overt claims that he remained a loyal subject of the crown and the church. Thus for example John Bramhall, Bishop of Derry, and one of Hobbes's most fierce critics, argued that although Hobbes formally claimed to believe in God, atheism was the necessary consequence of his doctrines.[6] Edward Hyde, Earl of Clarendon (and, like Hobbes himself, at one time a member of the intellectual circle at Great Tew) attacked Hobbes among other reasons for arguing that a subject in exile is no longer a subject at all. To Hyde this smacked of treason in a period when a great number of loyal royalists and Anglicans (not to mention the king himself) were in exile.[7]

In thinking about the subversive qualities of *Leviathan* it is worth considering how this text was received in relation to an earlier text, Machiavelli's *Prince.* While many of Hobbes's contemporaries sensed that something was afoot in *Leviathan,* the English reception was quite different from that of *The Prince.*[8] As Victoria Kahn shows quite clearly in her book *Machiavellian Rhetoric, The Prince* was read and understood by many English critics, both before and during Hobbes's lifetime, to be explicitly rhetorical in nature. As a rule, early English critics of Machiavelli did not take *The Prince* as being meant literally, but understood it to be structured in ways that, in Kahn's words, "fragment, subvert, or otherwise qualify the literal sense of [the] text."[9] Kahn writes that for many of Machiavelli's English contemporaries (give or take a generation or two), an appreciation of his rhetorical manipulations was "not simply the result of a naive misreading of Machiavelli but [was] rather attuned to the rhetorical dimension of his political theory in a way that later thematic readings of Machiavelli are not."[10] While many modern scholars of Machiavelli tend to see him as a secular republican, denying or playing down the rhetorical nature of *The Prince*, Kahn argues convincingly that his contemporaries, even in the guise of attacking or disagreeing with him, often reproduced Machiavelli's rhetorical style.[11]

Among Hobbes's own contemporary readers, there is, it is true, a suspicion that there is some rhetorical trickery going on in Hobbes's text as well. Both Clarendon and John Eachard make the point that Hobbes's style seduces readers away from the weakness of his central arguments. Thus Clarendon wrote, "Too many people who, pleased with [Hobbes's] *style*, have not taken notice of those downright conclusions which overthrow and undermine all those principles of Government which have preserved the Peace of this Kingdom through so many ages."[12] Eachard wrote that "Mr. Hobbes . . . by a starched mathematical method, by magisterial haughtiness . . . and the like hath cheated some people into a vast opinion of himself."[13] But such arguments address rhetoric only in its narrowest, Ramist sense, as a kind of sideshow meant to divert the eye from the real argument. This is quite different from the recognition of the rhetorical methods that were recognized to be employed by Machiavelli, methods that in some sense could be said to constitute the "real" argument of *The Prince* as opposed to the text that bears them.

In general, for those contemporaries who responded to *Leviathan*, one finds less a recognition of Hobbes's rhetorical powers than an anxiety that the text was somehow dangerous and slippery. Robert Filmer reveals this ambivalence when he wrote of Hobbes that "no man that I know, has so amply and judiciously handled [the topic of sovereignty]. I consent with him about the rights of exercising government, but I cannot agree to his means of acquiring it."[14] Filmer complained that Hobbes's theory of the state of nature was an affront to the authority of Adam and could possibly lead to anarchism.[15] John Whitehall said this even more plainly, arguing that "Mr *Hobbes* is generally for Positions that tend to unhinge all the foundations of Government."[16]

It is certainly true there are sentiments occasionally expressed in *Leviathan* that are markedly at odds with his stated allegiances. This includes his infamous passage at the end of part 4 that the "Independency" of his own time, caused by the disruption of the Anglican Church, "is perhaps the best."[17] This seemed to amount to a questioning of Anglican authority, and by extension the entire edifice of Stuart authority as well. At the same time, there is also a very controversial (and opposite) idea, which Hobbes promotes, that says the king or queen is not only the formal head of the Anglican Church, but, if they so choose, the rightful determinant of liturgy and doctrine as well.[18] Arguments such as these, as well as some of his more unorthodox doctrines—such as the idea that the soul was not immortal and that it "died" along with the body itself—pointed less to rhetorical subversion on Hobbes's part than outright unorthodoxy and even heresy. The doctrinal similarity between a nominal orthodox Anglican like Hobbes and a radical like Gerrard Winstanley might have been too much for the Anglican clergy and royalists of the time to bear, much less agree with or condone. Reeling as they were from the loss of king and the destabilization of the church, to them Hobbes's writings might have seemed like an ultimate act of treachery at a time when the crown and church most needed defending. After the restoration, angry Tories often picked Hobbes, of all people, to serve as a scapegoat for any persistent strains of radicalism. "Hobbism" became a pejorative term, and those accused of it sometimes had to recant Hobbes to save their livelihoods, if not their lives.[19]

Hobbes himself, in his not always candid responses to his many critics, in his comportment during the Engagement Controversy (1649–54), and in his general and often seemingly self-serving complexity, appeared to many contemporaries to be an untrustworthy fellow who could be counted on only to dissemble and save his own skin. This shored up the interpretive uncertainty of what *Leviathan* actually meant and how it should be read.

From the standpoint of the present, such readings of Hobbes seem quite alien. To accuse Hobbes of atheism, antimonarchicalism, and the like seems completely out of synch with the text that we hold in our hands. In passage after passage, Hobbes insists on his goodwill toward the king and the church; he insists on his obedience to those institutions and engages in a strenuous and lengthy attack on any and all of their foes. With several important exceptions, readers of Hobbes today are far more likely than his contemporaries were to read *Leviathan* more or less literally, to take the author at his word and either downplay or explain away any apparent discrepancies.

If he was indeed a good servant of king and church, it may be Hobbes's misfortune that *Leviathan* is such a slippery and complex text. One could argue that such a sprawling book could not help but contradict itself, regardless of the intentions of the author. One could claim that with passions so high, and meaning so fraught with tension throughout the upheavals of civil war and the Commonwealth and the restoration that was to follow, even small doctrinal slippages were grounds for great enmity and that Hobbes could not help but alienate some of his readers, although one must note that not many books have generated as much controversy—nor as many competing claims as to the meaning of a book as does *Leviathan*. One could even say that Hobbes, being a conservative at heart but worried about saving his own skin, tried to be deliberately ambiguous so as to cover his bets regardless of who ended up the victor in England's long years of conflict. (Certainly some of his behavior both in exile and back in Cromwell's England during the Engagement Controversy may support this view.)

And yet, even given all of these myriad possibilities that would account for *Leviathan*'s peculiar reception, it seems there is something else going on in this book, something that is not merely an accident or confusion about interpretation. There is a particular quality to the ambiguity of this text that gives more than enough ammunition for the complaints of Bramhall and others that somehow *Leviathan* isn't quite what it appears to be. This ambiguity, wherein for every claim to support the state and church there is a potential counterclaim, seems systematic, following a logic and rhythm of its own.

Indeed, as I will argue, this "something else" amounts to a full-scale self-subversion of the text, a calling into question not only of what this text says, but of whatever *any* text might say. It raises questions not only about Stuart or Anglican authority, but about authority in general and the authority of the writer in particular. The first readers of Hobbes's *Leviathan* saw in it a possibility, which it might now be time to reconsider. They understood that *Leviathan* is profoundly radical and that it offers its readers something quite different than what they might expect. While as a whole, Hobbes's contemporary critics recognized some of the paradoxes and contradictions of *Leviathan*, I would argue that to read *Leviathan* more along the lines of the way that *The Prince* was read and understood in the same time period might help to uncover and expose the rhetorical constructions that I believe are crucial to our interpretation of both texts. If *The Prince*, a text that is formally committed to the support of princes, can be shown, if not to subvert princes outright, than at least to expose the tools and means of their authority, perhaps it is time to read *Leviathan* in the same light, with the same purpose and possibly the same outcome.[20]

READING HOBBES TODAY

Generally speaking, Hobbes's reception in his own lifetime was markedly different from the way he is read today. There are extremely important variations within today's Hobbes scholarship but there seems to be a few basic conceptions that are widely shared. In terms of his reputation over most of the twentieth century, persisting into our own time, figures like Leo Strauss and C. B. MacPherson, although on opposite ends of an ideological spectrum, agree on a few basic parameters. Most central is Hobbes's role as a so called "proto-liberal," a precursor to liberalism (taken in its broadest sense as the doctrine that accompanied the rise of modern capitalism) as well as being one of the formative figures in instigating modernity itself. Accordingly, Hobbes's stature as a central canonical figure for political theory is very well established. As Strauss writes in his famous study of Hobbes:

> Hobbes . . . philosophized in the fertile moment when the classical and theological tradition was already shaken, and a tradition of modern science not yet formed and established. At this time he and he only posed the fundamental question of man's right life and of the right ordering of society. This

moment was decisive for the whole age to come; in it the foundation was laid, on which the modern development of political philosophy is wholly based, and it is the point from which every attempt at a thorough understanding of modern thought must start. This foundation has never again been visible as it was then.[21]

For Strauss, Hobbes breaks completely from the Christian and naturalistic traditions that predate him. As he sees it, Hobbes does nothing less than establish a radically new basis both for political authority—replacing a rule based on law with a notion of rights—and for individual subjectivity, whereby he abandons the traditional principle of honor and replaces it with a principle of fear (of death).[22]

MacPherson's interpretation of Hobbes as a capitalist apologist is quite critical. Strauss, albeit for very different reasons, seems—or is at least generally considered to be—critical of Hobbes as well.[23] One of the paradoxes of the celebration of Hobbes as the chief architect of early modernity and liberalism is how little Hobbes himself is esteemed, and not just by critics of liberalism like MacPherson, but even by many who admire and support liberalism.

In the more recent past, there have been several important attempts to read Hobbes in a more favorable light, although in nearly all cases, these attempts stop short of a full embrace. Several of these readings will be considered in some detail in this book. For example, Hanna Pitkin concedes in her treatment of Hobbes that his notion of political representation seems empty and antidemocratic, but her analysis of his text suggests that he acknowledges this—at least rhetorically—and allows for a wider and more desirable notion of representation after all. Similarly, Gregory S. Kavka argues that Hobbes is not as amoral as he seems to be insofar as there is a kind of voluntarist ethos discoverable in the pages of *Leviathan*. Yet, as we will see, Kavka is ambivalent about the value and extent of Hobbes's morality, offering for example that he gives us only a "Copper"—as opposed to golden—rule for ethics.[24] In both cases, the embrace of Hobbes is partial at best; Hobbes is depicted as being not as bad as we think, but still an ambiguous and deeply problematic figure.

One of the most important and useful readings of Hobbes in this regard is provided by Richard Flathman.[25] In *Thomas Hobbes: Skepticism, Individuality and Chastened Politics*, among other works, Flathman offers us a Hobbes who complicates and enriches the so-called "modernity" that we seem to have inherited from him. Rather than paint him either as a supporter of tyranny or a wholly benign rights-based liberal, Flathman recognizes a tension in Hobbes's theory between the autocratic nature of sovereignty on the one hand and the "self making," democratic features of his theory on the other. This tension, as Flathman reveals, lies at the center of liberalism itself. Much of Flathman's work is an attempt to reconcile these two features of liberalism; at the very least his writing serves as an appreciation of their productive tensions. Flathman argues that in Hobbes's system, although the sovereign—or in this particular instance God, who for Flathman serves Hobbes as a model for terrestrial sovereignty—is absolute in the sense of having no rival for power, this rule "not only permits but obliges [people] to rule themselves in some parts of their thought and action," leading to a form of government that might "accommodate their differences."[26] In several of his works, including his more recent *Reflections of a Would-Be Anarchist*, Flathman openly admires the most radical aspects of Hobbes's political theory and even, as the latter title implies, flirts with anarchism itself, a notion of radical democracy that is free of the constraints of liberalism and sovereignty altogether.[27] Yet when it comes to his reading of Hobbes, Flathman shares a tendency with other contemporary thinkers to hesitate, to draw back from his own most radical interpretations of this thinker. For all the "self-making" that he appreciates in Hobbes and possibly therefore in liberalism itself, as Flathman tells us quite plainly, sovereignty and the absolute form of authority it represents are required to prevent abject chaos: "Authority [for Hobbes] is necessarily absolute. The alternative to absolutism is not limited authority; it is anarchism if not radical antinomianism. However it is exercised or implemented, absolute authority is the basis of all systems of rule."[28]

Despite an implicit acknowledgment of the problems inherent even in its most benign liberal form, Flathman seems to choose sovereignty as a necessary basis for political authority—a basis that he discovers in the work of Hobbes himself. In this way, like Kavka and many others, Flathman appreciates a subversive tendency in Hobbes but does not pursue it beyond the confines of the liberal system.[29]

For all of this, there is nonetheless something quite radical in Flathman's courageous and open approach to the paradoxes of liberalism.[30] It may be that in his attempt to plumb the depths of Hobbes's theory and thereby liberalism itself, Flathman discovers something subversive, something that is perhaps evocative of the way Hobbes was read in his own lifetime. The nature of this subversion is such that it may indeed not even be the author's conscious decision to pursue it. It may simply be the result of the clarity of the predicament that Flathman presents us with (something that I will argue may also be the case with Hobbes himself).

What all of these contemporary thinkers about Hobbes seem to share—even thinkers who range as dramatically in their politics as Leo Strauss and Richard Flathman—is an accommodation with sovereignty and, by extension, an acceptance of Hobbes's "proto-liberal" status. This is a common denominator in nearly all contemporary Hobbesian scholarship on this matter. The argument here seems to be that given his radical skepticism, his fears about rhetoric as a tool for lies and propaganda, his pessimism about human nature, his break with religion as a basis for political authority, and his embrace of "science" and experience, Hobbes must turn to sovereignty as a bulwark against total chaos. Without this bulwark, it is generally believed, Hobbes sees us—or perhaps more accurately, we see ourselves, thanks to Hobbes's intervention—as being unable to prevent ourselves from being determined by our worst features as human beings: our greed, our fear, etc. The assumption is that we need one voice, however arbitrary, to determine some sense of order. Even if we don't believe in what the sovereign says in our private hearts, we must pay some lip service to sovereign decrees to have a world with some semblance of order, or simply to preserve our life. Of course, many contemporary Hobbes scholars suggest that this turn to sovereignty is not so bad, that the sovereign might in fact turn out to have our best interests at heart or at least might be forced not to completely obliterate our rights for the sake of its own self-interest. But in Flathman in particular, we see a recognition of the awful choice that we have made and of what such a choice forces us to give up.

In *Subverting the Leviathan* I contest this contemporary assessment, both
of Hobbes himself and of the broader question of politics and sovereignty
that such an understanding of Hobbes implies. Richard Flathman has always been in my opinion one of Hobbes's most astute readers, along with
Victoria Kahn, another author who will figure prominently in this analysis.
I aim to take Flathman's insight and pursue it to its logical (and rhetorical)
conclusions. Rather than try to rescue liberalism from the contradictions
that Hobbes himself may reveal about that system (and Flathman in turn
reveals via his own treatment of Hobbes), I seek to show how a reading of
Leviathan might have us instead dispense with liberalism and sovereignty
altogether. There are things that Flathman cherishes about liberalism that
he would not abandon; these include individualism and the very notion of
"self making" that he sees as the most attractive feature of Hobbes's system.
My argument is that we need not abandon such notions when we abandon
liberalism itself; in fact, as I read him, Hobbes is telling us that we can have
these features only when we have abandoned, not so much liberalism itself,
since that was to come in Hobbes's future, but rather sovereignty, that system which even Flathman seems to consider essential for any functioning
political entity. Hobbes himself shows us that the chaos that many argue
would occur if we took away the sovereign principle is in fact not deflected
but actually preserved by sovereignty itself. As we will see, sovereignty is the
source of chaos; it is the proverbial fox guarding the hen house.

Rereading Hobbes in this way allows us to revisit the dawn of early modernity without a sense of the inevitability of what actually transpired in
history. Rather than saddle him with an association with liberalism (which
is much more a product of thinkers like Locke and—albeit in a very con-
flicted and paradoxical way—Rousseau than Hobbes himself), I would
argue that Hobbes is alerting us to the cost that must be paid in obeisance
to sovereignty. Rather than align him with liberalism, I see Hobbes as actually participating in a much more radical political view; a view that we see
championed in more recent scholarship by figures like Hannah Arendt (we
will attempt to reconcile her with Hobbes, despite her frequent condemnation of him exactly because of his association, as she sees it, with sovereignty
itself) as well as Walter Benjamin. When we read Hobbes as being a radical

democrat, with some help from these later thinkers, we are able to access a radical alternative to liberalism itself; one that was offered at the dawn of modernity but not pursued.

SHOWING CODES

I propose to make these arguments by examining Hobbes's theory of reading and by showing the self-reflexive nature of *Leviathan* as a text. It is my basic claim that when we read *Leviathan* according to Hobbes's own instructions and prescriptions for reading, this radical democratic alternative emerges. As an analogy to explain what I mean by "self-reflexivity," it was once common with word-processing software to use a key to "show codes." This function made visible amid the text that one happened to be working on the various commands ("bold," "indent," etc.) that occurred around and within the text, structuring and constructing it. With those codes hidden, one saw a simple set of words, with all of the bold, indents, etc. as given, disguising the complicated processes behind what appears to be a "normal" text.

In a similar way, *Leviathan* offers us a chance to "show codes" in its own text, or, to put it in a more vernacular and political way, to reveal the conspiracy that the book potentially advocates. We can view and participate in the construction of the text through a greater awareness of metaphors, figures, and other rhetorical devices that form the backdrop to and grounding for the text itself.

In making this claim about rhetoric, I take a somewhat different position from a considerable and quite diverse number of contemporary scholars of Hobbes, ranging from Victoria Kahn to David Johnston, who claim that Hobbes disguises but depends upon rhetoric—those very codes that I have been referring to—in order to manipulate his readers and develop a workable theory of state power and political authority.[31] In this view, Hobbes's skepticism, and his fear that religion and traditional notions of authority no longer had the ability to compel obedience, lead to a portrayal wherein for Hobbes authority must literally be reconstructed from the ground up, produced, as it were, out of thin air. These authors claim that Hobbes's famous and outspoken dislike for rhetoric is a ruse, allowing him to practice it in

secret while denouncing the use of rhetoric by others (potentially dangerous rivals to his own rhetorical production of sovereign authority). Once he
produces this authority, it is argued, Hobbes then erases his tracks, leaving
only the authority itself visible, like a text with no codes "shown."

In this book I challenge the idea that *Leviathan* hides its rhetorical nature in order to produce political subservience. As I read it, *Leviathan* is not
a ruse to be foisted onto an unwary reading public. On the contrary, it is a
means by which a hitherto unwary reading public can learn how to access
the codes and rhetorical figures that form the basis of political authority
and belief itself. As I will argue further, Hobbes's denunciation of rhetoric
is not total; he is opposed to precisely the style of rhetoric that he is often
accused of practicing himself, wherein rhetoric is performed in secret, ma-
nipulating and obscuring for nefarious purposes (what he calls "demonology").[32] When, on the other hand, rhetoric is accomplished openly and in a
way that all can understand and share, Hobbes not only supports but enlists
it as a requirement for political life.

ORGANIZATION OF THE ARGUMENT

This book is organized by its attention to three overlapping modes of
representation that Hobbes considers: rhetorical, religious, and political.
Hobbes's observations about rhetorical and linguistic representation, as well
as his considerations of proper (and improper, or idolatrous) representations of God, are a key to understanding the modes of political authority
and political representation in *Leviathan*. As a rule, contemporary Hobbes
scholars tend to focus on the politics of *Leviathan* and subsume religious
and rhetorical considerations to that primary reading. However, I will argue,
in doing so many scholars end up with a relatively narrow understanding of
what constitutes politics in *Leviathan* in the first place. Even those authors
who do consider Hobbes's religious views (and there are many of these)
tend to accept the political views established in parts 1 and 2 as determinant.
(Hobbes's consideration of religion is generally understood, by Pocock and
others, as having an entirely different purpose and meaning.)[33]

Accordingly, most Hobbes scholars of our era focus on the genealogy of
sovereignty that Hobbes gives us toward the end of part 1 and throughout

part 2 of *Leviathan*. Yet the ahistorical, utterly secular, and fanciful story that Hobbes tells us about the state of nature and the social contract that is presided over by the sovereign is just one of his versions of the genesis of political authority. This book will consider an alternative genealogy for political authority involving Hobbes's consideration of the covenant between God and the Jews as well as the kingdoms and communities that that covenant forged and will forge. I will attempt to show how this alternative genealogy jibes much better with the radical and decentered interpretive approach Hobbes champions through his rhetoric than the story of sovereignty itself. When considered in tandem, the rhetorical and religious strands of *Leviathan* serve to exclude and undermine the story of sovereignty that the book (or at least part of it) formally supports. This in turn suggests a different sort of politics.

The first three chapters of *Subverting the Leviathan* establish Hobbes's theory and method of reading, beginning in chapter 1 with an examination of his use of rhetoric. Here I will contrast my own understanding of the role rhetoric plays in *Leviathan* with that of several prominent Hobbes scholars, including Quentin Skinner. Chapter 2 describes Hobbes's theory of reading and its relationship to authority, as well as the juxtaposition between "private" and public (i.e., sovereign) forms of interpretation. Although the text formally supports public sovereign readings over "private" individual ones, Hobbes subverts his own argument by stealthily favoring individual interpretation. We will also begin to explore Hobbes's alternative foundation of political authority established in the time of Moses. Chapter 3 concerns itself largely with Hobbes's readings of Scripture, most of which occur in the second half of *Leviathan*. I argue that when Hobbes reads Scripture, he instructs us in how to read any text, including *Leviathan* itself.

Chapters 4 through 6 concern the actual application of this theory of reading to a reinterpretation of *Leviathan*. Here questions of religious and political representation predominate. Chapter 4 explicitly compares Hobbes's notions of religious representation, especially his notion of idolatry, with his understanding of political representation (a comparison Hobbes himself invites us to make many points throughout the text). While many authors claim that as with his use of rhetoric, Hobbes is essentially disingenuous with his use of religion, I will argue that Hobbes's religious beliefs, however complicated, are neither in the service of his politics (as David Johnston for one claims), nor at odds with it (as J. G. A. Pocock claims). Instead, they illuminate and complicate his overt political message. For example, in the case of religious versus political representation I will try to establish how for Hobbes the sovereign is by his own argument an idolatrous figure (or what he also calls a "separated essence"), something that purports to stand in for but actually supplants what it represents.

In chapter 5, I compare Hobbes's treatment of promises and secular covenants to his treatment of religious covenants, largely by considering two "persons" or representations of God on earth, Moses and Jesus, and the forms of political authority they serve to instantiate. For Hobbes, these "persons" (as well as the figure of the Holy Spirit) serve as iterations of God's fulfillment of the covenant made with human beings. When we consider that the sovereign, unlike God, does not partake in making promises with its subjects, we see a sharp contrast between the kind of fixed, absolute promises that Hobbes attributes to secular covenants under sovereignty and the kind of fluid and ongoing relationships that are set up by the covenant with God. Here, too, an alternative form of politics (one I will argue works more along the lines of Arendt's notion of a politics of "contracts and treaties") is suggested via an exploration of religious considerations.[34]

Chapter 6 examines a central rhetorical figure in *Leviathan*, the Holy Spirit, which I argue serves for Hobbes as a guarantor of doctrinal decentralization, allowing rhetoric and interpretation to remain fluid and avoiding and challenging the sovereign monopoly over meaning and authority. The rhetorical, religious, and political implications of *Leviathan* are here brought most closely together. I also consider the kinds of alternative visions of radical democracy that Hobbes offers, particularly in his considerations of the early Christian church, a time when there was no overarching Christian sovereign to settle doctrinal matters.

In the conclusion I consider further Hobbes's implicit critique of sovereignty and in particular liberal sovereignty. Even if we cannot achieve a radical democratic alternative, this reading of *Leviathan* allows us to recognize that sovereignty is not inevitable and that the practice of politics is not only possible but far preferable without it.

There are a few points to make about nomenclature. Throughout this text, I will be considering sovereignty in several forms. For Hobbes, as we will see, sovereignty can be either divine (when God is King, as he claims was the case in ancient Israel) or terrestrial. I will argue that these two forms of sovereignty are utterly different in terms of the kinds of political authority that they produce, with divine sovereignty being far more radical in character. Generally, when I refer to sovereignty, it is terrestrial sovereignty that I will be referring to. If I mean to refer specifically to divine sovereignty, I will make that clear.

In terms of "terrestrial" sovereignty itself, I will refrain from speaking of *the people* insofar as such a term is redolent of sovereignty's invasion of a particular community (or, if I retain the term, I will use quotes—"the people"—to show that I mean a sovereign vision of community). To speak of "the people" implies an already sovereign population, a sense of unity of purpose and will that is the hallmark of sovereignty itself. Instead, I will simply use the term *people,* an admittedly less romantic term but one that does not bring the same baggage. If my usage of the term *people* is jarring in a political context, perhaps it informs us as to the ways in which a belief in and expectation for sovereignty runs deep in our language. In terms of the related term *the public,* I didn't come up with an alternative that worked as well, so I have resorted to the admittedly less helpful *a public* in the hopes that this term at least alters the notion of publicness from a sovereign form to a more ordinary sense of the term.[35]

SUBVERTING THE LEVIATHAN

In *Subverting the Leviathan*, I am not claiming that my reading of Hobbes's *Leviathan* is right and virtually every other reading of the text since 1651 (or at least since 1936 when Strauss's text on Hobbes was first published) is wrong. Nor am I claiming that I know for a fact that Hobbes himself was consciously subverting his own text. Instead, I am simply claiming that when we apply Hobbes's own theory of reading as presented in *Leviathan* to the text itself—a move that the text seems to invite on many levels—we can read *Leviathan* in a different way. As we will see, Hobbes's operative metaphor for politics is reading, a notion redolent of a multiplicity of views and arguments. As I will argue, the "meaning of *Leviathan*," rather than being foreclosed, does indeed permit a variety of readings, and I would like to add my interpretation to other readings of this text (with a great deal of help from Hobbes himself).

As may be appropriate given Hobbes's own radical nominalism and skepticism, I therefore adopt a position of agnosticism when it comes to the question of what Hobbes "really meant," a question I will return to at the conclusion of this book. Did Hobbes intend his book to be read in this way? In other words, are his instructions for reading Scripture and other texts actually intended to apply to *Leviathan* itself? Does he consciously enlist codes and parables to undermine his own text? I don't think this question can be demonstrated effectively, nor do I think it matters much anyway. Hobbes certainly paid lip service for most of his life to the sovereign that he claimed to uphold but he has his moments (including in controversial passages in *Leviathan*) when he seems to be talking to all sides at once. At any rate, whether Hobbes is a craven coward, as many imply, a man who paid lip service to whoever he felt could protect him, or whether he was a misunderstood loyalist to the Anglican Church and the Stuart monarchy, or whether he is even, as I like to think of him, a radical democrat who, in his writings, transcended his own conservatism, Hobbes offers us a book that can be read in this way (among others). The book *Leviathan*—if not the author—offers us this notion of reading. In *Subverting the Leviathan*, largely for the sake of simplicity, but also because I don't exclude the possibility of Hobbes intending to write the book in a deliberately subversive manner, I will treat author and text basically interchangeably without intending any concrete empirical or historical claim about the mind or intentions of Thomas Hobbes himself.

I will occasionally refer to other books by Hobbes, but I will concentrate on the English version of *Leviathan* in part because I don't want to make a broader claim about Hobbes than what is to be found in *Leviathan* itself, and in part in order to recognize, as many of his contemporaries did, that there was indeed something different about *Leviathan* than his earlier (and, for that matter, later) works.[36] Furthermore, I will focus mainly (but not exclusively) on parts 3 and 4, not because I find the religious part of the book more important or unrelated to the earlier parts of the book, but because in parts 3 and 4 Hobbes is engaged in reading Scripture and exemplifies the theories of reading and, by extension, rhetoric that he is setting forth throughout the book.

Hobbes's *Leviathan* is exquisitely attuned to the relationship between author and reader, between the "authority" of the text and the opinions and influences that a book has upon its audience. In this way, reading *Leviathan* becomes a commentary not simply on a literary or philosophical text, but on the way decisions are made, on the way we consider things, on who and what opinions we defer to and those that we do not. *Leviathan* transcends the usual perceived limits of reading when it comes to questions of politics in a way that only a very few books manage. Indeed, *Leviathan* is not only a book about politics, but, because of its own attention to questions of reading, authority, and power, is itself political, part of the very fabric from which our political lives are or could be constructed.[37] *Leviathan* tells us something about the power of rhetoric in general. As I read it *Leviathan*, is a parable about language, about how words can be used to rule and bind us and how just as easily those very agents of control can turn on their would-be masters and become agents of resistance, subversion, and reappropriation of political authority. *Leviathan* reminds us that words and images are not just things we passively receive but are empty, filled with promise. Through our reading of them, words exert a power of representation. This power does not belong to any of us; it is always available for new meanings and new possibilities.

I

Hobbes's Use of Rhetoric

THIS BOOK MAKES a claim about *Leviathan*'s rhetoric, about the act and art of reading as a critical exercise. It also makes a claim about the reception of such rhetoric, about how texts are interpreted and understood in a particular political community, and how a community can be changed by acts of reading and interpretation. To explore this, we must first understand the nature of rhetoric and the idea that rhetoric "does" something to a text. We must understand how that "doing" affects the reader(s) themselves.

Hobbes brings up this issue at the end of part 3 of *Leviathan* when he argues that a work (presumably any work, but certainly *Leviathan* itself) must be read in a particular way:

> For it is not the bare Words, but the Scope of the writer that giveth the true
> light, by which any writing is to bee interpreted; and they that insist upon
> single Texts, without considering the main Designe, can derive no thing from
> them cleerly; but rather by casting atomes of Scripture, as dust before mens
> eyes, make every thing more obscure than it is; an ordinary artifice of those
> that seek not the truth, but their own advantage.[1]

In speaking of the "Designe" of a text, Hobbes is echoing some of the most basic notions of rhetoric as articulated by Aristotle, Cicero, Quintilian, and other classical scholars. They express the idea that language contains not just a content but also a form (or "Designe"), which is indeed more informative than the "bare Words" of a given text. This notion invites us to consider the text not simply as it appears to us here and there, but also in terms of how it is constructed overall, how the parts are related to the whole. In speaking of the "Designe" of the text when we are already well into the book, Hobbes seems to be inviting a rhetorical reading of *Leviathan* after the fact, after we have already read most of his book in a different, more "ordinary" (i.e., nonrhetorical) way.

It has been argued that when Hobbes speaks of the "Designe" of the text, he is making an analogy to geometry, to the way that the analytic building blocks of his argument fit together in one seamless whole. Sheldon Wolin has commented on Hobbes's epic goal of producing a fixed and clear definition for everything.[2] Raia Prokhovnik makes similar arguments, as we will see. In *Leviathan*, Hobbes supplies us at one point with a schema for all human knowledges.[3] The early parts of the book in particular offer an assortment of definitions, serving as units of meaning that presumably then collectively compose the "meaning" of the entire text. Such a view seems the opposite of textual subversion. Reading *Leviathan* in *this* way suggests a viable basis by which a sovereign can make assertions and provide a foundation for lasting political authority.

For one level of reading and interpretation, this argument is persuasive. Hobbes's definitions do appear to be part of an effort to lay down a comprehensive basis for ratiocination and sovereign political authority. Yet the terms *Scope* and *Designe* also carry a second, more explicitly rhetorical sense, relating to the actual effect the interactions between various parts of *Leviathan* have on our reading and interpretation of the text. Rather than merely accept Hobbes's assertion that the various aspects of the book fit together as a perfect, geometric whole, we should actually look at those interactions. In them we will see a far more subversive and contentious process at work.

HOBBES, HUMANISM, AND RHETORIC

Hobbes's relationship with rhetoric is well documented, but the subject remains controversial. A great deal of scholarship argues that Hobbes, although schooled in classical rhetoric (as exemplified by his translation of Thucydides' *Peloponnesian War*), turned later in life, and certainly by the time he wrote *Leviathan*, to science and logic; he abandoned his earlier humanist education and, with the publication of *Leviathan* in particular, ushered in a new era of modernism.[4] Other scholars see a Hobbes who stayed true to his earlier roots in classicism, despite his avowed dislike for Aristotle in particular.[5] Still others argue that Hobbes briefly abandoned rhetoric and humanism but returned somewhat reluctantly by the time he sat down to write *Leviathan*. As David Johnston and others have argued, Hobbes, having been convinced by the English civil war that people were far less rational than he had suspected, realized that appeals to emotion, persuasion, and propaganda (i.e., rhetoric) were necessary if his ideas were to have any hearing at all.[6]

In *Leviathan*, Hobbes amply manifests the ambivalence that has fostered so many divergent views of how he felt about rhetoric. As the passage cited above indicates, Hobbes seems to call for an appreciation of the rhetorical structure of his own text. Elsewhere Hobbes also argues for the use of rhetoric, as in "A Review, and Conclusion" at the very end of *Leviathan:* "So also Reason, and Eloquence [rhetoric] . . . may stand very well together. For wheresoever there is place for adorning and preferring of Errour, there is much more place for adorning and preferring of Truth, if they have it to adorn."[7] In the service of "truth," the quality of which remains to be determined, rhetorical "adornment" can play its perhaps necessary part.

And yet even as he appreciates its uses, elsewhere in *Leviathan* Hobbes raises a concern about rhetoric, including his own. He indicates a strong desire that his work not be read through a perversion of what rhetoric can indeed "do" to a text:

> There is nothing I distrust more than my Elocution; which neverthelesse I am confident (excepting the Mischances of the Presse) is not obscure. That I have neglected the Ornament of quoting ancient Poets, Orators, and Philosophers, contrary to the custome of late time . . . proceedeth from my judgment, grounded on many reasons. (p. 490)

Here Hobbes considers rhetoric to be somewhat acceptable so long as one does not resort to "ornaments"—rhetorical gestures that are useless and possibly misleading. This seems to contradict his (previously cited) comment just a few pages earlier in the text about the positive virtues of rhetorical ornamentation.

In part 1, Hobbes similarly argues that when accompanied by the virtue of discretion the wielder of rhetoric "will be easily fitted with similitudes, that will please, not onely by illustration of his discourse, and adorning it with new and apt metaphors; but also, by the rarity of their invention" (1.8, p. 51). He distinguishes such discretion from "fancy," which he tells us, speaking in this case specifically of fanciful history, "has no place, but onely in adorning the stile" (p. 51). By his frequent and conflicting use of the term *adornment,* as well as *ornament* (as we shall see in our discussion of Quentin Skinner's work, these may be translations of classical terms), Hobbes expresses an ambivalence that seems to reflect his mixed views of rhetoric itself. Rhetorical adornment, it appears, is good or tolerable when it furthers a "truth" but bad when it is only a matter of "fancy" or "stile," a distinction that begs the question, crucial to Hobbes, of how we know a truth from a falsehood in the first place.

Given Hobbes's radical skepticism, his nominalism, and his attention to the fables, metaphors, and allegories that writers employ to deceive their audiences, it could and has been argued that *Leviathan* is a work of supreme hypocrisy. After all, here is a writer who complains that deceptive textual exegesis has mesmerized people into following a series of false prophets, leading to the English civil war. Yet Hobbes himself seems to claim that in *Leviathan* he and he alone offers a correct reading of Scripture and by extension of the world itself, which, if widely accepted, would remedy all of the ills of society and in the process quite possibly help prepare us for the second coming of Christ. Here he sounds like one of the many charlatans he is so quick to denounce. Furthermore, and as often noted, a book that worries about the nefarious uses of rhetoric employs a large amount of it itself. To understand how Hobbes may not be guilty of such hypocrisy, we need to better understand the idea that rhetoric "does" something in a text above and beyond the function of the text itself.

WHAT DOES RHETORIC DO?

If we accept that *Leviathan,* replete as it is with metaphors, imagery, allegories, and other tropes and figures, is a highly rhetorical work, we must still come to terms with what this means for our reading of the text. What do we learn, to use Hobbes's own parlance, when we consider not merely the "bare Words" but the "Designe" of *Leviathan* (taken in its rhetorical sense)? Three important works deal directly with the question of what rhetoric itself "does" in general and specifically in or to *Leviathan.* The three texts are Quentin Skinner's *Reason and Rhetoric in the Philosophy of Hobbes,*

Raia Prokhovnik's *Rhetoric and Philosophy in Hobbes' Leviathan,* and David Johnston's *The Rhetoric of Leviathan.*[8] Each of these makes an important contribution to our reading of *Leviathan,* but each stops short of realizing their own claims about how a rhetorical reading of *Leviathan* might radically alter our encounter with the text.

Quentin Skinner

In his monumental work on this subject, Quentin Skinner admonishes many authors on Hobbes for misusing the term *rhetoric.* Skinner claims that his own use matches Hobbes's. It is hard to argue with him, given the breadth and depth of his knowledge. For Skinner, rhetoric means "a distinctive set of linguistic techniques ... derived from the rhetorical doctrines of *inventio, dispositio,* and *elocutio.*"[9] Skinner argues that to understand Hobbes, we need to understand his use of *ornatus,* which can be loosely translated as the use of tropes and figures in persuasive speech. Skinner admonishes us not to think of *ornatus* as "ornaments" to truth (a correlation, as we have seen, that Hobbes himself seems to make), but rather as "weapons and accoutrements of war," used for "winning the war of words, and thus of gaining victory for [one's] side of the argument" (p. 49).

Skinner distinguishes between a focus on meaning (what the text says) and "the dimension of linguistic action" (what the text "does"), that is to say the dimension of rhetoric itself (p. 7). He writes: "The possibility that *Leviathan* may be replete with rhetorical codes has scarcely been entertained" (p. 13). He further states that "lack of attention to Hobbes's rhetorical strategies has arguably given rise to a number of over-simplified interpretations of his religious beliefs, especially his beliefs about the veracity of the Bible and the mysteries of the Christian faith" (pp. 13–14).

There is an exciting possibility behind these sentiments, one that promises indeed to "re-read" Hobbes, just the way Hobbes appears to ask us to. And yet Skinner's book, which offers a magnificent categorization of all of the tropes and figures, particularly those involving irony and satire, in my opinion does not fully live up to its claims.

Skinner offers many examples of tropes and figures that Hobbes enlists largely for the purposes of satire. For example, he shows how Hobbes employs the trope of *aestismus,* which takes advantage of double meanings of words or phrases. Thus, given that the term *egregious* in Hobbes's time could either mean "exceptional" or "exceptionally absurd," Hobbes calls members of the "school divines" (a group of scholastic admirers of Aristotle) "Egregious persons" (p. 410).

Another example given by Skinner is Hobbes's use of *apodioxis,* which belittles by negating ludicrous assertions attributed to one's adversary. Thus Hobbes attacks the scriptural basis for the Enthusiast's claim that they had direct access to God through visions and dreams. Whereas the Enthusiasts pointed to chapter 28 of Exodus, which has God saying, "Thou shalt speak unto all that are wise hearted, whom I have filled with the spirit of wisdom, that they may make Aaron's garments to consecrate him," Hobbes renders this passage ludicrous by writing that this cannot mean "a spirit put into them, that can make garments" (pp. 420–21).

Skinner clearly establishes a pattern of rhetorical maneuvers in *Leviathan* that are far more common than in Hobbes's earlier texts. In *The Elements of Law,* Hobbes had also discussed the passage concerning Aaron's garments. But rather than employ the figure of *apodioxis,* he had merely argued that the Enthusiast's interpretation of that passage was wrong. So Hobbes is doing something different in *Leviathan.* But what has this difference accomplished? What is altered by the turn to rhetoric?

In the examples above, we get no real sense of any change in meaning by the addition of the rhetorical tropes and figures that Hobbes employs. For each argument cited above—the attack on scholasticism, and on Enthusiasm—Hobbes openly (nonrhetorically) professes these very same ideas throughout the text. For example, from virtually the very first page he attacks Aristotle's influence on scholarship of *Leviathan.*[10] He also openly denounces belief in possession, visions and the like. Thus Skinner's distinction between "meaning" and "doing" becomes less clear, at least given the examples that he offers. The rhetorical examples don't necessarily seem to "do" anything that the text itself doesn't also "say." Through his focus on satire, Skinner mainly depicts Hobbes as employing figures and tropes to make his point better or more cruelly, but not to the degree that these tools escape being "ornaments" altogether. Such figures and tropes are weapons, yes, but very much in service to the meaning that has already been established in the text.

If Skinner were merely saying that rhetoric is more persuasive than simple argument, one could hardly argue against that. But throughout his text, Skinner insists that although it can be a purely manipulative and amoral force, rhetoric can also be something else: part of the basis for an ethical order, the classical ideal of the *vir civilis* that by implication both Hobbes and Skinner appreciate. Therefore, the question of what, if anything, rhetoric "does" to the meaning or effect of the text becomes not simply a linguistic or indeed a rhetorical matter, but also one of ethics and politics.

If we accept the possibilities that Skinner suggests are inherent in rhetoric (as I believe we should), we might want to think of other ways in which Hobbes's rhetoric functions. The examples Skinner furnishes are possibly suggestive of the "dimension of linguistic action," but it is difficult to understand them as such without a clearer sense of what a "nonornamental" (in the ordinary sense of the word) rhetorical function would look like. One author who illustrates such an approach is Raia Prokhovnik, whose work complements Skinner's project in many ways.

Raia Prokhovnik

Of the three books considered here, Prokhovnik's has perhaps the best fit between claims for rhetoric's power and an analysis of what rhetoric actually "does" in *Leviathan*. For Prokhovnik, the rhetoric Hobbes uses "not merely reflects (like a static mirror reflection) his thinking but expresses and organises his thinking."[11] Here, as with Skinner, there is an implicit claim that rhetoric is not mere "adornment."

Prokhovnik fleshes out her claims somewhat more than Skinner does by looking at what she calls the "texture" of meaning in the text. She writes:

> Any philosophical work which seeks to present a view as a whole, a coherent unity, contains in its use of language metaphors whose significance are particular to that specific work. The texture of meaning that hangs on such metaphors operates like the allegory of the Leviathan, and the philosophical character of the whole text requires the understanding of that texture.[12]

For Prokhovnik, in *Leviathan* rhetorical figures, especially allegorical ones (and in particular the allegory of the Leviathan itself), serve as a way to knit the text together, to present a complex and multifaceted argument that would not otherwise be possible. For example, she argues that part of this "texture" in *Leviathan* comes from Hobbes's use of mechanical and organic imagery. For Prokhovnik, the way Hobbes juxtaposes images of machines and bodies to describe the political community does more than simply poetically describe that community in ways that are aesthetically pleasing. Rather, these descriptions perform the rhetorical task of enabling the argument Hobbes seeks to make. Hobbes's portrayal of naturalistic and artificial bodies as occupying the same space organizes (and produces) the notion of the "body politic" so that it can be both an artificial creation (a commonwealth) and a zone occupied by (natural) bodies at the same time. Furthermore, Prokhovnik claims, by speaking of the "body politic" and by supplying the amazing visual image on the frontispiece to exemplify and produce this notion in the reader's mind, Hobbes can "show" how sovereignty actually works.[13]

This then is the "texture" of *Leviathan* that Prokhovnik refers to, a form of argument that can only be accomplished and produced by the use of rhetoric itself. Of the texture provided by the allegory of the Leviathan itself, Prokhovnik writes:

> What would *Leviathan* be without the allegory? Without the language that forms the allegory, the work (no longer to be called *Leviathan*) would consist of a set of doctrines without a cohering philosophy, and its rhetoric would lack its central feature.[14]

Perhaps even more intriguingly, in terms of her larger claims of what rhetoric accomplishes, Prokhovnik offers a few insights into how the actual structure (i.e., "Designe") of *Leviathan* may in fact influence our reading of the text. For example, she argues that the very organizational pattern of *Leviathan* is an exemplification of Hobbes's methodology, whereby he "identif[ies] the simplest element analytically and abstractly considered, and reconstitut[es] civil society from there" (p. 167). She implies that this pattern whereby the whole is constituted from the parts is indicative of the synechdochal nature of the Leviathan itself whereby the parts, as we have already seen, function to model and explain the entirety. For Prokhovnik, the metaphors that Hobbes employs to describe and speak of the Leviathan reinforce this synechdochal structure (p. 174).

This whole-from-its-parts pattern stems from what Prokhovnik calls Hobbes's "statement of procedure," namely his famous admonishment in the introduction to *"Read thy self."* She writes: "In rhetorical terms, then, Hobbes stresses that conviction arises from agreement (based on personal experience—which, because it can, and must, be 'read' is a kind of book . . .) on the first elements and their subsequent constructions" (pp. 174–75). Thus for Hobbes, the reader must be convinced of the validity of "first elements," the "initial components" of an argument and then be led rhetorically toward the (now inevitable) conclusion (p. 175). In other words, "reading" us as readers of his book, Hobbes's metaphor organizes that act of reading itself—it is written in a style that focuses very much on the act (or anticipation) of being read in order to manipulate those readers into reading what he wants us to read.

Reading Hobbes as she does, Prokhovnik does indeed expand upon Skinner's notions about the "dimension of linguistic action." For her, rhetoric is not merely ornamental insofar as without it the very argument of the book could not be made. Rhetoric, she claims, allows Hobbes to link together very disparate ideas into an argument that announces its coherence via certain central allegorical and metaphorical "textures."

Prokhovnik's reading of the text is indeed convincing in that it conforms very nicely to the kinds of rhetorical activities that she describes. Yet Prokhovnik herself suggests that the rhetoric of *Leviathan* isn't necessarily uniform in its effect or in its structuring of the meaning of the text:

> In Leviathan, the impression that each word has been wrenched out of a severe and arduously logical train of systematic thought, is accompanied by another, quite different impression, that of a writer who keeps his predominantly 'poetic' instinct under restraint but cannot prevent a wealth of imagery flowering into a full-blown allegory which provides one level of continuity in the work. . . . In Hobbes [rhetorical structures] work toward different effects, and it is this conjunction that causes *Leviathan* to strike the reader as both fascinating and ambiguous. (p. 185)

This claim for *Leviathan*'s ambiguity suggests that Hobbes's use of rhetoric may produce deeper conflicts in the text than Prokhovnik's analysis might generally suggest, interfering with her own claims (and Hobbes's as well) that the book conforms to a very clear and consistent logic. In her own genealogy of Hobbes's ongoing relationship between rhetoric, poetry, and "fancy" on the one hand and science, logic, and "judgment" on the other, Prokhovnik suggests that there is a steady movement toward the latter and an increasing suspicion toward the former. She goes on to claim that given this tension within Hobbes, his work can be, and has been, misleading and misunderstood. As she puts it herself, Hobbes is a figure who epitomizes a transition between medieval and renaissance notions of imagery and text on the one hand, and later modern notions on the other, and so in many ways his work remains unresolved.

The figure of Hobbes that Prokhovnik sketches in this passage seems to be far more complicated than the perfectly symmetrical rhetorician that she claims to read in *Leviathan* more generally. The upshot of Prokhovnik's rhetorical reading of *Leviathan* is, as with Skinner as well, hardly out of tune with the overt message of the text; namely that *Leviathan* is what we think it is, a text supporting our capitulation to the sovereign. Like Skinner, Prokhovnik does offer one conclusion that slightly deviates from what the text appears to argue—namely that *Leviathan* performs a subversion of religious doctrines in the guise of promulgating them. She argues that *Leviathan* rhetorically undercuts and reduces the saliency of religion as a threat to the secular state. Yet this argument is not necessarily all that hidden in the actual text itself; despite his pose of orthodoxy, Hobbes makes many open statements that appear to undermine the Anglican Church if not religion itself. Certainly, as we have already seen, many of his contemporaries spotted this ambiguity even without benefit of any explicitly rhetorical analysis.

Thus Prokhovnik's discovery of deeper structural meanings in *Leviathan* does not seem to actually intrude all that much upon the overt or nearly overt message of the text, which she seems to readily accept. As compelling as her reading of *Leviathan* is, much of its power comes from its conformity to what the text already appears to say, an appearance that may be enabled by rhetoric but that indeed functions as little more than the bearer of a message relayed by the "bare Words" of that text. This is puzzling because Prokhovnik really does seem to offer ways of reading *Leviathan* that suggests the ability to access a metatextual level of reading and understanding. Inasmuch as Prokhovnik herself alerts us to the fact that the "Designe' of *Leviathan* may be more complicated than we think, the consequences of Hobbes's admonition to read his text according to the "Scope" and "Designe" of the book may lead in directions neither she nor he anticipates.

David Johnston

David Johnston's book, *The Rhetoric of Leviathan*, makes fewer claims than Skinner's about the power of rhetoric and so has less at stake in its treatment of *Leviathan*. Like Skinner and Prokhovnik, Johnson makes a persuasive case that Hobbes appreciates and deliberately employs rhetoric. Johnston claims that Hobbes, believing that public opinion was the cause of the English civil war, had no choice but to embrace rhetoric so that he could not merely describe but also persuade others to his position.[15] Accordingly, Johnston denies that Hobbes's increased interest in sciences like geometry came at the expense of rhetoric. He claims further that Hobbes saw that science could not match rhetoric's power to evoke mental images ("perspicuity") before a reader's eyes; science and logic cannot produce images (like the frontispiece) that greatly increase the persuasive power of a text.

Given Hobbes's (re)turn to rhetoric, what does Johnston say this means for his (and our) reading of *Leviathan*? Are the differences that Johnston notes in *Leviathan* vis-à-vis other earlier works by Hobbes (in particular *The Elements of Law*) the result of Hobbes's (different) use of rhetoric? Or does he simply employ rhetoric in order to push a message that might seem different in *Leviathan* but is essentially unchanged from previous works?

Johnston's book both suggests and resists the notion that Hobbes's engagement with rhetoric somehow changes the meaning of the text. Although he appreciates the ways in which the turn to rhetoric engages with a completely different sort of vocabulary, Johnston nonetheless seeks to portray this turn as being largely in the service of science itself. This becomes particularly clear when Johnston turns to questions of Hobbes's reading of Scripture. Johnston parts company with J. G. A. Pocock's position that parts 3 and 4 of *Leviathan*—those sections that deal most with religion and Scripture—are almost a separate book unto themselves. Instead, he argues:

> If . . .we focus upon the effects Hobbes's words seem designed to produce, we find that (Pocock's investigations notwithstanding) there is a close, even intimate, relationship between the argumentation of the second half of the book and that of its first half. The second half of *Leviathan* is designed to shape the thoughts and opinions of its readers in ways that will make the argumentation of the first half persuasive and compelling.[16]

Here we see a view of rhetoric as serving mainly to promote or enhance the persuasive powers of the text itself. At the same time, Johnston appreciates how for Hobbes, rhetoric engages on a deeper, or prior level, than a "scientific" approach to a text. Johnston argues that *Leviathan* is rhetorical insofar as it seeks not only to convince by the power of its logic (as his earlier works did) but also on a more metatextual level, to employ rhetoric to convince the reader of the value of logic and science itself. Citing Hobbes in the Introduction to *Leviathan,* where he writes "for this kind of Doctrine, admitteth no other Demonstration," Johnston surmises that "the vigor and vividness of Hobbes's language in *Leviathan,* as well as the extremely polemical cast of his theological argumentation, are designed to [persuade his readers to accept scientific principles as truth]" (pp. 131–32).

By implication, for Johnston, Hobbes flirts with (even as he distrusts) the powers of rhetoric to make truths out of thin air, to establish authority where there was none before. Yet once having done so, Hobbes retreats (or attempts to retreat) into the world, in this case the world of reason and science, that his rhetorical endeavors have helped to create. Johnston writes:

> Hence the change in form and methods that distinguishes the argumentation of *Leviathan* from that of his earlier works of political philosophy represents neither an abandonment nor in any essential sense a modification of his original purposes. . . . The final aim—to bring into being a commonwealth based upon firmer, more rational foundations than any that had ever existed before—remained unchanged. (p. 133)

However, to achieve this "unchanged" objective (i.e., an objective that is not changed by the turn to rhetoric, only enhanced by it), Hobbes has to bring about a "prior cultural transformation" and to engage with "metaphysical, prophetic and historical dimensions of human existence," something that can only be done by engaging with rhetoric in a way that makes it more than simply a tool of science (p. 133).

In his notions of how rhetoric works in *Leviathan*, Johnston chastises Pocock for his appreciation for Hobbes's religious arguments (p. 118). He claims that Pocock loses sight of the strictly rhetorical character of parts 3 and 4 and that Pocock literalizes where he should be reading the book for its structure and its style, that is to say, for its rhetorical effects. Here we see, in effect, Johnston himself acknowledging how rhetoric can transform the meaning of a text, making the second half of *Leviathan* not mean what it appears to at all.

But how can we be sure that Johnston, in arguing for this reading, has not been captured by the "meaning" of the text that he has already decided is correct? Not unlike Prokhovnik, Johnston claims that the "rhetoric" of *Leviathan* favors the meaning of parts 1 and 2 at the expense of parts 3 and 4 or, perhaps more precisely, that parts 3 and 4 are important but only to the degree they subsume religion and lay the ground for accepting parts 1 and 2, which constitute the "real" meaning of *Leviathan*.

In making the claims that he does, Johnston opens up the possibility—which he does not acknowledge—that not only might a rhetorical reading change the meaning of parts 3 and 4, but it might just as easily change the meaning of parts 1 and 2 as well. At this point we must ask whether the meaning of the text is leading the rhetoric or whether it is the other way around.

The "Meaning of Meaning"

Here we face the very slippery nature of rhetoric and the way it can elude or resist even the most convincing arguments as to its true "meaning." Once the power of rhetoric to shift and alter meanings is acknowledged, it becomes a matter of employing rhetoric oneself to convince others that one's own reading is authoritative (as opposed to a different view of reading in which scholars simply argue over which of their readings is right, which is actually correctly identifying the true and only meaning of the text).

If we are to acknowledge the full effect of rhetoric, does this necessarily mean that in order to read a book "correctly," one must read it in a way that is in discord with the overt message of the text? If one finds that the "rhetorical codes" of a text offer up the same ideas as the text itself, does this mean that one must have read these codes wrongly? Rather than argue this, I would make a different claim: that a reader be open to other possible readings, to avoid being utterly captured by the meaning of the text as it is presented. Only when we are open to rhetorical codes not being captured by the overt meaning of a text, can we begin to appreciate the radically unmoored style of reading that Hobbes offers us.

Skinner, Prokhovnik, and Johnston offer important readings of Hobbes's use of rhetoric and yet, as I see it, their analyses share the characteristic of pulling back from their own insight (especially the first two). These three books mainly furnish *examples* of rhetoric in *Leviathan* rather than fully developed explanations of what rhetoric does or can do. As I see it, the authors that I have examined do not entirely fulfill their promise to understand what rhetoric does as a system of organization of texts; they do not fully address what the design of the text itself performs or does to that text and to our reading of it. When "meaning" itself is put into question by the very rhetorical devices that appear to support and produce it, then conversations about the meaning of texts, about the "correct" reading, becomes a matter, just as Skinner tells us, of reading, interpreting, and arguing over "rhetorical codes."

REFERENTIAL ABERRATION(S)

Hobbes himself was clearly aware of the quality whereby rhetoric cannot command persuasion but must cajole or seduce us if it is to succeed. Throughout *Leviathan,* Hobbes acknowledges that the author can't force people to read what she or he intends them to read into a text. Hobbes furnishes many examples of people being forced to utter untruths but readily acknowledges that personal belief is untouched by such demands.[17]

One of Hobbes's complaints about rhetoric is that even as it constructs a particular meaning, it can just as easily multiply the meanings that we read into a text. It may or may not have been Hobbes's intent to have

Leviathan be read in one particular way, but there is much in this text that suggests that he knew that it could be read in many other ways as well. If rhetoric can set multiple meanings against one another, then it seems that what rhetoric "does" is often quite the contrary of serving the "meaning" of the text. Indeed, such an understanding of rhetoric suggests that it serves if anything to undermine any one particular meaning.

This idea of multiplication of meanings is of course not an idea unique to Hobbes and in fact lies at the very basis of rhetoric, going back to Aristotle himself.[18] Contemporary thinking (at least in the continental tradition) has often embraced this feature of rhetoric. As Paul de Man tells us in *Allegories of Reading:*

> Considered as persuasion, rhetoric is performative, but when considered as a system of tropes, it deconstructs its own performance. Rhetoric is a *text* in that it allows for two incompatible, mutually self-destructive points of view, and therefore puts an insurmountable obstacle in the way of any reading or understanding.[19]

De Man famously offers us an example of how rhetoric can do more, something quite different than the text that contains it, by examining, believe it or not, a moment from the 1970s American TV show *All in the Family:*

> Asked by his wife whether he wants to have his bowling shoes laced over or laced under, Archie Bunker answers with a question: "What's the difference?" Being a reader of sublime simplicity, his wife replies by patiently explaining the difference between lacing over and lacing under, whatever this may be, but provokes only ire. "What's the difference?" did not ask for difference but means instead "I don't give a damn what the difference is." (p. 9)

As de Man explains it, the "rhetorical question" Archie Bunker poses indicates how there is a difference between a literal and figurative meaning: "the literal meaning asks for a concept (difference) whose existence is denied by the figurative meaning" (p. 9) Hence the two readings are at odds with one another, are in fact "different" albeit in a complicated way. For de Man, however, it is not the case that the figurative meaning is somehow the "real" meaning and the literal meaning is only a kind of platform for the figure to be read on. Rather for de Man, what is in fact the heart of what he (in a clearly very different spirit than Skinner) calls "rhetoric" is in some sense the interrelationship of these states and the difficulty or impossibility of distinguishing the "real" meaning at all. As he puts it:

> The grammatical model of the question [i.e., what's the difference?] becomes rhetorical not when we have, on the one hand, a literal meaning and on the other hand a figural meaning, but when it is impossible to decide by grammatical or other linguistic devices which of the two meanings (that can be entirely incompatible) prevails. Rhetoric radically suspends logic and opens up vertiginous possibilities of referential aberration. (p. 10)

Thus, even as rhetoric produces a legible reading in the text, it simultaneously undercuts that reading, suggesting other readings, unsettling and disturbing our narrative conventions in the process. In this view, rhetoric does more than simply persuade, it also invites a "referential aberration" into the mix. Like the sorcerer's apprentice, rhetoric may seem useful or desirable as a tool, an ornament for the author's "meaning," but it can also take on a life of its own and alter that meaning and the readings that result from its engagement.

Turning this analysis to the question of politics, when we consider the *aporias* that rhetoric produces, we can see that rather than argue (as Johnston does) that secular authority is being promoted over religious authority (or the other way around), we could just as easily say that Hobbes's turn to rhetoric doesn't simply favor one authority over another at all. Instead we can read *Leviathan* as calling into question authority itself, our use and belief in it.

One could make an argument that rhetoric cannot help but be subversive. Indeed this seems to be at the heart of de Man's claim. Such a notion is (seemingly in a less appreciative sense than de Man) the basis of a great deal of Hobbes's own stated suspicion of rhetoric, his conviction that rhetoric often leads to abuses, to what he calls "the kingdome of darknesse" where lies and deceit take the place of any semblance of truth.

Even granted this danger inherent in rhetoric, as I see it, *Leviathan*, as a text and more precisely as a series of rhetorical performances, enacts and embraces the very *aporias* Hobbes seems anxious to avoid. As we shall see, this does not mean that *Leviathan* becomes reduced to meaninglessness—

as we have already seen with de Man, meaning and its undoing are twin born. Rather, I will be arguing that *Leviathan* takes advantage of these *aporias* in order to potentially challenge and redirect our interpretations. As I've already stated, I read *Leviathan* as a highly self-reflexive text. Accordingly, my claim is that in *Leviathan*, rhetoric serves not merely to persuade, but also to change the nature of persuasion; it serves not simply to unfurl its argument within the context of a given set of facts or thoughts, but rather to call that set of preconditions into question. It shows how authority is produced and enabled and also how it can be given away, subverted, lost, and retrieved. *Leviathan* also shows us not just how to interpret, but what interpretation consists of; it allows us to resist interpretation, to expose the *aporias* and "referential aberration" of the text.

Skinner, Prokhovnik, and Johnston are helpful in alerting us to the possibilities of rhetoric and then, particularly in Prokhovnik's case, alerting us to just how one might go about searching for the function and power of rhetoric in this text. With all due respect to Skinner, the definition of rhetoric that I will be using is broader than the one he uses (and is probably also a broader definition than the one Hobbes himself uses). My own working definition of rhetoric includes the classical basis that Skinner relies on, a conception that focuses on the construction of an argument, the structure and the use of tropes and figures. But as de Man shows us, rhetoric does more than this.

At the risk of overburdening the term *rhetoric*, I would emphasize yet another layer, which may be implicit in both Skinner and de Man's definition but is worth saying plainly. As I see it, rhetoric is also (and perhaps principally) concerned with its effect on its audience, on its reception in a particular speech community and on the act of reading (or, in other forms of media, seeing, listening) itself. While rhetoric often serves to make the act of reading appear natural and seamless, so that the great effort and construction that goes into it disappears into a now naturalized and authoritative text, it can just as easily reveal the inner workings of all texts, exposing and subverting the creation of exactly that selfsame textual authority. In this way, the reader becomes aware of the power of rhetoric to seduce, to convince, to manipulate. It is in this last sense in particular that I consider *Leviathan* to be a supremely rhetorical text and for this reason (despite all the great weight of readings that the book has already been subject to) end-lessly productive and highly worthy of further reading and interpretation.

The great achievement of *Leviathan* is to enable its readers to catch the author in the act of producing his own textual authority and furthermore, the authority of the sovereign. Having so been exposed, the authority that is produced through rhetoric becomes as legible as the tropes and figures that produce it. What remains in the wake of such an exposure is the reader's awareness of their own role and participation in the promulgation of au-thority as well as the possibility that the reader will learn to employ the codes and meanings of rhetoric deliberately rather than passively, with im-portant consequences for the types of political authority we subscribe to (and those we don't).

With this in mind, let us turn in the next few chapters to the question of reading more directly, examining this idea from an explicitly rhetorical perspective. When reading is understood as a specifically rhetorical activity, we gain a fuller perspective on the "dimension of linguistic action," namely what rhetoric "does" to a text, and what our reading of that rhetoric "does" in having an effect on its audience.

2

Public & Private Reading

IN LOOKING AT the chaos and disruption of the English civil war, Hobbes presents us with a conundrum. In *Leviathan* and elsewhere he lays blame for the war largely on the faulty interpretation of Scripture.[1] Competing interpretations of the Bible by, among others, the Church of England, Puritan radicals, Quakers, even Catholics, were all claimed as correct by their respective adherents, and with these claims was a commensurate political vision that many were ready to fight and die for. For Hobbes, there may be as many scriptural interpretations as there are interpreters of Scripture. The conundrum is that for Hobbes, God is unknowable. God does not (with very few, very special exceptions) ever speak directly to us. Instead we must imagine and represent what God might say. For Hobbes, Scripture, although authored by God, is not literally God's word but stands in for those words, and is thus unfortunately subject to interpretation (hence the troubles of the English civil war).[2] Thus Hobbes tells us that "men had need to be very circumspect" in following a prophet or claimant to speak for God, for "he that pretends to teach men the way of so great felicity, pretends to govern them; that is to say, to rule, and reign over them. . . ."[3] Yet paradoxically Hobbes insists that Scripture is and must be the basis for any notion of truth or justice, a foundation for epistemology.[4] He tells us that God is the author of natural law, without which human law is empty. For Hobbes, it seems as if we can't live with Scripture as a basis for politics and yet we can't live without it, either. What, he asks us, is to be done?

In "Of a Christian Common-wealth," the third of four parts of *Leviathan* and at 160 pages (in the Cambridge edition) a book within a book, Hobbes offers us a complete and substantial interpretation of Scripture of his own. He begins "Of a Christian Commonwealth" by telling us that although the possibility of a Christian commonwealth "dependeth much" on revelation and the "Will of God," we ought not despair that God has chosen of late to remain silent.[5] He concludes:

> Nevertheless, we are not to renounce our Senses, and Experience; nor (that which is the undoubted Word of God) our naturall Reason. For they are the talents which he hath put into our hands to negotiate, till the coming again of our blessed Saviour; and therefore not to be folded up in the Napkin of an Implicite Faith, but employed in the purchase of Justice, Peace, and true Religion.[6]

For Hobbes, the absence of a clear and authoritative divine voice, far from being the cause of our woes, enables and even requires the possibility of human agency. Our reason is a gift from God, a "talent" that God has given us to negotiate a world now bereft of divine revelation. Rather than despair, we must endeavor to become aware of our own power to produce truths in God's name. This talent is not meant to supplant Scripture but rather to enable us to learn how and what Scripture teaches us.[7]

If Hobbes is saying that we can and must know truth(s) through Scripture, but that there are many false claimants for that truth, how are we to distinguish the true from the false? In particular, why should we take Hobbes's word for what the correct reading of Scripture is, when he is, by his own argument, just another claimant? Indeed, Hobbes's own version of "the truth" is quite unpleasant (to modern ears, certainly, but also to many of his contemporaries). To end dissention and war, he argues for the supremacy of the Church of England over all other churches and tells us that this church itself must be subjugated to the English king. English citizens may believe in their hearts what they like, but they must obey their terrestrial sovereign in all their actions.[8]

Hobbes's "answer," like the national sovereign he is advocating as part of that answer, seems absolute and unimpeachable. And yet, by raising the issue of scriptural interpretation, he seems to have laid a trap for his own authority; in suggesting that claims for truth (necessarily including even his own claims) are always suspect, this seemingly authoritarian writer evinces a distinctly anti-authoritarian streak. At the very least, he seems to invite a kind of scrutiny that his strong claims for sovereign power would seem to disfavor.

To look at *Leviathan* in this way implicitly raises questions about how a book that remains deeply skeptical about truth claims can say anything at all, much less serve as the basis for lasting and absolute sovereign authority. How do we interpret such a book when the question of interpretation itself is such a central motif? Whence comes the authority of a book that ceaselessly exposes and calls into question the very notion of authority and relatedly, of authorship? And how does Hobbes reconcile his reading of Scripture, supposedly the basis of that authority, with his own insight that God is absolutely silent and unknowable?

In this chapter, I will be arguing that Hobbes does indeed offer us a reading of Scripture but one that avoids the pose of its own sanctity or correctness. Rather than pretend that his reading is right while all others are wrong, Hobbes offers us a notion of reading that we can all participate in, one that opens up the question of reading itself, complicating and subverting notions of truth, authority, and sovereignty in the process. In keeping with the understanding of rhetoric described in the previous chapter, I will be arguing that in his concept of reading, Hobbes offers an allegory about reading (conveyed through the figure of the reader who "reads her or himself") that is in effect metafigurative. This is an allegory about its own allegorization; we read about reading, we are included in and participate in this metaphor for politics, thus becoming ourselves politicized. Rather than describing and expounding upon reading as a method of surveillance and monopoly of meaning and interpretation, or making the claim that his own "reading" (or the sovereign's) is authoritative and all others are not, Hobbes' allegorization of reading depicts resistance to sovereign authority even in the guise of apparent (and enthusiastic) submission. *Leviathan* thus models an act of textual (and civil) disobedience to the authority and law it supposedly supports and even produces.

In the last half of the chapter, I will change focus from reading as a rhetorical performance, to reading as a kind of messianic delivery, one that produces an alternative political authority in its wake. Here, I will seek to juxtapose Hobbes's notions of religious representation with his rhetorical arguments. In considering specifically Aryeh Botwinick's discussion of Moses, reading, and authority for Hobbes, I will consider the metafigurative nature of reading not only as an allegory, but as an eschatological event, one that contains and structures all future acts of interpretation. For Hobbes, the messianic aspects of Moses's actions is evident in the fact that, although itself a mere moment of "reading" (i.e., Moses's interpretation of the "Sinaitic events," and the Israelites' ratification of this reading), this act transcends its human origins, serving not only as an instance of reading but the instantiation of "reading" itself, defining what reading will mean forever after. As we will see, Hobbes's understanding of the messianic origin of reading becomes important because it suggests that reading is not an endlessly relative business, where, in looking for meaning we find nothing at all. Rather we can see how meaning and interpretation are developed, produced, and resisted, all the while contained within the epistemological framework that was produced by the particular acts of reading we attribute to Moses and, in turn, the Israelites.

READING OURSELVES

To make these arguments, we must determine what Hobbes means by reading and what his theory of reading tells us about how to read *Leviathan* itself. The question of reading is one that Hobbes takes very seriously, as best exemplified by his famous statement in the introduction to *Leviathan:*

> There is a saying much usurped of late, That *Wisedom* is acquired, not by reading of *Books*, but of *Men*. Consequently whereunto, those persons, that for the most part can give no other proof of being wise, take great delight to shew what they think they have read in men, by uncharitable censures of one another behind their backs. But there is another saying not of late understood, by which they might learn truly to read one another, if they would take the pains; and that is, *Nosce teipsum, Read thy self:* which . . . teach[es] us, that for the similitude of the thoughts, and Passions of one man, to the thoughts, and Passions of another, whosoever looketh into himself, and considereth what he doth, when he does *think, opine, reason, hope, feare,* &c, and upon what grounds; he shall thereby read and know, what are the thoughts, and Passions of all other men, upon the like occasions.[9]

We can already see how for Hobbes reading is an inherently political act, because by reading ourselves, we are reading one another. The act of reading is therefore not an isolated and nonpolitical activity but apparently the necessary basis for politics itself. Reading ourselves, it seems, connects us to "the thoughts, and Passions of all other men." But as soon as he writes this, Hobbes seems to quash or at least overwrite such an authorization of private readings by declaring in turn that all such readings—including, as we shall see, his own—must be subordinated to a public figure: "But let one man read another by his actions never so perfectly, it serves him onely with his acquaintance, which are but few. He that is to govern a whole Nation, must read in himself, not this, or that particular man; but Man-kind."[10] Here Hobbes seems to subsume the private act of reading to a "public" one. This passage suggests that private readings are important only to the extent that reading serves as a site to be overwritten by the public, sovereign pronouncement. This textual overwriting seems to occur quite literally: in the first passage, Hobbes tells us that in reading ourselves we are reading "all other men," but with the arrival of the sovereign's reading in the second passage, we can read (that is to say have knowledge of) only our own personal acquaintances, so that the potential political implications of the first passage have now been withdrawn.[11]

Indeed, large portions of *Leviathan* are devoted to contesting private readings of all sorts, ranging from interpreting Scripture to the meaning of laws. For Hobbes, private readings, especially of books, can be the source of subversion and misinterpretation of words and power:

> From the reading, I say, of [various Greek and Latin] books, men have undertaken to kill their Kings, because the Greek and Latine writers, in their books, and discourses of Policy, make it lawfull, and laudable, for any man so to do; provided before he do it, he call him Tyrant. For they say not *Regicide*, that is, killing of a King, but *Tyrannicide*, that is, killing of a Tyrant is lawfull. . . . In summe, I cannot imagine, how any thing can be more prejudiciall to a Monarchy, than the allowing of such books to be publikely read.[12]

Hobbes thus returns us to the question of interpretation. A private reader might, encouraged by their reading of a particular book, take regicide for tyrannicide, or by extension take anything for anything else. Books seem to open a kind of maw in the delicate fabric of socially ordered meaning whereby the very private, internal, and inchoate experience of reading itself becomes mapped onto the world, to deleterious effect.

For sentiments such as these, Hobbes has an obvious answer to the problem of interpretation of texts. Because he acknowledges that Scripture is endlessly interpretable, Hobbes claims that when it comes to the interpretation of Scripture the real question we should be asking is "*By what Authority* [is Scripture] *made Law*."[13] In other words, for all intents and purposes Scripture must "mean" whatever the sovereign says it does. Although he readily calls the sovereign "arbitrary," Hobbes nevertheless insists that this figure must have the last word in matters of interpretation in order to avoid chaos.[14] The rest of us, it seems, should not be interpreting at all:

> To look upon [Scripture], and therein to behold the wondrous works of God, and learn to fear him is allowed; but to interpret them; that is, to pry into what God saith to him whom he appointeth to govern under him, and make themselves Judges whether he governs them as God commandeth him, or not, is to transgresse the bounds God hath set us, and to gaze upon God irreverently.[15]

We see here another version of Hobbes's notion that the sovereign should "read ... Man-kind," that its reading not only trump but in a sense replace our private readings of ourselves and of one another.

But how does this declaration of subjugation sit with Hobbes's own authority in this text since, after all, he is performing an act of interpretation himself? Indeed, he is "interpreting" Scripture to offer a justification for the sovereign's monopoly on interpretation. What is the foundation for Hobbes's authorization of sovereign power when such an act of authorization removes his own ground or right to make such a pronouncement in the first place?

Rather than settle such a question definitively, Hobbes consistently revisits this dilemma of authority. He periodically insists that everything he writes is duly submitted to his civil sovereign. In the very beginning of the *Leviathan*, he tells us, for example: "That which perhaps may most offend, are certain Texts of Holy Scripture, alledged by me to other purpose than ordinarily they use to be by others. But I have done it with due submission, and also (in order to my Subject) necessarily; for they are the Outworks of the Enemy, from whence they impugne the Civill Power."[16] How can Hobbes be so definitive about his own scriptural interpretation when it seems that his reading of texts is contingent on sovereign approval ("due submission")? Who, we must ask, is the true author of *Leviathan* or the interpretations contained therein? Are we to infer that Hobbes has "checked" or cleared his ideas with the sovereign? As we have already seen, *Leviathan* is replete with notions that, upon the book's publication, managed to alienate many of the Anglicans and royalists that were his erstwhile allies to the point where he came to feel safer in Cromwell's England than in exile with the court in France.[17] Furthermore, as Hobbes himself would later point out, at the time that *Leviathan* was being written, the question of just who or whether there was a sovereign was a contentious point.[18] So in a sense, this "submission" suggests more the absence or problematization of sovereignty than its being a solution to the question of authority in the text and nation.

The question of Hobbes's submission to the sovereign is further complicated when we realize that right after Hobbes admonishes the sovereign to "read . . . Man-kind," he allows that such a reading could be best accomplished by a careful perusal of *Leviathan* itself. "Yet, when I shall have set down my own reading orderly, and perspicuously, the pains left another [i.e., the sovereign], will be onely to consider, if he also find not the same in himself. For this kind of Doctrine, admitteth no other Demonstration."[19] What does it mean that Hobbes tells the sovereign to "read" the subjects of the commonwealth by reading a book written by one of those subjects (in the process, rendering the sovereign into a "private reader")? In a sense, Hobbes plays with the double meaning of reading in this passage, moving from a notion of reading as an active stance—examining and learning about one's fellow human beings—to a passive one, learning and following everything that Hobbes has already discovered.

In passages such as this one (and there are many others), Hobbes seems to be appropriating the sovereign "last word" even while appearing to defer to that sovereign authority. He seems to be surrendering to something that he is in the process of creating or authoring. Rhetorically speaking, these "submissions" may be an example of the figure of *epitrope* (in Latin *permissio*), which in its ironic form consists of apparently turning over something (in this case authority) to an audience (in this case the sovereign "reader") only to imply something negative or derisive in so doing. Yet in this case, the butt of his joke seems to be not the sovereign, but rather the subject/ reader, who is bound by an authority that is produced before their eyes. Is Hobbes trying to pull something over on us, his readers, making authority out of nothing, creating "truth" as a sleight of hand? In reading (for) the sovereign is Hobbes "reading" (in the more contemporary and pejorative sense) us all?

READING *LEVIATHAN*

In much of the contemporary literature on Hobbes, the general consensus seems to be that Hobbes is indeed tricking us. Victoria Kahn argues that the many instances of Hobbes appearing to give away his authority as a writer are part of a disguised agenda. She writes, "Hobbes explicitly acknowledges that since he is not the sovereign, he can make no assertions."[20] Kahn goes on to suggest that Hobbes may be disguising not only his authority but his use of rhetoric as well, seeming to cede the one (authority) to the sovereign and the other (rhetoric) to the humanist writers who preceded him, but in fact preserving both powers for himself by this gesture. Because rhetoric for Hobbes is redolent of deception and misinterpretation, it is to be formally shunned and yet he realizes it is necessary to resort to it if he wants to have any influence at all in his writings (i.e., any authority). Kahn writes: "the naked truth has no authority of its own; in fact, it cannot be seen at all, for truth itself is an effect of the belief . . . in authority."[21] In other words, Hobbes sees himself not as the subject of sovereignty, but, as we have seen too, as the *author* of it. Since there is no "truth" to this authority, Hobbes sets out on a project of creating this authority the only way he can, rhetori- cally. But of course Hobbes cannot do this openly, for the realization that the sovereign authority is a rhetorical product (much less a product of one of its citizens, i.e., Hobbes) would be devastating to that authority. Hence Hobbes must disguise the fact that he is not describing but producing that authority by denouncing both his rhetorical talents and, of course his au- thority as an author, ceding it to the sovereign itself.[22] Hobbes's text is pro- ducing the very sovereign authority it appears to be merely describing (and submitting itself to).

In a very different vein from Kahn, Tracy Strong argues that Hobbes mostly eschews rhetoric and seeks to generate authority by making his own authorship invisible or at least irrelevant. He writes that Hobbes's goal in *Leviathan* is nothing less than the creation of a secular version of Scripture itself.[23] In *Leviathan,* claims Strong, Hobbes sought to reproduce the experience of reading Scripture as articulated by Luther and earlier Protestant thinkers. Those thinkers presumed that reading Scripture was, as Strong explains it, like reading a computer manual in which "in the end it means one thing only."[24] In this view, there is no interpretation per se, just meaning that one finds or doesn't find. For Strong, the way Hobbes achieves this (or attempts to, anyway) is to have a book that is essentially authorless, or at least one in which the author hardly matters. Strong writes: "For Hobbes there is a formal parallel between truth arrived at by reason (as in *Leviathan*) and truth arrived at by Scripture. *The author is of no significance for understanding in either*" (Strong's emphasis).[25] The meaning of *Leviathan* isn't Hobbes's own, then, it is just "there," in the text.[26]

In a parallel argument, Strong writes that the notion of authority and authorship in *Leviathan* works similarly: "The sovereign—the Leviathan— is then a (written) text of which each individual is the author, but it is a text for which the author is no longer available."[27] In the social contract, each individual lays down their natural rights, that is, makes an authorization to every other individual, resulting in the sovereign, an artificial being. It might seem to make sense that in the text of *Leviathan*, Hobbes is authoring the sovereign, too, laying down his own authority or right as author in the process, as a model for the subjects of the *Leviathan* to follow.

This is an elegant and compelling argument. Yet the very idea of a text that needs no interpretation (not to mention a text that "has no author") is itself a rhetorical production. It suggests (although Strong would not put it in this way) a kind of ruse or sleight of hand—one that Hobbes himself would be very quick to denounce in others. Are we to believe, for example, that Hobbes himself didn't write *Leviathan*, but that his "reason" did? Or that Hobbes the author is no longer "meaningfully" available in this text? In *Leviathan*, Strong argues that the covenant effectively removes us from active authority in the commonwealth, but Hobbes himself has made no such covenant as author of *Leviathan*. Does he then really achieve, even rhetorically, the status of the author(s) of Scripture?

If Strong is right and it is Hobbes's intent to disappear into his text, this hardly seems a suitable or effective solution to the problem of the text's authority. Disappearing in this context means something like "covering his tracks," which implies the danger of those tracks being rediscovered. At any rate, certainly no one did buy this ruse and it does not seem, given his many worries, that Hobbes expected them to. And anyway, if this is really what he is doing, Hobbes makes a strange job of it. Strong suggests that it is even possible that Hobbes put his own face on top of the Leviathan's image in the frontispiece. If this is the case, Hobbes may be calling our attention (however coyly) to his own authorship of the book. If his goal is a text that is "authorless," why then draw attention to that author, even if indirectly, whether by putting his face on the frontispiece—if that is what he is doing—or merely by repeatedly focusing on the question of authors and authority?[28]

In her response to Strong's claims, Victoria Silver suggests that neither Hobbes nor Luther are as resistant to interpretation as Strong suggests. Her claim is that interpretation is necessary for these thinkers because of their conviction that God is quite literally not understandable.[29] Instead of Scripture being like computer manual and us needing simply to figure it out, Silver argues quite convincingly that for Hobbes we interpret because as human beings we must make some sense out of God's impenetrability. Interpretation doesn't mean "figuring out" so much as it offers a way for us to accept our lot in the universe as God's subjects.[30] She argues, for example, that Hobbes's use of imagery from Job (including the image of the Leviathan itself) suggests very strongly a God who is not to be rationally understood but trembled before and simply obeyed. She writes, "Thus what is given in Job is not the legibility of God's authority and intent but, if the Leviathan qualifies as 'king over all the sons of pride,' the opposite."[31] Where Strong suggests that Hobbes sought a literal and nonmetaphorical reading of the Bible, Silver sees that paradox and metaphor are all we have by which to "know" God. Likewise, the sovereign that stems from such a theology is not a gentle Whiggish creature as Strong reads it, but a cruel Tory (I picture Margaret Thatcher). It is something that Hobbes doesn't necessarily expect us to like, but that we are stuck with, in the manner of Job.

Silver challenges Strong's reading of Hobbes' famous mistranslation of "*Nosce teipsum*" (translated as "read thyself" instead of "know thyself") in the Introduction to *Leviathan*. For Strong, this "reading" of oneself means "having a text and finding that text in oneself," that is, reading *is* (or becomes) knowing and hence perhaps this is not so much of a mistranslation after all.[32] Silver reminds us that "reading" is not the same as "finding" and that (although she doesn't quite say it this way) the mistranslation itself is evidence that reading is not about sureties but is indeed about the act of interpretation. The problem, Silver surmises, is that we can't know ourselves—there is nothing certain or clear to know. If we could know something absolutely, we wouldn't need to read *Leviathan* to show us who we are meant (or who Hobbes means us) to be.

In these readings of Hobbes we get various assertions of how Hobbes intends to transcend himself as author of a text and establish authority *malgré lui*. Strong's argument, although nicely structured, seems to me to be the least convincing of the three. The claim that Hobbes seeks literalness in texts and in the world around us would be more plausible if he didn't continuously subvert this project by complicating his relationship to the truth that he claims to "find" in his text. His strange relationship to sovereign authority, his calling our attention to his own authorship, seems to suggest that Hobbes's goal is not to disappear into the text but to challenge and complicate the way that we read a text in the first place.

Kahn's reading is more nuanced in part because, like Silver, she accepts the fundamentally rhetorical tone of Hobbes's writing. Kahn essentially argues that Hobbes, acknowledging the power and danger of rhetoric, uses rhetoric as a weapon against itself, exposing its own arbitrariness (and, as she sees it, the arbitrariness of Scripture, too).[33] She writes: "Hobbes's intention is to use . . . rhetoric . . . in order to purge the commonwealth of its most dangerous rivals for the subject's obedience."[34] In this way, Hobbes leaves us with no choice but to embrace the arbitrary sovereign as being the least of all evils, the "prudent" choice.[35]

Contested Readings

Whereas Strong implicitly argues for a sleight of hand on Hobbes's part, Kahn does so openly. Yet here too we come to a problem of textual authority, even as it is based on an act of deception. If Hobbes were indeed so determined to fool us, you'd think he would not invite the kind of scrutiny that he does, especially when it comes to his notion of reading. Crucially, Hobbes admonishes us that an overly rapid, or immediate grasping at a text (or anything else for that matter) leads not to knowledge but, as we will see further, to idolatry and false doctrines. We have already noted how Hobbes distinguishes between the "bare Words" of a text and the "Scope" of the author. His concern that we read Scripture carefully might be further evidence of his wish that *Leviathan* be slowly pondered as well:

> Whereas there be, that pretend Divine Inspiration, to be a supernaturall entring of the Holy Ghost into a man, and not an acquisition of Gods graces, by doctrine, and study; I think they are in a very dangerous Dilemma. . . . The safest way is to beleeve, that by the Descending of the Dove upon the Apostles; and by Christs Breathing on them, when hee gave them the Holy Ghost; and by the giving of it by Imposition of Hands, are understood the signes which God hath been pleased to use, or ordain to bee used, of his promise to assist those persons in their study to Preach his Kingdome, and in their Conversation, that it might not be Scandalous, but Edifying to others.[36]

Hobbes requires the reader to suspend his or her immediate first impressions of a text, and instead study and acquire inspiration slowly over time. (We will return to this passage on two occasions later in this book.) It seems that for Hobbes only the more careful perusal of texts can really be said to constitute "reading" at all; in his view, to read otherwise is to commit a form of idolatry, a misinterpretation and misuse of signs.

Hobbes's understanding of reading defeats any sleight of hand—even ones that the author himself might seek to perform. Instead, his text makes us all too aware of the act and process of reading itself, precisely because we would otherwise succumb to the manipulations of rhetoric that convey the "meaning" of the text.

Hobbes informs us that when we read a text carefully, when we are aware of the "Scope" or "Designe" of a text, our reading might not be what we expect it to be. At the very end of the book, in the last paragraphs of "A Review, and Conclusion" (and speaking in this case specifically of his analysis of ecclesiastical power), Hobbes claims that his arguments are "consonant to the Scope of the whole Scripture," which is to say bound not by this or that word but by the structure of Scripture itself (p. 489). Accordingly, Hobbes writes, "And therefore [I] am perswaded, that he that shall read [*Leviathan*] with a purpose onely to be informed, shall be informed by it" (p. 489). The passage that contains this sentence is full of the usual claims of sovereign power and natural law, but it also suggests that the text might surprise us as to its meaning. This passage could either mean that those who seek only information will get exactly what they expected, or it could mean those who read the book "onely to be informed" shall in fact *be* informed, presumably in unanticipated ways.

Hobbes goes on to parse more closely the question of reading and being read:

> But for those that by Writing, or Publique Discourse, or by their eminent actions, have already engaged themselves to the maintaining of contrary opinions, they will not bee so easily satisfied. For in such cases, it is naturall for men, at one and the same time, both to proceed in reading, and to lose their attention, in the search of objections to that they had read before. (p. 489)

Here Hobbes challenges the style of reading wherein the truth is known before the reading occurs. If this is the case, we can return to our consideration of the prior passage, concluding that being "informed" by *Leviathan* probably means in ways that are unanticipated and not already known or presumed. Hobbes seems to insist that reading happen in real time, that the reader be open to a future understanding different than that of the present moment in which the act of reading begins. Hobbes disclaims the preset opinions of those who read his book planning to disagree with his own conclusions, but the passage may also be read as an indictment of precisely the sort of "sovereign" style of reading (arbitrarily determining the meaning of a text in advance of actually reading it, or purely because of prior readings) that one must employ in order to reach those conclusions in the first place.

Such a view of reading seems quite different from and even at odds with the kind of pro-sovereign pronouncements that Hobbes seems to make so often. If the sovereign is going to tell us what Scripture and other words mean, if the sovereign "already knows" what our reading will mean and be, what is the value of our own study and perusal? Why demand a careful and thoughtful reading of a text if we are only going to suspend our private acts of interpretation anyway and acquiesce to whatever and however the sovereign tells us to read? If rhetoric is really a tool of the state to promulgate its authority and laws over the rest of us (or perhaps more accurately, a tool that Hobbes uses on behalf of the state), why is Hobbes demonstrating the inner workings of that style to us, the readers, and subjects of this text?

One way to reconcile different notions of Hobbes's understanding of reading is to claim that for Hobbes, we can and must believe what we like, but in our formal actions and pronouncements, we must claim to believe and actually follow the sovereign's pronouncements. Hobbes acknowledges this possibility, as when he allows for what he calls the "licence [of] Namaan" (3.43, p. 414). In the biblical story to which this refers, Naaman was asked by an "Infidel King" to bow before an idol and did so to save his life. For Hobbes Naaman's actions are excusable; because Naaman still believed in his heart, he remained obedient to God (3.43, p. 414; 3.42, p. 344). The example here is of an "Infidel" king, but the argument clearly can extend to any other sovereign. Does this mean that for Hobbes private acts of reading are permissible, but only *qua* private acts, interior and nonpolitical, not challenging the sovereign's power or authority in any meaningful way?

But if so, why allow for our own power to read at all? Why evoke a competing notion of interpretation, another notion of reading than the sovereign's own? If Hobbes really wanted to preclude any public disagreement with the sovereign, would it not make sense to begin by forbidding private disagreement as well? (Or if not forbid it—since that wouldn't make much sense—at least not condone and ardently and openly defend it the way Hobbes does?) Once again, Hobbes's common usage of the term *reading* for both models of politics (i.e., both individual and sovereign forms of interpretation) suggests that Hobbes does not intend for reading to remain a merely private or personal activity. If a private reading is meant simply to serve as a vehicle for the public reading of the sovereign, then why call it "reading" at all (i.e., why choose this particular metaphor)? The collective label of "reading" Hobbes places both individual and sovereign powers of interpretation on a common plain of contest. Indeed, extending the metaphor of reading to the sovereign brings that seemingly unreachable figure into the interpretive domain of the private reader/citizen. This implies that the private readings are not nonpolitical after all, not simply applying to one's personal acquaintances, and allows us a reading that, as Hobbes tells us himself (before he retracts this claim), is informed by "what are the thoughts, and Passions of all other men."

Reading Out Loud

We get a better sense of the political implications of private reading when we further consider how for Hobbes, all forms of reading, both private and public, are necessarily connected to the social and political contexts in which they occur.[37] For Hobbes the externalization and concordance of our interpretations is a necessary precondition for those interpretations to gain anything more than a subjective (or truly "private") quality. As Hobbes notes in the early parts of *Leviathan*, in our deliberations we seek "the foresight of a long chain of consequences, of which very seldome any man is able to see to the end."[38] It is indeed only when our private musings are subjected to public scrutiny that such deliberations take on any certainty at all:

> The secret thoughts of a man run over all things, holy, prophane, clean, obscene, grave, and light, without shame, or blame; which verball discourse cannot do, farther than the Judgement shall approve of the Time, Place, and Persons.... Again, in profest remissnesse of mind, and familiar company, a man may play with the sounds, and aequivocall significations of words; and that many times with encounters of extraordinary Fancy: but in a Sermon, or in publique, or before persons unknown, or whom we ought to reverence, there is no Gingling of words that will not be accounted folly.[39]

If we consider "reading" as the metaphor that Hobbes is using for the organization and interpretation of ourselves and our thoughts, we see that we must in effect "read aloud" in order to make sense or make order out of the subjective chaos of our thoughts; in other words, we must submit our private readings to a kind of collective conversation that, very much like Arendt, serves as the basis for what will constitute "reality" to each of us. The interior space of thought is insufficient for Hobbes to constitute actual "reading"; it does not in itself produce meaning or authority. For Hobbes there must be a "public" component to reading, perhaps the very public that Hobbes evokes in his notion of our ability to read "all other men." This "alternative public" (an idea that I will return to at greater length in chapter 6) is different from and possibly in contention with the notion of the sovereign who stands in for (or simply is) "the public"—this is a public composed of mutually aware and engaged individual readers. Reading for Hobbes is therefore never a truly private isolated act, never truly apolitical; even when we are reading a book by ourselves, that reading becomes incorporated into a political and collective context and necessarily is effected by and effects that context; while reading, our thoughts anticipate future discussions and are informed (but not determined) by discussions and events that have already occurred.

As usual, Hobbes tends to promote such an idea through a consistent formal subservience to the notion of sovereignty. In a later passage in *Leviathan* (to take just one example), Hobbes considers "reading" aloud in a different sense, as in a public declaration of sovereign intentions:

> The Law of Nature excepted, it belongeth to the essence of all other Lawes, to be made known, to every man that shall be obliged to obey them, either by word, or writing, or some other act, known to proceed from the Soveraign Authority. For the will of another, cannot be understood, but by his own word, or act, or by conjecture taken from his scope and purpose; which in the person of the Common-wealth, is to be supposed alwaies consonant to Equity and Reason. And in antient time, before letters were in common use, the Lawes were many times put into verse . . . And for the Law which *Moses* gave to the people of *Israel* at the renewing of the Covenant, he biddeth them to teach it their Children, by discoursing of it both at home, and upon the way; at going to bed, and at rising from bed; and to write it upon the posts, and dores of their houses; and to assemble the people, man, woman, and child, to heare it read.[40]

In one paragraph we find two competing notions of reading: one in which our private moments of reading become the basis for collective discussions about meaning, and another in which the sovereign trumps such conversations and tells us basically what to think. We see this distinction being demonstrated very literally: the laws of Israel were both 'discours[ed] . . . at home, and upon the way" even as assemblies of people gathered "to heare it read." Is it such a foregone conclusion that our "private" discussions of the law will always coincide with the sovereign's interpretation? What if it doesn't? What happens to the kinds of interpretations and social meanings that are "privately produced" when they are trumped and replaced by the sovereign's pronouncements? While, as is so often the case in *Leviathan*, the sovereign's public reading seems, by virtue of its very publicity, intended to counter any private readings that may obscure or obstruct the sovereign's definition of meaning, this passage serves to remind us that the sovereign's "public" reading relies on the acquiescence of that other public, a reading (or in this case, listening) public. The public reading of the sovereign's word is a rhetorical performance, intended to construct, authorize, or produce our belief, a belief that we can give or withhold.

Of the sorts of beliefs that are produced from these or any other acts of reading, Hobbes writes that

> when wee believe any saying whatsoever it be, to be true, from arguments taken, not from the thing it selfe, or from the principles of naturall Reason, but from the Authority, and good opinion wee have, of him that hath sayd it; then is the speaker, or person we believe in, or trust in, and whose word we take, the object of our Faith; and the Honour done in Believing, is done to him onely.[41]

This passage is itself masterfully rhetorical, its construction implying that in those instances when we do know the "thing it selfe" or do have principles of "naturall Reason," we can dispense with any subjectively based judgments of belief. Yet, given that for Hobbes "[n]o Discourse whatsoever, can End in absolute knowledge of Fact, past, or to come," we never can know "the thing it selfe" and cannot even be absolutely sure about the "principles of naturall Reason" either.[42] Therefore a claim that seemed to describe an exception actually establishes a rule: we have no source of authority but our belief and trust. Belief, far more than knowledge, is the basis of politics for Hobbes. In pointing to the direct relationship between our beliefs and our opinions about the person or authority that we "Honour," Hobbes complicates the style of passive obedience he is normally seen as advocating. He reminds us that the sovereign is an "object of our Faith"; it really does matter how we think about it; without a sense of trust and "taking their word," sovereign authority disappears. Even when it is used to perpetuate sovereign rule, belief depends upon (and Hobbes reminds us of the fact of) our personal and collective interpretations-or indeed readings—insofar as he tells us "Beleef, and Unbeleef never follow mens Commands."[43]

It's clear that Hobbes is acutely aware of the importance that belief and faith serve as cornerstones of authority, obedience, or political power. As Kahn, following Kenneth Burke, points out, authority must be based on belief, and belief is therefore a battleground, an explicitly political question.[44] The question to ask here is whether Hobbes's description of belief as a kind of reading has enhanced or reduced our individual powers to participate in this battle ourselves. Does his exposure of the rhetorical performance of authority merely permit us the "licence [of] Naaman"? Or does it enable the private reader to better engage in the rhetorical maneuvers that constitute a battle over truth, law, and authority?

For all of the reasons cited above, I would argue that reading is a poor choice of metaphor if Hobbes's intention is in fact the promotion of absolute sovereign authority at the expense of private or individual judgment (i.e., the judgment of that "other public"), precisely because as a metaphor, it is not redolent of singular meaning but is inherently open to and indicative of a plurality of meanings. Metaphors of seeing, knowing, or simply commanding might have better applied. Indeed, even Hobbes's mistranslation of *Nosce teipsum*, suggests a deliberate, and possibly subversive, misreading of just what constitutes knowledge and power in the first place. By choosing reading as his operative political metaphor, Hobbes seems to have done more than simply applied a metaphor to illustrate his notions of obedience and rule. By calling our attention to the act of reading and setting it against the sovereign's own monopoly of meaning (via the use of one metaphor to describe two distinct—and possibly contesting—political orientations), Hobbes may be challenging the sovereign's definitive reading, not only by supplanting it with a reading of his own (as he does quite openly), but also by allowing for all of our own readings to similarly challenge and clash with sovereign pronouncements (as well as Hobbes's own "authorial" pronouncements in the text).

The Allegory of Reading in Leviathan

In addition to providing a metaphor for the kind of authority and power that Hobbes seeks to (rhetorically) produce, Hobbes's understanding of reading can be seen as providing or performing as an allegory, one that complicates and illuminates the entire text of *Leviathan*. This allegory is implicit in the figure of the reader that Hobbes evokes in the introduction to *Leviathan*. As with any allegory, the figure of the reader, the subject who "*Read*[s her or him] *self*" is a sustained metaphor or image, which runs throughout the length of the book. This figure is encountered for so long as we are actually reading this book and is periodically reinforced by the book's intense attention to the question of reading.

By virtue of its subject, this allegory works somewhat differently than other allegories might, in that the figure of the reader allegorizes the activity of reading that the reader is actually doing. The self-reflexivity of telling the reader to "*Read thy self*" even as the reader is in the process of reading these very words, turns the reader into a figure within the very text they are encountering. As such, we can consider this allegory to be "metafigural" (which de Man tells us means to "[write] figuratively about figures.")[45] Thus, the reader of *Leviathan* becomes potentially aware of their own self as reader, becomes aware of participating in the act of rhetorical performance so that "*Read thy self*" becomes both an authorial command and a performative description indicating our participation in the text.

Throughout *Leviathan*, this allegory, the figure of the reader that the reader encounters when they read this book, serves to challenge and complicate the readings and interpretations that we engage with; figured into the text itself, we surrender our foreknowledge of what the text "means" and become aware of our role and powers as interpreters. We cease merely to gaze upon the text as it is and become involved in the ongoing production of meaning that occurs within and beyond the text itself.

To give a clearer sense of what I mean by this treatment of reading as a self-reflexive allegorical activity, let me again contrast my arguments with those of Raia Prokhovnik. As we have seen, in her own analysis Prokhovnik also focuses on the importance of Hobbes's notion of reading, calling his call to *"Read thy self"* his "statement of procedure," a central premise that organizes his entire epistemology.[46] She writes that in his rejection of standard empiricist claims about knowledge "it is clear that for Hobbes it is not the physical senses, but sense as perception, that is important."[47] In other words, for Hobbes it is not that our senses bring the world to us, but rather it is our reading of the world (via those senses) that makes the world what it is to and for us.[48]

Here once again, reading, perception, understanding, and interpretation become the privileged modes of knowing. (all organized under the metaphor of reading itself. This is opposed to those modes of knowing in which the senses "give" the world and its meaning to us whole, without need of examination or interpretation. In light of this, Hobbes's mistranslation of *Nosce teipsum* becomes more interesting because the very quality of knowing is informed by knowledge's transformation into reading. As Prokhovnik implies, knowing for Hobbes *is* reading; reading offers us the only kind of knowledge that we can ever have (this is not unlike Silver's claim and is almost exactly the opposite of what Strong claims about the distinction between reading and knowledge).

Accordingly, Prokhovnik considers Hobbes's "statement of procedure" to be a metaphor, but as she reads it, a metaphor with certain limitations. She writes:

> Hobbes' metaphor [i.e., *"Read thy self"*] . . . expresses . . . in shorthand form, his epistemological position that the only way to knowledge is through one's own experience, and presents the image of experience as an intelligible account which can be read. . . .Knowledge cannot be gained through external means such as the authority of books, but only through the fruits of (in prudence) and right ordering of names (in science) in experience.[49]

Prokhovnik reads Hobbes's metaphor in part as a comment on the limits of books as a source of knowledge. She does not, however, note the paradoxical nature of such a claim coming as it does at the beginning of a book that is in fact already being read; we read that we should not trust "reading" as it is normally understood (i.e., reading books), that we should trust our experience rather than books (even though it is a book that tells us to read and trust ourselves in this way). In other words, we cannot help but "read" the world, but we mustn't trust what we "read" in books (presumably including *Leviathan*) to advance the knowledge gained by such a reading. Perhaps even more to the point, reading of books cannot constitute what reading as a form of knowledge might or should be; here the metaphor becomes unmoored from the very activity that spawns it.[50]

Prokhovnik does not completely ignore the fact that both the metaphorical reading of the world and the literal reading of the book share one name ("reading"). It's worth returning to part of a passage of hers quoted in chapter 1: "In rhetorical terms, then, Hobbes stresses that conviction arises from agreement (based on personal experience—which, because it can, and must, be 'read' is a kind of book from which his general condemnation [presumably of reading and trusting in books] is excepted)."[51] At least when considered metaphorically, "books" (i.e., as a "kind of book") seem to be part of reading, an exception to Hobbes's general (and literal) condemnation of reading actual books.

Yet when it comes to the reading of actual books, Prokhovnik draws a line, refusing the metafigural implications of his "statement of procedure." She stresses the purely metaphorical nature of Hobbes's call to *"Read thy self"* by exempting it from its literal (and literary) form. She accepts Hobbes's condemnation of books as being unironic and in this way, I think misses some of the most important implications of Hobbes's theory of reading, even as she otherwise offers us a very rich view of what reading might entail for Hobbes. For Prokhovnik, reading as a metaphor is "shorthand" for what the book says in general, it is not a comment on reading so much as an example of reading (we could say an ornament).

When Hobbes's own subversive treatment of reading is excluded, we are left, like Prokhovnik, with no alternative but to conclude that the only "person" capable of offering a basis for meaning must be the sovereign.[52] It is only when we recognize that this is a text that authorizes us to read, but at the same time demands that we believe nothing that we read in books (even *Leviathan,* which is the source of that authority), that reading becomes more of a question than an answer. We cease to read the phrase *"Read thy self"* as a grammatical command (whereby we already know what reading is and now we simply must do it) and it becomes instead a rhetorical question (a "referential aberration"). The phrase *"Read thy self"* inaugurates an allegory that calls its own meaning into question. In this moment, so early in *Leviathan*, Hobbes has already helped to establish the conflict between textual authority and our own "authorship" as readers.

Benjamin and Allegorization

In his own analysis of allegories and their uses, Walter Benjamin helps us shed more light on what might be happening in the pages of *Leviathan*. In his well-known treatment, *The Origin of German Tragic Drama*, Benjamin describes the difference between an allegory and a symbol. Benjamin states that while allegory is much derided for being abstract, purely representative without any reference to a specific object or idea, the symbol tends to be praised as a real instantiation of meaning, wherein "the beautiful is supposed to merge with the divine in an unbroken whole."[53] For Benjamin, however, the power and promise of allegory lie precisely in the fact that it is so clearly representative, not a claim to any sort of instantiation but instead an instance of mere allusion. By their nature, allegories create a distance between what they claim to speak for and what they "are." Benjamin, speaking in particular of the German baroque allegorists who wrote "mourning plays" in the seventeenth century (and who were therefore contemporaries of Hobbes), points out how their allegories are often grotesque or absurd. These dramatists are in love with the sounds and images they engage with in a way that collides with the supposed message or intention of the allegory itself.

For Benjamin, then, allegory is a kind of "ruin," only a suggestion of what it was thought or intended to be.[54] He writes, "Where man is drawn towards the symbol, allegory emerges from the depths of being to intercept the intention, and to triumph over it."[55] The allegory thereby becomes a part of the production of meaning, rather than just a delivery system for it. If we understand Benjamin's treatment along the lines of Skinner's "dimension of linguistic action," we can see how allegory accomplishes this function handily. The object, once allegorized, "is now quite incapable of emanating any meaning or significance of its own."[56]

While the allegory is normally deemed abstract and unrelated to the object, Benjamin sees that it is the symbol that is truly unrelated—truly, to use Hobbes's term, a "separated essence." The allegory exposes and affects the materiality of our relationship to the object; it reflects the "truth" of representation, the fact that we are dealing merely with representation itself, and doesn't pretend, as the symbol does, to be "the thing itself."

If we apply such conceptions of allegory to Hobbes's own usage, we can see how helpful Benjamin's interpretation is for our own purposes (this will become even clearer over the course of the next two chapters). Through the allegorical figure of the reader, Hobbes is in effect enacting a distinction between our reading as a symbolized instantiation of the "meaning of the book" on the one hand and the material inscrutability of the text on the other. As object (or "ruin"), the allegorized text interferes with and distorts the sense of immanence and "truth" that the text simultaneously symbolizes. The allegorization of our own act of reading allows us a distance from our own experience of reading; it thematizes that experience and renders it legible to us. This "ruins" our reading of the text by forcing us to respond to the materiality and "scope" of the text as a whole.

Benjamin considers the political implications of such a reading of allegory, including the kinds of authority that such readings produce. He writes that "[the allegory is an] expression of authority, which is secret in accordance with the dignity of its origin, but public in accordance with the extent of its validity" (p. 175). In other words, although its source is mysterious, the allegory has a tangible effect in the world; it occurs, as he tells us, in public, reflecting and responding to the political and social context from which it is produced. It is in part for this reason that Benjamin opposes the conviction that a turn to allegorization is a turn to meaninglessness (a theme we will be taking up more with Hobbes later in this chapter). Although Benjamin concedes that with allegory "[a]ny person, any object, any relationship can mean absolutely anything else," he denies that allegory produces total relativity (p. 175). On the contrary, he appreciates this quality of allegorization in no small part because he sees that politics itself is built out of the various unexpected and constantly surprising associations that the use of allegories makes possible.

Insofar as Benjamin's own politics are informed by a consistent strain of messianism, allegory can be said to serve as a conduit for divine expression (or more accurately, a conduit for divine *aporia*). Ultimately, for Benjamin it is allegory and not the symbol that anticipates and "represents" the divine:

> It will be unmistakably apparent, especially to anyone who is familiar with allegorical textual exegesis, that all of the things which are used to signify derive, from the very fact of their pointing to something else, a power which makes them appear no longer commensurable with profane things, which raises them onto a higher plane, and which can, indeed, sanctify them. Considered in allegorical terms, then, the profane world is both elevated and devalued. This religious dialectic of content has its formal correlative in the dialectic of convention and expression. For allegory is both: convention *and* expression. (p. 175)

As I will be arguing further in chapter 4, this characterization of the divine as it is produced and suggested via allegory is almost precisely what Hobbes describes as "worship," a nonidolatrous mode of representation. (Thus for both Benjamin and Hobbes, as we will see, rhetorical and religious sensibilities are mutually reinforcing.) The fact that an allegorized object is "only" an empty, purely representational figure makes the object seem devalued, but, as we will see more clearly with Hobbes, too, the profane world is also "elevated" in that it becomes infused with what Benjamin calls the "'rhetorical' arts," that is, with the power of allegory itself (p. 177). Even if allegory is "only" what it is ("convention"), it is also an unpredictable and ever-changing mode of representation ("expression"), a dialectical engagement that allows the possibility of newness—even, as we will see further, of messianic self-delivery.

READERS AND AUTHORS

Having considered the question of reading in general, as well as the nature of allegories and their effect on the "meaning" of a text in particular, we can now focus more closely on a related question: the relationship that is produced between the readers of a text and its "author," in this case Hobbes himself. This is a relationship to which Hobbes pays a great deal of careful attention. It is critical for him because it determines whether or not the reader is persuaded or affected by a book. Hobbes explicitly links "authorship" (presumably including his own) to "authority" and in this way suggests a connection between the question of his own textual authority and the authority of the sovereign. Thus a better understanding of the relationship that Hobbes sets up between himself and his readers helps illuminate the sorts of political obedience (and disobedience) that *Leviathan* may potentially demonstrate.

Hobbes reminds us that authority—the foundation of political rule—is itself derived from the term *author*. Hobbes famously tells us in chapter16:

> Of Persons Artificiall, some have their words and actions *Owned* by those whom they represent. And then the Person is the *Actor*; and he that owneth his words and actions, is the AUTHOR: In which case the Actor acteth by Authority . . . [S]o the right of doing any Action, is called AUTHORITY and sometimes *warrant*. So that by Authority, is always understood a Right of doing any act: and *done by Authority*, done by Commission, or Licence from him whose right it is.[57]

In this passage, the ordinary citizen is the "AUTHOR" of the artificial person, the Leviathan itself. The authority of the sovereign is "authored" by people when they transfer their rights to it. Those rights become disembodied, reformulated in the person of the sovereign itself so that the author becomes subordinated to the "actor."

As with the more general issue of reading, the notion of authorship and authority has a particularly self-reflexive quality here. To speak of "authors" in a book that we are reading implicitly raises the question of *Leviathan*'s author and the authority he commands over us, his readers. Calling the reader "authors" and connecting this to the question of political authority creates an analogy that links text, author, and readers to nation, sovereign, and people. This linkage complicates rather than resolves the question of authority, whether of the textual or national sort. If people are "authors" of the sovereign's power, is Hobbes too just the "actor" in this text and not the author of *Leviathan* after all? Or are the readers themselves now also "authors" of this text? By calling people authors, is Hobbes exposing the rhetorical sources of his own authority and thereby the authority of the sovereign as well?

As we have seen with Strong's analysis, the question of just who is author is an important one for *Leviathan*. Strong too suggests that *Leviathan* is structured by an analogy between text and nation. In Strong's terms, it seems that calling people authors is once more a ruse since they have no real power, no real authority either in the text or nation. In a sense, Hobbes merges with the sovereign, becoming "sovereign of the text" (this quite literally insofar as he claims that to "Read . . . Man-kind" the sovereign simply needs to read *Leviathan* itself), leaving the reader bereft of the very authorship that Hobbes has seemingly bestowed upon them.

Hobbes's distinction between authors and actors initially suggests, as Prokhovnik has argued, that Hobbes can maintain the covenants and consent of the members of the commonwealth (wherein people remain "authors," the basis of authority) while still keeping all real power in the hands of the sovereign (the "actor" who acts on behalf of those who "author" its behavior).[58] This discussion of people as "authors" seems intended to produce the appearance of democratic involvement while it in fact delivers the opposite. Indeed, the sentence that follows the passage about authorship strongly suggests this is what Hobbes is up to: "From hence it followeth, that when the Actor maketh a Covenant by Authority, he bindeth thereby the Author, no lesse than if he had made it himselfe; and no lesse subjecteth him to all the consequences of the same."[59] This conveys a "passive" vision of authorship (and hence, of the authority that it produces,) just as we have a seemingly passive understanding of reading; it seems that in both cases, the sovereign trumps us. By implication, if we are also "authors" of *Leviathan*, the authority we receive from this title is bogus since Hobbes himself continues to determine the "meaning" of his own book. Once again, Hobbes seems to offer a "power" to the reader (whether as "readers" or as "authors") only to retract it.

Nevertheless, as I have already argued in the case of reading in general, we can see that for Hobbes such promotions of sovereign authority, while paid a great deal of lip service, are potentially subverted and challenged: the authority he appears to "give over to the sovereign" is undermined by the very same gesture. In bringing to our attention the fact that the word *author* is at the root of authority, Hobbes may be rhetorically suggesting that the sovereign merely executes or enacts an authority that doesn't belong to it; if there is a trick involved here, it may well be at the sovereign's expense. When we read *Leviathan* with an eye toward its rhetorical effects (Skinner's "dimension of linguistic action") it's clear that even if it were Hobbes's intention to mislead his readers, the rhetorical effect of such pronouncements may turn against his "intentions."

Calling people authors allows for a potentially subversive interpretation that cannot be read out of *Leviathan*. If we can catch Hobbes in the act of producing sovereign authority out of thin air (as Kahn so compellingly demonstrates), or see him giving the sovereign carte blanche authority that (by his own rhetorical construction of calling the reader/subjects "authors") doesn't belong to it, then the source of authority itself comes into question. Accordingly, we might read the question of *"By what Authority* [Scripture is] *made Law"* as open-ended rather than a settled statement about whose authority is actually operative in this text.[60]

Even in the paragraphs that follow his extrapolation of authority early on in chapter 16, Hobbes gives some teeth to the claim that being an author is not an empty or meaningless category. For example, Hobbes tells us that without the author's "Counter-assurance," no covenant made with the actor is valid by the actor's mere word alone; the author has some role to play, even if it is a limited one.[61] Hobbes even considers a situation in which an actor *is* the author, self-authoring her or his own deeds:

> But if he that so Covenanteth, knew before hand he was to expect no other assurance, than the Actors word; then is the Covenant valid; because the Actor in this case maketh himselfe the Author. And therefore, as when the Authority is evident, the Covenant obligeth the Author, not the Actor; so when the Authority is feigned, it obligeth the Actor onely; there being no Author but himselfe.[62]

Although this is presented as a kind of rare event or exception, the idea that the actor can be self-authoring suggests a crucial point: authors may give power over to sovereigns, but they also might not. As with the notion of reading, for Hobbes the power of the author is not something we necessarily give over once and for all but instead remains something of our own, something we wield whether we realize it or not. People's authorship and authority remain question marks, a possibility that the sovereignty of the text cannot quite erase.

MOSES'S AUTHORITY AND THE "SINAITIC EVENTS"

If Hobbes's understanding of reading and authority is more complicated than what first meets the eye, if authorship and the authority it produces do not permanently transfer the right to act on one's own behalf, then what kind of authority are we left with? In looking at Hobbes's radical nominalism and skepticism (a question I will be revisiting in the next chapter), many scholars have concluded that for Hobbes the only alternative to sovereign authority is chaos. If Hobbes is really reinterpreting or subverting authority in the way I have been suggesting, does this not invite precisely the sort of epistemological and political indeterminacy that the entirety of *Leviathan* seems determined to avoid?

As I will argue further, the idea that we are limited to a choice between sovereignty and chaos is one of the prime conceits of much of contemporary liberalism. One of the main points I would like to establish in my reading of Hobbes is that the subversion of sovereignty does not lead to such chaos. I will be arguing that the theories of reading and interpretation that Hobbes supplies for us bring with them a kind of authority that is meaningful even as it partakes of a radical decentralization of authority itself.

Hobbes makes this argument not only through his theory of reading but just as crucially through his consideration of a religious, largely Christian eschatology. As stated earlier, although most scholars of Hobbes focus almost exclusively on the genealogy of sovereignty that he describes in parts 1 and 2 of *Leviathan*, it is important to recognize that Hobbes offers us a second genealogy as well. Whereas the first genealogy is familiar to most of us, that of a sovereign who emerges out of the chaos of the state of nature, the second genealogy is less often considered. This other genealogy of sovereignty, considered mainly in part 3, begins with what for Hobbes is the paradigmatic moment of authority and authorship, set up by the relationship between

Moses and the Israelites subsequent to the events on Mount Sinai. The remainder of this chapter will consider this other genealogy. My claim is that the authority that it produces is far more conducive to the "Scope" and "Designe" of *Leviathan* than the story that is usually considered; it is more in keeping with the radical epistemology and theories of reading that Hobbes subversively espouses throughout the book (including the first half).

Essentially, there are two models for sovereignty, and consequently two models of authority being demonstrated in *Leviathan*. "Terrestrial" or secular sovereignty, as we already know, is established by the social contract. Divine sovereignty is established by Moses in God's name. For Hobbes, Moses established the first "kingdom of God," making God the king of ancient Israel (the second kingdom will come after the second coming of Christ).

These two sorts of sovereignty have a completely different character in terms of the political authority that derives from them. For Hobbes, when God was/will be sovereign, the authority that is produced comes not from God (since God, even when king, is utterly unknowable) but rather from people. In this situation people are truly "authors" in a meaningful way. Rather than have one voice announce one meaning (and reading) for all of us, we have a source of authority that is itself radically decentered (without, however, collapsing into chaos and meaninglessness).

This alternative source of authority, as I will seek to show over the next few chapters, does not stop when God's sovereignty is supplanted by earthly kings (for Hobbes this moment coincides with the election of Saul as king of Israel). Instead this authority remains, saving us from having no choice but the arbitrary authority of secular sovereigns. Although Hobbes's depiction of secular sovereigns makes it seem like he is tricking us when he tells us that people are "authors," I will argue that his depiction of the messianic instantiation of authority that occurs in the time of Moses makes this claim potentially meaningful after all. Hobbes's eschatological history therefore bolsters and supports his rhetorical understandings. Taken together, as we will see further, Hobbes's religious and rhetorical considerations allow for more radical readings of *Leviathan*.

To better understand Hobbes's reading of Moses, I will draw on Aryeh Botwinick's *Skepticism, Belief, and the Modern: Maimonides to Nietzsche.*

While I do not share many of Botwinick's findings about Hobbes, he frames the notion of Moses's authority in a way that I think is very illuminating of the nature, powers, and limitation of authority for Hobbes as well.[63] By examining this moment in some detail, we might see how authority works for Hobbes, how it is produced, how it can be given or even withdrawn. Above all, we can find a sense of how for Hobbes authority can be meaningful even (or especially) when it exists outside the confines of earthly sovereigns.

Hobbes and "Negative Theology"

In his book Botwinick often compares Hobbes with Maimonides, and argues that both partake in what he calls "negative theology."[64] According to Botwinick, Hobbes shares Maimonides' belief that "holiness is not what God does to our consciousness in a moment of ecstatic embrace of him, but what we do to ourselves by way of acknowledging the unbridgeable distance that separates us from him" (p. 119).

For Botwinick, the political upshot of this "negative theology"—for Hobbes even more than Maimonides—is subservience, both to God and to the political community to which we belong. Thus negative theology becomes the basis of political authority. This stems from the nature of our submission to God: "Since God's idiom of 'speech' is his will—his mind or essence or attributes remaining totally rationally inaccessible to us—our only appropriate response is a corresponding act of will indicating and sustaining conformity to divine authority" (p. 132). In other words, since God's will must be our own (i.e., a political decision as to what God's will consists of), when we decide on what "God wills" we are also inherently deciding our own will and must therefore conform to that decision. In a complicated way, then, to think about God allows us to author our own decision (this is similar to what Flathman argues about the role of theology in Hobbes's political theory). The empty or unknowable name of "God" serves as a vehicle by which we can produce authority out of thin air. Thus what for Kahn amounts to a trick or rhetorical production, for Botwinick is more of a theological conviction on Hobbes's part—albeit one that is no less rhetorical in character.

Reading and Ratification

In Botwinick's view, for Hobbes politics was born when Moses decided to accept the word of God, or more accurately, the moment when Moses interpreted what he was hearing and receiving as indeed the word of God. Botwinick writes: "Thus, outside of the context of Moses's acquiescence in interpreting 'the created voice' as the voice of God, there would no revelation to speak of. In other words, on a primary religious level authority is grounded in consent" (p. 4). This consent goes beyond Moses's own personal decision to interpret for God (or to interpret his experience on Mount Sinai as being an experience of God). In a crucial statement, Botwinick writes that "Moses chose to read the Sinaitic events in a certain way, and his reading was ratified by the rest of the Jewish people" (p. 136). Through this act of reading, and in its ratification by the Jews (who "authorize" that interpretation), Moses gains his authority over (even as he produces) the nation of Israel.

In this version of the story, it is not God but the people of Israel who are the "authors" of Moses's authority. Although Moses is normally seen as merely a passive vehicle of God's own authority, because of Hobbes's devotion to negative theology Botwinick sees this moment as being an act of human agency, in this case enacted in the context of representing the (unknowable yet necessarily true) divine authority. Here we see the power of authority, not as a passive stance but as an active and basically human-centered phenomenon.

Botwinick's interpretation can be supported by any number of passages in *Leviathan* itself, especially in chapter 40. There Hobbes writes:

> But seeing Moses had no authority to govern the Israelites, as a successor to the right of Abraham, because he could not claim it by inheritance; it appeareth not yet, that the people were obliged to take him for Gods Lieutenant, longer than they beleeved that God spake unto him. And therefore his authority (notwithstanding the Covenant they made with God) depended yet merely upon the opinion they had of his Sanctity, and of the reality of his Conferences with God.[65]

For Hobbes, this belief or "opinion" that God has spoken to Moses is not itself the basis of law or the Jews' obligation, since "opinion com[es] to

change," as subsequent events clearly indicate (p. 324). Nor can this authority come directly from God, because as Hobbes notes, "God spake not to
them immediately, but by the mediation of Moses himself" (p. 324). Pointing to the human origins of Moses's authority, Hobbes writes: "[Moses's]
authority therefore, as the authority of all other Princes, must be grounded
on the Consent of the People, and their Promise to obey him" (p. 324). To
better demonstrate this, Hobbes cites the biblical passage (Exodus 20.18)
where Israelites say to Moses "*speak thou with us, and we will hear, but let
not God speak with us lest we die*" (p. 324). Hobbes writes, "Here was their
promise of obedience, and by this it was they obliged themselves to obey
whatsoever he should deliver unto them for the Commandment of God"
(3.40, pp. 324–25).

In other words, the Israelites don't simply agree with Moses's reading,
they actually designate him as the one who will interpret or read on their
behalf. In this way, people do indeed serve as the authors of Moses's power.
Their "ratification" constitutes a promise to accept (if not always believe)
subsequent readings by Moses.

Moses and Future Sovereigns

True to his tendency to undercut any subversive implications of his doctrine
by an act of formal textual obedience to the principle of (secular) sovereignty, Hobbes tries to establish that Moses's right to read "for" people who
author his authority extends beyond the life and office of Moses himself.
Directly following his consideration of Moses, Hobbes tells us that "no man
ought in the interpretation of the Scripture to proceed further than the
bounds which are set by their severall Soveraigns" (p. 326).

Hobbes seems to be arguing that just as Moses was the sole authorized
reader in his own lifetime, so too must we abstain from any interpretation
ourselves, leaving that job to our "severall Soveraigns" who follow in Moses's
wake. Once again it appears (and Botwinick himself certainly seems to read
him this way) that Hobbes's theory of reading and authority is a passive one
after all. Here too "reading" seems to mean having our own interpretations
be replaced by a sovereign intrusion. Once the people of Israel agreed to let

Moses "read" for them, future generations of humans have all, it seems, been bound by this decision as well.

But we can make such an argument only when we forget the unique, indeed messianic nature of Moses's reading in Hobbes's genealogy, as well as the unique nature of the people's authorship or ratification of that reading. This moment of reading is not like any other; it establishes the meaning and nature of reading and authority ever after, and as such is not so much a model as it is the envelope for future acts of reading. Future acts of reading thus cannot have the same significance as for Moses and the Jews because they are not foundational but rather occur within the context of this original interpretive moment.

Hobbes's claim that future sovereigns read for us in the same way that Moses read for the people of Israel seems strange, given that it is preceded by a lengthy digression on the unique nature of Moses himself. First of all, for Hobbes, although he calls Moses the "Civill" sovereign, Moses's sovereignty is clearly inferior and subject to God's. God is the king; Moses is merely God's "Lieutenant" (3.40, p. 324). His authority is a reflection of God's, which is in turn produced by the "authors," i.e., the Israelites themselves. Thus Moses is not actually a model for future sovereigns but holds a unique position (serving, as we will see, as one of God's three "persons" or representatives for Hobbes) (3.42, p. 339).

Furthermore, the nature of Moses's "reading" is unlike any future sovereign act of reading. For Hobbes, Moses is not only the sole interpreter of God for his time, but sets a standard of interpretation that is unmatched in subsequent history (with the possible exception of Jesus). Indeed, Hobbes tells us that the "Sinaitic events" serve as the model or even essence of what reading is and means, so that they literally come to serve as not a sign of but *the* sign for textual authority: "For the Scriptures since God now speaketh in them, are the Mount Sinai; the bounds whereof are the Laws of them that represent Gods Person on Earth" (3.40, p. 326).

By arguing that God "now speaketh in [Scripture]," Hobbes presumably means "now that Moses has performed his act of interpretation." Moses's reading of the events of Mount Sinai allows an unknowable notion such as the authority of God to become expressed and understandable so that indeed "God now speaketh in them." Here we have a rhetorical representation in the place of God's actual speaking (which people feared to hear). This "Mount Sinai" stands in the text in the same way that Mount Sinai itself stands in the face of the Jews huddled at its feet; it does not require interpretation but serves as the meaning of interpretation itself. It can suffer no further deconstruction—it is (has become) the very ground of meaning itself.

The "Spirit of Moses"

Botwinick also makes much of the notion that Moses's act of reading is unique (although, as we will soon see, he draws a different conclusion on the political relevance of this uniqueness). In an exemplary interpretation of this question, Botwinick claims that for Hobbes what Moses does is essentially foreclose the meaning and nature of revelation for all time, leaving that question essentially sealed, and ushering in instead a new question as to the nature of the political order that comes out of such meanings and revelations.[66] Botwinick claims that all further prophecies after Moses "are a function of the scheme of authority relations introduced by Moses rather than religious phenomena in their own right."[67]

Once again, we can find ample textual evidence for this claim in the pages of *Leviathan*. Hobbes describes how Moses allowed "*seventy . . . Elders of Israel*" to go up to Mount Sinai for themselves to witness the presence of God:

> Yet this was not till after Moses had been with God before, and had brought to the people the words which God had said to him. He onely went for the businesse of the people; the others, as the Nobles of his retinue, were admitted for honour to that speciall grace, which was not allowed to the people; which was . . . to see God and live . . . but did not carry any commandement from him to the people.[68]

Thus by the time the elders of Israel "see" God, the meaning and reading and authority of God has already been established by Moses himself. There is no subsequent commandment that ensues from nobles to people, as there is from Moses himself; there no establishing authority in this case because the Israelites have already ratified or authorized Moses's own reading (binding the seventy elders as much as anyone else). The readings of the elders can only be made within the context of that larger, prior reading; once the meaning of "reading" has been established, it only remains to engage in specific acts of reading.

Hobbes's version of this story supports Botwinick's claim that Moses does not perform *an* act of revelation, but *the* act. All who follow in his "spirit" are, by definition, in a different epistemological category from Moses himself. Hobbes tells us that the "Spirit of Moses"

> signifieth nothing but the Mind and Disposition to obey, and assist Moses in the administration of the Government. For if it were meant they had the substantiall Spirit of God; that is, Divine nature, inspired into them, then they had it in no lesse manner than Christ himself, in whom onely the spirit of God dwelt bodily. It is meant therefore of the Gift and Grace of God, that guided them to co-operate with Moses; from whom their Spirit was derived.[69]

Shortly afterward he calls this spirit only an "Inclination to Gods service."[70] For Hobbes, this spirit is explicitly *not* a religious visitation, not a kind of divine presence that is transmitted from one figure to another (wherein Moses's sanctity becomes the sanctity of all future kings), but is a sign of human agency, albeit an agency bound by the "Sinaitic events."

For Botwinick himself, though, this "spirit" extends from Moses's authority and connects it to subsequent sovereign authority; this first genealogy of sovereignty in effect authorizes the second. In other words, the religious grounds of authority we find in Hobbes's treatment of Moses becomes transformed into the secular grounds of authority we read about in parts 1 and 2 of *Leviathan*. Botwinick has some help here from Hobbes himself, who writes that "whosoever in a Christian Common-wealth holdeth the place of Moses, is the sole Messenger of God, and Interpreter of his Commandements."[71] Yet despite Hobbes's own overt claims, the logic of his depiction of Mosaic authority does not make this connection possible. On the contrary, I will claim that the authority of Moses serves as a ground to *defy* and subvert the authority of subsequent sovereigns.

We have already seen how Moses's act of reading is the basis for the possibility of other readings, but those future readings must of necessity be arbitrary, whereas his own reading is, by a unique and unrepeated (and unrepeatable) act of political decision and consent, not so. Thus the authority that derives from such later readings must by necessity have a different form of authority than that which stems from Moses himself.[72]

As we have also already seen, for Hobbes sovereign authority after Moses is self-producing (something that many of Hobbes's most astute readers, including Botwinick, Johnston, and Kahn, have noted). But therein lies the key difference between Moses's authority and that of subsequent sovereign rulers: Moses's authority is *not self-produced:* it miraculously, impossibly, and indeed messianically comes from God, or rather from Moses's own interpretation and from the Jews' ratification of that interpretation. Their belief that it really was God who gave Moses the Ten Commandments—that the divine presence really was seen and really did speak—exceeds its own possibility of representation; it really, impossibly, and unrepeatably becomes "true," that is to say, a basis for whatever truth will be on earth. This moment of reading by Moses, however "humanly contrived," miraculously exceeds its human origins, becoming the envelope for all future human acts of interpretation.

Moses's act of reading and the authority produced in its wake are less self-producing than self-enclosing; this reading is an act that allows no escaping from its consequences. We are indeed eternally and absolutely bound by this moment; it is the basis of all subsequent authority. Yet future iterations of this act are lacking precisely this kind of self-enclosing authority; they are indeed arbitrary in a way that Moses's act was not, because Moses's reading sets the meaning of what meaning is and thereby transcends its own possibility of being arbitrary. As we will see, Moses's authority and the "kingdom of God" that it ushers in are the only "nonarbitrary" authority the earth will see until the future kingdom of Christ on earth. By contrast, future terrestrial sovereign authorities are exposed as tautological in the sense that they are self-declared, not introducing something new into the world, not changing time and meaning, but simply asserting themselves without any foundational substance.

Although Moses's power to read for the Israelites resembles the power that Hobbes confers on subsequent sovereignty, we can see that this resemblance is misleading (hence, it is crucial to recall that Moses himself is not a full-fledged sovereign in his own right). As I read Hobbes here, he is saying that Moses establishes the possibility of reading and interpretation but at the same time forecloses the possibility of any correct, definitive, or absolutely authoritative reading for the future insofar as there is only one constitutive act of reading (Moses's own). Authorizing Moses to read on their behalf, the Jews are in effect authorizing themselves (as well as their future generations) and, by the same token, de-authorizing—at least potentially—future sovereign readings and pronouncements.

What bound the Israelites together during the Sinaitic events was not so much what actually happened (since we can never really know) but what they decided had happened. Since it was ratified by the Israelites as a proper instance of God's speech, we no longer have the power to judge the form of speech itself, only its content. Although Moses's own authority is absolute and unimpeachable, a "Mount Sinai" that simply stands for what authority is and means forever after, future iterations of authority are not so irrevocable; the authority that is produced in future moments remains a matter not of form but of content and is thus subject to the very sorts of struggles over interpretation and meaning that a Hobbesian scheme of authority initially seems intended to disallow.

Politically speaking, the upshot of the story of Moses in Hobbes's rendition is subversive when we compare it to the other genealogy of sovereign authority that we are more used to considering in *Leviathan*. Insofar as we moderns do not live in Moses's own time(i.e., we do not live in a "kingdom of God") our sources of political authority have become far more dispersed. The direct authority Moses enjoyed serves as a contrast to the types of power and authority that we find in our own age, undermining Hobbes's own assertions about the nature and extent of contemporary sovereign power. In our own time the "Spirit of Moses" serves, I would argue, not to bolster kings but to deny them the totalizing power to speak "the truth." It serves to ensure that, epistemologically speaking, no amount of false sovereign authority can supplant the possibility of meaning and authority established by the "Sinaitic events" themselves. In this way, we do not have to fear that chaos will certainly ensue if we abandon sovereignty; we are held together not by sovereign fiat but by the "Spirit of Moses" itself.

"The Leviathan State"

Botwinick draws a different conclusion. He accepts Hobbes's connection between the two genealogies of sovereignty, and so the political gist of Moses's "revelation" in Hobbes's system is what he calls the "Leviathan state," itself the basis of contemporary liberalism: "The Leviathan state projected by Hobbes as harboring the prospect of lasting forever embodies a vision of endless deferral: it displaces truth, ultimate value, and sovereignty from the monotheistic God to man to successive generations of men."[73] For Botwinick, the value of liberalism is that nothing is final or ever settled. The only "braking mechanisms" on liberalism's radical openness, he tells us, are the processes and rights that determine and organize liberalism in the first place, those things that "allow existing democratic outcomes to be reconsidered and revised."[74] In other words the very dynamism of liberalism, its nature as a supposedly democratic system, comes from its agnosticism and negative theological roots, from the fact that things are never fixed and can be endlessly refigured. This, Botwinick claims, is the result precisely of the particular, unsettled, and unsettling nature of authority as it issues from the Sinaitic events themselves, as conveyed to us by Hobbes, among others.

In my own view, however, to see modern liberalism as stemming from Hobbes's political theory is to neglect Botwinick's own crucial insight of reading Moses as a metafigurative prophet. Although Botwinick seems to suggest that a liberal political order is required for the ongoing practice of such openness, as I see it (in part from my reading of Botwinick himself) such openness comes despite rather than because of liberalism. The radical openness that Botwinick appreciates is indeed a result of Moses's instantiation of meaning, but liberalism as a practice shares no part in this. Subsequent sovereign powers, including liberal ones, serve as mere iterations of meaning rather than the grounds—however contested—of meaning itself.

Liberalism, when contrasted to the kind of authority produced during the time of Moses, is hardly as circular or open as initially appears. For Botwinick, the liberal state, despite its monopoly of force and authority, is determined by its lack of closure and hence preferable to other more authoritarian forms of political sovereignty. Yet it remains true that even the liberal state must, via this very monopoly, seek to do that which Moses alone could do. In other words, even a liberal state must take authority upon itself and speak, as it were, for God, even while denying (which seems a particular, and peculiar, feature of liberalism) that it has done so. As we will see later, Hobbes argues strenuously that our own time does not constitute a "kingdom of God." In his—or our—own time, regardless of how it is articulated, a sovereign state, be it liberal or absolutist, will and indeed must supplant the uniqueness of Moses's absolute authority with a bogus "right to read," that is, with a supposedly absolute authority of its own. If the liberal state chooses to disavow much of its power, it yet remains within it purview to define what is properly within its power and what isn't. This is a closure which appears to be something else, a political decision in the guise of not deciding, and hence does not partake of the radical possibilities of democratic political authority inherent in the "Sinaitic events" themselves (I will return to these arguments in the conclusion of this book).

The next two chapters will take up the notion of reading and authority in greater detail, examining the nature of representation itself as it pertains to the acts of reading and authorization, and particularly as it is illuminated by Hobbes's discussion of religious (and political) representation in parts 3 and 4 of *Leviathan*. We will see that in his actual practice of reading Scripture—and in particular in his reading of eschatological history—Hobbes reveals instructions and prescriptions for reading that might better inform our own reading of *Leviathan* itself.

3

A Skeptical Theology?

THE NEXT TWO chapters form a two-part exploration of Hobbes's theory of representation. Here, I will attempt to follow Hobbes as he reads Scripture, taking his model for reading the Bible as a model for reading in general. This chapter concerns itself with Hobbes's demonstrated preference for the blank or empty sign. Hobbes consistently reads Scripture in ways that deny any kind of literal or true meaning, emphasizing instead the rhetorical construction of those texts. In the next chapter, I will link this reading style to Hobbes's attacks on idolatry and what he calls "demonology," to argue that his understanding of representation has enormous political and religious connotations (some of which we have already begun to see). Taken together, these two chapters demarcate Hobbes's specific instructions for how to read a text—including *Leviathan* itself. Hobbes's treatment of signs, symbols, and language teaches us about the building blocks of reading and interpretation, which in turn form for him the bases of political authority. Once again, we are not going to take Hobbes's own authorial word for what the "Scope" and "Designe" of *Leviathan* might be but rather we will set out to discover those things for ourselves , using his reading as a model for ours.

In the pages that follow, I will attempt to pinpoint Hobbes's understanding of language and meaning in part by comparing and contrasting him to Puritan radicals and reformers of his day and earlier. These groups shared Hobbes's interest in the exposition of signs as being empty (in order to combat idolatry), but whereas they saw this exposition as an opportunity for divine immanence to be made manifest, for Hobbes it merely serves as a moment of representation (a view more in keeping with Benjamin's approach). Likewise, I will seek to defend Hobbes against the attacks of

Hannah Arendt, who argues that he epitomizes the modern conceit that
nothing has meaning unless we make that meaning ourselves. The eschatological history that Hobbes offers us in parts 3 and 4 of *Leviathan* reveals
that he is not arguing for purely arbitrary human-derived meanings any
more than he is arguing for meaning that is present or immanent in language. By positioning Hobbes between these various claims by the Puritans
and Arendt, we can see that what Hobbes offers is a theory of meaning
and interpretation that is neither wholly arbitrary nor wholly determined
by externalities such as the divine. While the content of meaning is up to
our own choosing, rhetoric itself (as produced from Hobbes's eschatological history) constructs and structures meaning in ways that give it consistency and persuasiveness; becoming more aware of the rhetorical structure
of language (as Hobbes sets out to do) frees us from the phantasms of total
submission to one authorizing voice (the conceit of sovereignty) and of the
total right of each of us to mean and say whatever we like, at our whim.

For Hobbes, the realization of a sign's rhetorical nature is crucial. When
we fail to note this and instead imagine that the sign has a value or content
of its own (i.e., as symbol), we easily fall under the sway of those who make
claims as to what those values or contents are. When, on the other hand,
we learn to read in a fashion that is explicitly aware of the rhetorical and
representational nature of language (i.e., as allegory), we become able to
participate in, rather than simply suffer from, the use of signs in the world.
In this way, Hobbes's theory of representation provides an inherently democratic method of interpretation.

HOBBESIAN NEGATIVITY

To explore these questions, we must delve further into the concept, introduced in the last chapter, of Hobbes's "negative theology." This concept,
along with the related notions of nominalism and skepticism, collectively
describes an attitude toward language, truth, and God on Hobbes's part.
These three terms suggest Hobbes's refusal to concede that anything can
be known as itself, along with the related notion that all so-called "reality"
must be filtered by signs that are, by their nature, imperfect and incapable

THE BLANK

It is this notion of the pure sign, or blank, an image of imagelessness much beloved by Protestant (especially Puritan) theologians of his day, that Hobbes brings to bear upon matters of politics and representation. To understand this concept better, let us review the ways that Puritan and more mainstream Anglican theologians from the mid sixteenth to the mid seventeenth century thought about God, representation, and the meaning of an "empty" sign.

To get a clear sense of the animus against images that continued to be manifest in Hobbes's time, it is helpful to focus on a period slightly predating (but also overlapping with) Hobbes's own birth and early years. Anti-imagism was a strong feature of English religious life from the earliest moments of the Reformation (and even before that).[18] Margaret Aston tells us that the anti-imagist forces in England during the Reformation divided between iconomachs, who were merely hostile to images (but tolerated their presence to some, limited extent) and iconoclasts, who wished to destroy them wherever they saw them.[19] Patrick Collinson speaks of "iconophobia," wherein opposition to imagery was such that essentially all images, even secular ones, were forbidden.[20]

The question of which images, if any, were licit was one of the most vexing problems of the sixteenth and seventeenth centuries, both for religious and political leaders. Peter Goodrich sees the use of the blank as one Protestant Reformer solution to the problem of the image. To make his argument, Goodrich looks at the painting *Edward VI and the Pope; or, An Allegory of the Reformation* (c. 1568–1571) as an early example of artwork in which blank pages were featured prominently amid other elements. In that painting, the pope is shown bent over below the figure of Edward VI as the latter sits beside his dying father, Henry VIII. While the painting is filled with visual images and with words—including having"all fleshe is grasse" written across the pope's chest—Goodrich points out that there are five blank frames set amid the context of this picture. For Goodrich, the blank squares are themselves more telling than any of the words or images actually expressed. While the painting is a self-announced "allegory" against idolatry and papistry, the blank images not only deliver this message but complicate the meaning of the painting itself.

For Goodrich, the blank "figures" in the painting perform several simultaneous functions, challenging the traditional usage and interpretation of images. Since the blanks are themselves "figures" in that they are set alongside other images (which are figures in the more conventional sense), their very blankness points to the ephemera of figurativeness. That is, they serve to call into question and undermine the "meaning" of a figure qua figure; they question the very status of the image, its nature and its interpretability.

Furthermore, revealing a Protestant attention to the second commandment against graven images (a question that I will return to in the next chapter), the blank image represents for Goodrich a transformation "from image to imageless writing."[21] The blank is thus an image of imagelessness produced as an implied overwriting of other (presumably Catholic) images.[22] The blank is thus an overwriting and a purifying of a visual text—dramatizing in this "purification" the very arrival and power of what it represents (in Goodrich's argument, law). The blank represents in effect an erasure and at the same time a turn toward that which cannot be represented at all but must be simply asserted.

This understanding of blankness does not of course exclude its possibility of being read. As already stated, the blank is clearly also an image of sorts; it is not "nothing," but is rather an image (or "iconography") of nothing, which is something quite different. Goodrich writes, "What marks the difference between blank tablet or bare wood and the image, what distinguishes the iconic from the mundane, is precisely the status or legality of the image" (p. 104). The blank in this and other paintings still employs the language and legally established context of imagery, but in so doing it becomes in a sense metafigural, too: it becomes a commentary on image and what image can and cannot do or represent.

Accordingly, it might seem that we are witnessing a kind of deception. The very way in which this image of imagelessness announces that it (unlike prior, Roman or Roman Catholic images) has "solved" the problem of imagery, according to the strictures of the second commandment, suggests the Protestant Reformers had a cleverer means than the Catholics of rhetorically depicting their own sanctity, while in fact actually engaging with

much the same material (i.e., imagery) as their religious adversaries. By determining what is image and what is not (i.e., blankness), one finds that
only Catholics and their Anglican sympathizers use "images" and somehow
the Reformers do not. Here, the Reformers seem to be practicing a form of
rhetorical deception often ascribed to Hobbes himself.

But to see this as pure deception is to overlook some of the ways in
which the blank was understood by Protestant Reformers. Goodrich tells
us that "the blank space is neither innocent nor indifferent," alluding to the
possibility that the use of blank can be a trick ("not innocent") but can also
be something else ("not indifferent") (p. 92). Goodrich calls this "nonfigura-
tive figure" a "negative sign of a future or external power that irrupts within
the frame of painting" (p. 91). This external power may be the power of the
law (as is clearly figured in Goodrich's readings of these paintings), but as
many Reformers hoped, it might also allow for a (nonidolatrous) expression
of God. As such, the blank promises new possibilities of representation altogether. As Goodrich puts it,

> For the Reformers the blank panel represented the possibility, the threat as
> well as the potential, of an image that had as yet no significance in itself: the
> blank panel was *tabula nuda*, free of any phantasm that might confuse the eye
> of the soul by conflating sense and reference, sign and substance. (p. 106)

This is the wish for pure, perfect representation, even as the materials it enlists (images, figures) are redolent of idolatry itself. This contradiction is at
the heart of an ongoing anxiety and struggle in sixteenth- and seventeenth-
century England; representation was both a threat and a promise.

The Blankness of the Text

As a result of this ambivalence about imagery, much of the aesthetic of
Protestant Reformers was oriented toward a kind of ladder of representation, ranking means of representation that are decreasingly idolatrous in
form. For example, the oral was preferred over the visual.[23] Within the visual realm itself, Margaret Aston tells us that during this period "sculpture
was generally regarded as more harmful [i.e., more idolatrous] than painting; stained-glass windows came at the bottom of the danger scale."[24]

Another preference among Protestant Reformers was for text over pictorial imagery. Like the pictorial image of blankness we have already considered, the text offers another form of "blankness." In a sense, text becomes imagery once removed, hence a more permissible form of representation. Goodrich points out,

> The emphasis upon the scriptures was thus secondary to a conception of an oratorical word. . . . Writing was in this respect artificial memory, a visual image—though a permitted one—of a precedent sound or speech. The dual nature of all signs was thus transmitted from the visual to the verbal, from the imagistic to the rhetorical and graphic, but the structure of seeing and reading were analogous.[25]

We thus return to the question of reading, which becomes a way of "seeing" the unrepresentable presence of God. The text in its apparent imagelessness allows a safer, more licit "seeing" of God than any interfering visual images would.

Looking at reading in relation to the rise of printed texts, Goodrich may shed some light on the importance of Hobbes's call to "*Read thy self*," since a basis is suggested for Hobbes's use of reading as a metaphor for politics. For Goodrich, with the notion that the text is "less idolatrous" than the image, the "image [becomes] an aspect of, and internal to, the text."[26] Furthermore, Goodrich argues, "Where in civil law previously the image took the place of knowing how to read, the text now took the place of knowing how to see."[27] During this period then, reading becomes a metaphor for organizing and "seeing" the world, as a result of the advent of printing and a growing, Protestant, appreciation for the "imageless imagery" of text. Once seeing becomes reinterpreted as reading, it is not such a stretch for Hobbes to turn reading into a model for politics itself—the way we "see" and respond to the world around us.

As in our discussion of blank images, the notion of the text as imageless comes, not from some intrinsic quality of the text itself, but from the historical struggles over imagery and heresy that took place during the English Reformation. Aston tells us that from the time of Elizabeth I, passages from Scripture, in particular the Ten Commandments and more particularly still the second commandment, were used to adorn churches in lieu of "idolatrous" imagery, replacing icons that had been removed or destroyed.[28] This took place in a very deliberate (and politically charged) way.[29] For example, Aston cites this church instruction: "See that you set up the table of the commandments in the place where the Sacrament did hang."[30] Often banners announced that they were replacing former idolatrous images in a church. This essentially rhetorical gesture tells the congregation that the text/Scripture they see before them is in fact a sign of the removal of idolatry; thus it does not merely allow us to view the second commandment, it performs it.

During the first decade or so of Elizabeth's reign, this was more a matter of state policy than the product of a genuine popular movement. Eamon Duffy tells us that even at this stage in the Reformation, such acts were "not in most cases the result of a landslide of Protestant fervour, but of weary obedience to unpopular measures."[31] By the 1570s, however, a new generation that had grown up in an atmosphere of state-sponsored iconoclasm came to embrace it more sincerely.[32] A widespread (but of course not unanimous) enthusiasm for iconoclasm was to persist well into Hobbes's own lifetime.

Interestingly, not all replacements of icons were purely textual. During Elizabeth's reign, as well as after, royal emblems of power were often displayed along with text from Scripture. The "rood lofts" of churches—elevated areas containing often very elaborate displays of Christ on the cross—were often covered with canvas painted over with royal coats of arms (or the Ten Commandments, or both).[33] John Phillips argues that "the destruction of the sacred image of Christ and his saints was paralleled by the curious rise of the 'sacred' image of Elizabeth the Queen."[34] Parishioners long used to worshipping images of Christ and Mary now could pay homage to the "Virgin Queen" instead. In this way the state both sought to codify and benefit from the anti-imagism of Protestant Reformism, an attitude that would break down dramatically during the reign of the Stuart kings.

As a result of these movements, both political and religious, text is transformed from being merely another form of image to being an image of imagelessness, not unlike the blank panels in *Edward VI and the Pope*.[35] Deemed nonimage, text rhetorically achieves the status of being "blank," a conduit to the unrepresentable itself.[36] As imagery moves from "figure to word," the text becomes the site of blankness, and so paradoxically the chance of "seeing" (that is to say, reading) God is enhanced. For the Reformers, "reading" becomes a privileged activity exactly because it contains less risk of idolatry, and offers more possibility of loving the "truth" itself and not the images and signs that convey it.

HOBBES AND THE SIGN

As we turn from a consideration of more radical Protestant Reformer conceptions of representation to focus on Hobbes himself (and his own time), there are some important differences to note. In his own position on images and their uses, Hobbes is both less and more radical than the iconoclasts and iconomachs of his own and earlier times. As a "nominal" Anglican (quite literally in his case), Hobbes tends to be much less aggressively anti-image. Though Hobbes offered many positions that were out of line with Anglican orthodoxy, he did tend to follow the mainstream Anglican line of his day on imagery, such as it was. In fact, the Anglicans were never of one mind on the issue: Anglicanism included considerable suspicion of imagery and a great deal of internal debate over the proper use of images so as to distinguish it both from increasingly radical Puritanism and from Catholicism. But for Anglicans in general, images and figures were deemed acceptable so long as they were not treated as idols, a vague accommodation that gave them no end of trouble. Hobbes himself is hardly a shirker at using imagery, as the cover of *Leviathan*, with its quasi-religious, quasi-political looming figure attests. Such use of figures distinguishes him from most Puritans of his day.

And yet, Hobbes's defense of Anglican orthodoxy disguises or at least allows for a far more radical position than those of the Reformers or more radical Puritans who followed. This position amounts to a rejection of the notion of blankness as a sign of something real, of the discernible presence of God in the page that the Protestant Reformers seem to argue (or hope) for. Instead, for Hobbes the blank is a purely human (and rhetorical) contrivance, a self-reflexive representative construction that shows us only our desire to represent God rather than the actuality of God (commensurate with his "negative theology" and radical nominalism). For Hobbes, then, as we have already seen, "God" exists only as a series of signs or attributes that we have chosen for ourselves; whatever this concept of "God" can tell us about the true God can only be indicated by the failure of representation itself. Hobbes's stance here is more radical than the various iconoclastic stances (at least in terms of its political implications, as I will explain at length in chapter 6), for it does not depend on any external truth. Rather than claim that the blank or text serves as a conduit to the true God (producing a vacuum of authority that can be surreptitiously filled by some earthly claimant), Hobbes's stance gives the power of representation entirely to people that wield it, allowing them to read God as they see fit (within, of course, the confines determined by the "Sinaitic events").

Professing Inconstancy

Hobbes's skepticism, nominalism, and negative theology together amount to a preference for a certain style of reading. This style is marked, as we have already seen, by a penchant for negativity, a tendency to revel in the exposure of things not being what they appear. Again, Hobbes does not believe that words themselves hold some intrinsic meaning. He offers, "One man calleth *Wisdome,* what another calleth *feare*; and one *cruelty*, what another *justice.* . . . And therefore such names can never be true grounds of any ratiocination."[37] But the solution to this miasma of meaning, it appears, is not to be found in an appeal to the truth (since it cannot be known), but rather in a turn to rhetoric itself. He follows this passage by arguing, "No more can Metaphors, and Tropes of speech [be the true grounds of ratiocination, either]: but these are less dangerous, because they profess their inconstancy; which the other do not."[38]

Of course, Hobbes continues typically to display great ambivalence about rhetoric and its uses. Just a few chapters later, he claims that when it comes to "all rigorous search[es] of Truth . . . Metaphors . . . are in this case utterly excluded. For seeing they openly professe deceit; to admit them into Councell, or Reasoning, were manifest folly."[39] The similarity of language between "profess[ing] inconstancy" and "profess[ing] deceit" is marked. But, this is not necessarily a contradiction on Hobbes's part, since metaphors and other rhetorical tropes do in fact profess both "inconstancy" and/or "deceipt," depending on how they relate to the overall rhetorical structure of a text.

The notion that for Hobbes, metaphors "profess their inconstancy" may seem at best a backhanded compliment, but it suggests the very penchant for negativity that Hobbes so deeply appreciates elsewhere. In that passage he tells us that the use of "Metaphors and Tropes of speech" is "less dangerous"; unlike "bare Words," these elements of the "Designe" of a text are more easily exposed as purely rhetorical, whereas words that are not explicitly and evidently rhetorical (i.e., words that are neither metaphors nor other easily recognizable tropes or figures) appear to be truthful by their very nature. Although potentially "deceipt[ful]," metaphors always retain the possibility of being exposed for what they are, alerting us to the very rhetorical or negative dimension of language that for Hobbes can be said to constitute the essence of reading and authority.

Hobbes's most subversive uses of rhetoric (taken more in Skinner's sense of rhetoric) are those associated with figures of omission, marking absence and absent meanings: those figures and "Tropes of speech" that most specifically and especially "profess their inconstancy." An example is when Hobbes deliberately mistranslates *Nosce teipsum* as "*Read thy self*," using what might be called the figure of mistranslation. Other figures we have seen him possibly employ include *epitrope*, when Hobbes makes one of his suspect "submissions" to sovereign authority. Figures that we have yet to encounter include *anacoluthon*, where the grammar or structure of a sentence or textual construction leads one to expect something that is not there. (An example of this will be examined later in this book wherein Hobbes offers us three "Persons of God" [the Father, the Son, and the Church and Apostles, the last of which corresponds to the figure of the Holy Spirit], but only offers a parallel kingdom for the Father and the Son., leaving the question of the "kingdom of the Holy Spirit" unanswered.) Finally, although this is hardly an exhaustive list, Hobbes makes extensive use of *paralipsis*, the act of drawing attention to something in the guise of ignoring it (which is also a form of irony). We have already possibly seen Hobbes employ *paralipsis* in the not entirely straightforward treatment of his own authority and authorship.

All of these figures tend to partake of irony, of appearing to mean something they do not. In its rhetorical sense, irony plays with literal and figurative meanings in a way that deliberately engenders ambiguity and even con-fusion. But irony also plays into the kind of metatextual rhetoric that Paul de Man describes.[40] As such, irony does not simply suggest a "secret mean-ing" that is being merely occluded or hinted at, but also calls into question how meaning itself is produced. The power of irony indeed comes from its own "profess[ion of] inconstancy."

In general, if we move from a strict Skinner-style accounting of Hobbes's rhetoric to a larger consideration of his use of representation, whether of a rhetorical or religious (or, as I will try to show, political) sort, Hobbes's ten-dency is to question the content of a thing by focusing on and revealing its representational form. This practice of negative theology (or just plain negativism) extends not only to discussions of God and religion but to all matters of human life and language. It is the key, I believe, to reading *Levia-than* according to Hobbes's own prescripts and instructions.

While Hobbes appreciates the blankness of text, he, unlike the Prot-estant Reformers discussed earlier, doesn't try to assert that it becomes full (even potentially) with what it cannot express. Hobbes guards the blankness of the text, exposes it as such, in order to guard against the ten-dency to fill words with meaning. In this way he preserves God's mystery as aporia, focusing instead on human strivings for representation, on the inconstancy of language. Here we see him (in Benjaminian terms) at his most purely allegorical, asserting the ruin of language rather than its pose as truth. This becomes even clearer when we look at how Hobbes actually reads a text.

READING WITH HOBBES

To see how this allegorical or negative style works in practice for Hobbes, in other words, how he reads, it is easiest to focus on the second half of the book, where Hobbes makes most of his religious arguments and where most of his instructions for reading are to be found. Given that for Hobbes God in particular is marked as unknowable (and hence any clear referent or object is absent), the markers that we use for God and religious questions are particularly evident qua signs, and are thus most useful to illuminate Hobbes's practice of reading. In the rest of this chapter and the following one we will turn to that practice of reading and its political, religious, and interpretive connotations.

To begin this analysis of Hobbes's reading of Scripture, let's focus on a few terms he considers that are commonly associated with God, namely the *Word* and *Spirit* of God. For Hobbes, the misreading of such terms was directly responsible for what he saw as dangerous phenomena in his own time, such as Enthusiasm. Rhetorically speaking, terms like the *Word* and *Spirit* of God can be seen as hypostatizations, figures wherein a real existence is attributed to some concept by turning it into a noun. *Justice* and *Being* are hypostatizations insofar as they assert the reality of these concepts by virtue of their very nominal quality. For Hobbes to speak of God at all is to hypostatize: the very name *God* must be a rhetorical performance insofar as it is an attempt at representation that must produce its own object. In this way, the inference of God's reality (i.e., that God *is*) is, as we have already seen, given, or delivered by the name itself (this is how we "know" that God is).

"The Word of God"

As he does in his reading in general, Hobbes seeks to radically narrow the connotations of the term "Word of God." He tells us that the *Word* as a noun means only those "actual" words that God has spoken (as depicted in Scripture). This stands in contrast to the notion of the Word as a kind of separate entity from God—a hypostatization that begins to take on a life of its own (a "separated essence").[41]

Even in this more limited sense, for Hobbes it becomes very difficult to conceptualize God's *Word* in the absence of a clear sense of God as speaker. What does it mean to claim that God has spoken words when, as we have already seen, we cannot even presume that God has a voice or a mouth to speak with? For Hobbes, we must understand the concept of the Word of God as having meaning only to the extent it is revealed to be purely metaphorical in nature. Hobbes writes that the Word of God could be considered to mean on the one hand "the words that God hath spoken" and on the other the "Doctrine of Religion" (i.e., a metaphor for what has been attributed to God by the church).[42] He concludes:

Considering these two significations of the WORD OF GOD, as it is taken in Scripture, it is manifest in this later sense (where it is taken for the Doctrine of the Christian Religion,) that the whole Scripture is the Word of God: but in the former sense [i.e., the actual "words that God hath spoken"] not so.[43]

While Hobbes distinguishes between God speaking *"Properly"* and *"Metaphorically"* as depicted in Scripture, he acknowledges that all of God's speech in the Bible is of necessity representative. When we are reading the Bible, even when God is depicted as actually speaking we have no direct experience or knowledge of that speech.[44] In this case, even God's "proper" words have to be read as metaphors.

When God says to Moses *"I am the Lord thy God,"* and although in the Bible it is written that *"God spake these words and said,"* still Hobbes tells us it "is to be understood for the Words of him that wrote the holy History."[45] In other words it is not God who actually speaks in this text, but rather the author of the book of Moses (which Hobbes points out is not even Moses himself) imagining what God said.[46]

Even when God is depicted as "speaking" to prophets, Hobbes similarly argues that we cannot interpret this is an act of speech in the ordinary sense of the term:

> And hereupon a question may be asked, in what manner God speaketh to such a Prophet. Can it (may some say) be properly said, that God hath voice and language, when it cannot be properly said, he hath a tongue, or other organs, as a man? The Prophet David argueth thus, *Shall he that made the eye, not see? or he that made the ear, not hear?* But this may be spoken, not (as usually) to signifie Gods nature, but to signifie our intention to honor him. For to *see,* and *hear,* are Honorable Attributes, and may be given to God, to declare (as far as our capacity can conceive) his Almighty power. (3.36, p. 292)

Here again Hobbes turns to the argument that we know nothing of God and that when speaking of God, we seek "to honor him." To speak of "seeing" and "hearing" God signifies that we have, as it were, rendered God into a sensible being. But Hobbes warns us that it is not the true "God" we are sensing, but only our own rhetorical performance (i.e., hypostatization) of

God's being. Hobbes is intent on exposing what seems to be a straightforward account of God's presence as being merely an instance of representation (in metaphor, by "profess[ing the] inconstancy" of Scriptural language).

Otherwise, Hobbes is highly dismissive of the descriptions of visions
and visitations (the actual "seeing and hearing" of God and God's "Word")
in Scripture. Thus, for example, in a passage often cited to show that Hobbes
is in fact an atheist or at least a great discounter of religious certainty, he
writes:

> Seeing then all Prophecy supposeth Vision, or Dream, (which two, when they
> be naturall, are the same,) or some especiall gift of God, so rarely observed in
> mankind . . . there is need of Reason and Judgment to discern between natu-
> rall, and supernaturall Gifts, and between naturall, and supernaturall Visions,
> or Dreams. (3.36, p. 297)

This applies even with Moses. Hobbes admonishes us that we must not
take literally the passage that says, "*The Lord spake to Moses face to face, as a
man speaketh to his friend*" (Exodus 33.11). To presume a literal interpretation would, among other blasphemies, presume that God actually has a face.
Hobbes tells us even this speech "was by mediation of an Angel, or Angels
. . . and was therefore a Vision, though a more cleer Vision than was given
to other Prophets" (p. 293)

The Effect of the Word

According to Hobbes, the "Word of God" could also refer to some "effect"
that God or the notion of God has had on human beings: the effect of the
rhetorical performance of naming God (p. 288). For example, Hobbes interprets Psalm 105.19—"where Joseph is said to have been kept in prison, *till*
[God's] *Word was come*"—as meaning "till that was to come to passe which
he had . . . foretold to Pharoahs Butler, concerning his being restored to his
office: for there by *his word was come,* is meant, the thing it self was come
to passe" (pp. 288–89). Likewise, in Ezekiel 12:28, Hobbes reads "*There shall
none of my Words be prolonged any more*" as meaning "by *words* are understood
those *things,* which God promised to his people" (p. 289). The word here is
read as an "effect" because the focus is on the way the word was read and

was made manifest in the political life of a particular community. To those who tend to read Hobbes as dismissive of the spiritual impact of Scripture, it is worth noting the extent to which he believes that Scripture depicts and effects real, political consequences; that is indeed the "rhetorical" valence Hobbes gives to Scripture in the first place.

Hobbes's nominalism is radical: what he says about the "Word of God" also pertains to human speech. After all, for Hobbes all notions of God are only instances of human speech, and so all speech, whether "human" or "divine," can only be understood by the effect that it has in the world, by how it is "read" and interpreted:

> The *Word of God,* or of *Man* . . . doth not signifie a part of Speech, such as Grammarians call a Nown, or a Verb . . . without a contexture with other words to make it significative; but a perfect Speech or Discourse, whereby the speaker *affirmeth, denieth, commandeth, promiseth, threatneth, wisheth or interrogateth*. In which sense it is not *Vocabulum*, that signifies a *Word*; but *Sermo* . . . that is, some *Speech, Discourse*, or *Saying*. (p. 287)

For Hobbes, we cannot take a word in its singularity out of context; rather, we must see it as a speech act, an insertion of the speaker into the community that receives her or his words. In this sense, we can think of words as actions or performances. While Hobbes does occasionally use the language of speech as performance, he probably does not mean this in precisely the same way that contemporary performativity theorists do; still, it is instructive that Hobbes focuses on what speech "does" rather than on what it is (or what it "means").[47]

In this way, even as Hobbes narrows the meaning of the term *the Word of God*—and, by extension, any other term—almost to nothing, he also focuses on the power and effect of those words. God may be a cipher and the Word of God may be utterly mysterious, but by it the world is made, or unmade.

The "Spirit of God"

In addition to God's "Word," Hobbes discusses another frequent hypostatization in Scripture: "the Spirit of God" (reminiscent of our earlier discussion of the "Spirit of Moses"). As with the "Word," Hobbes here too denies much of the metaphysical and theological meaning attached, and ridicules such usages as superstitious:

> [Of the] signification of *Spirit* I find no where any; and where none of these can satisfie the sense of that word in Scripture, the place falleth not under humane Understandings; and our Faith therein consisteth not in our Opinion, but in our Submission; as in all places where God is said to be a *Spirit;* or where by the *Spirit of God*, is meant God himselfe.[48]

Hobbes insists that the use of the term *Spirit* is mainly figurative when used in Scripture, because "for metaphoricall significations [of 'Spirit'] there be many."[49] And speaking of the related term "inspiration," he tells us, "That word therefore is used in the Scripture metaphorically onely."[50] Thus when interpreting various specific uses of the term "the Spirit of God" in the Bible, Hobbes writes: "*as long as the Spirit of God is in my nostrils* [Job 27:3], is no more then to say, *as long as I live.*"[51] And he interprets "*the Spirit entred into me, and set me on my feet* [Ezekiel 2.30]" as meaning "*I recovered my vitall strength.*"[52]

As with the "Word," Hobbes denies any singular, inherent meaning to "Spirit"; he attacks the belief in exorcism, possession, and ghosts as a debased reading of metaphor, as the error of separated essences. But once again, to deny a literal reading of spirits (in the sense of supernatural beings) does not imply that the word "Spirit" is truly empty or utterly pointless. Like the blank panels in *Edward VI and the Pope*, the exposition of a metaphor as "blank" or empty allows Hobbes to metafiguratively reread its meaning. To speak of God as a "Spirit" not only implies the "wind" or "strength" or "life" that a straightforward reading of spirit as metaphor might imply, but also allows for God's spirit to be represented in a way that resists its own idolatry, so long as it is understood as a "metaphor . . . onely."

It might be argued that in "reducing" spirit to a metaphor, in exposing the sign as figurative, Hobbes has turned a spiritual notion into a rather mundane one (where the term describes not divine things but ordinary ones). Revealing the terms *Spirit* and *Word* as hypostatizations seems to take away their religious function. Yet it could just as easily be the case that Hobbes has brought a consideration of spirit into our everyday lives. In figuring spirit as unknowable, spirit becomes more than something restricted to the Bible, it becomes something that we can understand and honor in all aspects of human existence. Recall how in *The Origin of German Tragic Drama*, Benjamin tells us that "considered in allegorical terms, then, the profane world is both elevated and devalued."[53] The same thing happens in Hobbes. The same gesture of "profess[ing] inconstancy" exposes ("devalues") but also sanctifies ("elevates") whatever is being considered, rendering a sign both less and more than we consider it to be.

Miracles

In terms of God's "signs" in the world more generally, Hobbes is consistent in his tendency to read everything rhetorically. This is clearly the case with miracles. Most Hobbes scholars claim that Hobbes does not believe in miracles, those moments of God's direct effect in and interference with the natural world. There is much in Hobbes's understanding of miracles that supports this view. For Hobbes, if we do not understand the cause of a thing, and it appears miraculous to us, then that, he tells us, makes it a "Miracle":

> The first Rainbow that was seen in the world, was a Miracle, because the first; and consequently strange; and served for a sign from God. . . . But at this day, because they are frequent, they are not Miracles, neither to them that know their naturall causes, nor to them who know them not.[54]

The language here does suggest that a miracle is nothing but a fallible perception. Yet such an interpretation misses the point of what miracles mean for Hobbes.[55] As we have seen, religion, and in particular the notion and representation of God, functions to limit or at least inform Hobbes's skepticism. A particular miracle may or may not occur in reality, but what matters for Hobbes is less the event of the miracle itself than the reading of that event as a miracle, a reading that, in its effects, binds us as mightily as any "real" miracle might have.

For Hobbes, the ability to do amazing things is not inherently miraculous and God does not have a monopoly on this power. Considering that all of the "miracles" that God produced in Egypt could have been (and often were) feigned by Egyptian "magicians," Hobbes writes:

For it is evident enough, that Words have no effect, but on those that understand them; and then they have no other, but to signifie the intentions, or
passions of them that speak. . . . Therefore when a Rod seemeth a Serpent, or
the Waters Bloud, or any other Miracle seemeth done by Enchantment; if it
not be to the edification of Gods people, not the Rod, nor the Water, nor any
other thing is enchanted.[56]

A miracle, then, is a form of communication; to be considered miraculous,
a phenomenon must be understood (or read) as such ("[they] have no effect
but on those that understand them"). Thus miracles are conveyed to us rhetorically, that is to say not (only) as a literal thing but (also) figuratively, as a
form of persuasion. Or perhaps more accurately, the miracle is itself rhetorical, and not as empty symbolism ("when a Rod seemeth a Serpent, or the
Waters Bloud") but as a representation of God's intention to speak to us.

In this way, Hobbes can be said to "believe" in miracles after all. Thus
when Hobbes tells us that "the first Rainbow . . . was a Miracle," he may
mean this sincerely. It *was* a miracle the first time a rainbow was seen; an
entire system of belief was born out of this vision. By reading events as miraculous, we pay homage to God and in the process organize ourselves as a
community.

Hobbes's focus on the reception of a miracle has important implications.
If we take the "burning bush," for example, what is miraculous is not so
much that a bush spontaneously bursts into flame, but that the burning
bush signifies something to a particular political community. In arguing as
he does, Hobbes has undertaken a rather miraculous transformation of his
own. If a rhetorical figure is seen merely as an "ornament," it is nothing
more than a means to deliver a point better. In this way of thinking, the
burning bush would be only a sign of God's power and the real power, the
real meaning or point of the thing, would lie in God's ability to make a bush
spontaneously burst into flame (i.e., power lies in tangible things, in bodies,
in fire). However, in my reading of Hobbes, the power lies not in the physical thing but in the rhetorical figure itself, in signs qua signs. Rhetoric, far
from being ornamental, here shapes and even rules the world.

To be sure, Hobbes credits the phenomenon itself; it's not as if bushes
spontaneously burst into flame all the time. In order to reveal the divine

presence to the Hebrews, God had to do something extraordinary (or had to be *said* to have done something extraordinary). In this way, future rainbows are not miracles, and bushes that do not burst into flames are also not miracles. But the extraordinariness only offers an opportunity for the event to be read as a miracle. And the very definition of extraordinariness itself entirely depends on the human community, the would-be "readers" of God's actions in the world (as the case of the first rainbow clearly demonstrates). As with the notion of the Word and Spirit of God, in Hobbes's treatment of miracles the inexpressible becomes expressed, becomes readable without resolving itself into some absolute truth. Taken as a sign, the miracle serves to produce the very power it supposedly only represents.[57]

Is Hobbes Religious?

We are now in a position to ask if all of this amounts to anything like religion on Hobbes's part, or whether "religion" and questions of "God" are rhetorical devices with political and social purposes only. Ultimately this becomes a question about the nature and degree of Hobbes's skepticism, nominalism, and "negative theology." Does a "negative theology" imply no theology at all? What, after all, does "God" mean or do if God is, as Hobbes tells us, utterly unknowable?

We also must contend with the fact that if for Hobbes God is unknowable, then it seems hard to suggest we can know anything from Scripture either, a crucial concern when the interpretation of Scripture forms the backbone of parts 3 and 4 of *Leviathan* (and when for my own purposes, it serves as a model for how to read and interpret the entirety of *Leviathan*). Does Hobbes's skepticism defeat us from the outset? Is his turn to religion itself just another ruse?

In both Silver's and Kahn's view, Hobbes sees a world abandoned by God (for Kahn in particular, it does not seem to matter if God exists at all—certainly we would never know one way or the other). Without any certainty, all we are left with is rhetoric and arbitrary power and we need to be tricked into believing in something so that we do not tear ourselves apart as a society. This is not unlike the idea we find in Machiavelli, who praises Numa as the true founder of Rome because he established a religious basis for Roman law and social practices by pretending to get his inspiration from a divine source.[58]

Yet it is worth noting that for Hobbes, God's "abandonment" of the world is temporary: according to his eschatology, we live in a time between God's overt ruling of the world (as "king" of ancient Israel with Moses as lieutenant) and God's rule over an eternal kingdom after the second coming of Christ.

During this in-between time, Hobbes tells us, "Christian men doe not know, but onely beleeve the Scripture to be the Word of God. . . ."[59] Yet this belief is not empty. As Victoria Silver writes of Hobbes's "religion" (lumping it in with Luther's), the

> deity or the reality of things nonetheless remains a crucial postulate for these writers, manifest not as a knowledge or practice but as an incongruity. . . . Furthermore, the ways Scripture itself fails to mean tends to imply such a God, which is why faith and the sense of the text faith apprehends are peculiarly positional and episodic in practice.[60]

The understandings of God into which we rhetorically maneuver ourselves are "positional and episodic in practice." Our faith is a product of the particularities and context of our position. But this does not mean that such beliefs are somehow false or meaningless, ruses that we use to trick ourselves (or get tricked) for the sake of political and social order. The failure of Scripture to "mean" anything is what allows meaning, reading, and interpretation to remain an ongoing project, what saves us from ossified truth, from ruses.

Much scholarship (with Pocock being an important exception) discounts Hobbes's religiosity, arguing that his discussion of religion is merely "rhetorical."[61] While I do not disagree, I would challenge this sense of the term "rhetorical." Rather than meaning "empty" or "meaningless," rhetoric for Hobbes is the basis of his religious vision. Hobbes offers us a "negative theology" indeed, one that puts divinity at the center of his thought without in any way inferring something about God. Does this mean that we can say definitively that Hobbes "believes in God"? As it may now be clear to see, the answer depends on what we mean by belief. If we mean what Hobbes means by this term, then yes, he does believe in God, because belief is an artifact of our ability to construct rhetorical meanings out of thin air. Clearly (or "Daemonology") as that "fabulous Doctrine concerning Daemons, which are but Idols, or Phantasms of the braine, without any reall nature of their own, distinct from humane fancy" (4.44, p. 418). In short, demonology is the mistaking of things that are not for things that are. Demonologists demonstrate a confusion about reality that for Hobbes lies at the heart of the dangerous practice of politics in his own day. This confusion is a more or less deliberate policy by corrupt political and religious leaders in order to mislead citizens into subservience. Yet while misleading the rest of us, these demonologists are themselves misled; mired in their own web of deceit, they become incapable of recognizing anything but their own fantasies.

Hobbes calls the political power consequent from the practice of de-monology the "Kingdome of Darknesse." This kingdom is, he tells us, "*[A] Confederacy of Deceivers, that to obtain dominion over men in this present world, endeavour by dark, and erroneous Doctrines, to extinguish in them the Light, both of Nature, and of the Gospell; and so to dis-prepare them for the Kingdome of God to come*" (pp. 417–18). The enormous power in this "kingdom" tends to sweep away other forms of power: having no need to make recourse to "reality," its practitioners have an almost infinite ability to manipulate and dis-semble. Once these demonologists hold sway over the appearance of things, almost nothing, it seems, can stand in their path.

Hobbes furnishes many concrete examples of this "kingdom," beginning with his intense dislike for the Roman Catholic Church. However, demon-ology begins not with Rome but with Athens, with the "Heathen Poets" and the "vain and erroneous Philosophy of the Greeks, especially of Aris-totle" (p. 418). Demonology is, in a sense, a basis for Western thought, and hence Hobbes's challenge to it has radical implications.

The "True" Church

If we remain for a moment with the religious implications of Hobbes's theory of demonology, we can see how it affects his considerations of actual churches in his day. For Hobbes, any church that claims it is in fact the true church (the one church that is in a position to speak for God) is a practi-tioner of demonology and a danger to Christendom itself (hence his dislike for Roman Catholicism). For Hobbes, the best church is the one that knows that its doctrines are wrong (i.e., one that "profess[es its own] inconstancy"), or at least one that does not claim to have doctrinal infallibility.

In part 3 of *Leviathan*, Hobbes lays out his reasons for denouncing a church that associates itself with the one, true "Kingdome of God" (3.31, p. 245). He tells us that the kingdom of God does not exist in heaven, nor currently on earth. Although God is absolute in the universe, Hobbes insists that to use a human term like *king* to apply to God, God must have an actual, terrestrial kingdom. For Hobbes, the kingdom of God has had only one incarnation so far, as we have already seen. After Moses, this kingdom flickered in and out existence, depending on the comportment of the Jews. Eventually, with the election of Saul, the kingdom of God vanished from the earth, ushering in our present state of "kingdomlessness."

For Hobbes, the second incarnation of the kingdom of God will not appear until Christ's return (3.41, p. 333). For Hobbes, we live in an in-between time (between the two kingdoms of God) in which we have only the church and the figure of the Holy Spirit to comfort and guide us. In the vacuum left by God's absent kingdom we have instead the "Kingdome of Darknesse." Hence for Hobbes it is particularly anathema for a church to consider itself as actually speaking for the kingdom of God, because, as we will see further, the very existence of the church serves as a "person of God," a marker for the absence of the kingdom of God itself (we won't need a church when Christ is our king on earth). This is why the kingdom of darkness "*dis-prepare[s]*" us for the coming of Christ—it substitutes a false kingdom for a real (both no longer and not yet existent) one. The presence of this dark kingdom prevents us from realizing God's absence as king and hence prevents the real kingdom from (eventually) manifesting itself.

Demonology and the Church of England

Hobbes's insistence that all churches must more or less openly profess their subjectivism might seem to complicate his stated preference for the Anglican Church and the entire structure of church authority upon which he seems to rely so heavily (and perhaps this did not escape his critics who accused him of heresy and atheism). If Hobbes is a devoted Anglican, must he not consider the Anglican Church the "true church," the church whose interpretation is not subjective?

On the contrary, for Hobbes it seems that when considered on its own, even the Anglican Church is insufficiently subjective, not entirely free of the demonological practices of Rome. This could be the basis of his complaint that the church was imperfectly subservient to the state. In his genealogy of the Anglican Church, he tells us:

> First, the Power of the Popes was dissolved totally by Queen Elizabeth; and the Bishops, who before exercised their Functions in Right of the Pope, did afterwards exercise the same in Right of the Queen and her Successours; though by retaining the phrase of *Iure Divino*, they were thought to demand it by immediate Right from God. (4.47, p. 479)

Although this is presented in a positive light, we see that even in Anglicanism there remains a bit of the fallacy that the kingdom of God is already come, as represented by the power of God as invested in the Anglican bishops.

Although he acknowledges that the "Exorcisme" of Henry VIII and Elizabeth of the "Spirit of Rome" had "clean swept" the house of England, Hobbes still saw that spirit as threatening the nation (p. 482). He writes: "For it is not the Romane Clergy onely, that pretends the Kingdome of God to be of this World, and thereby to have a Power therein, distinct from that of the Civill State" (p. 482). Warning us that the "Spirit of Rome" may lurk even in England as an ever-present threat, we see demonology as a danger to be resisted at all costs.

For these reasons, Hobbes's support of a state church seems to come, not from his belief that such a church has more access to truth than its rivals, but rather from the belief that such a church is beneath the authority of the civil sovereign and thus its doctrine is more openly human-derived and fallible. The state (at least the English state) has no pretense to divine truths. Hobbes seems to appreciate the way that states are more or less openly arbitrary:

> And that which offendeth the People, is no other thing, but that they are governed, not as every one of them would himselfe, but as the Publique

Representant, be it one Man, or an Assembly of men thinks fit; that is, by an Arbitrary government: for which they give evill names to their Superiors; never knowing (till perhaps a little after a Civill warre) that without such Arbitrary government, such Warre must be perpetuall; and that it is Men, and Arms, not Words, and Promises, that make the Force and Power of the Laws. (4.46, p. 471)

Thus the state, unlike the church, apparently "profess[es its] inconstancy" in a way that helps to better avoid the error of demonology.

We see the outlines of a now familiar argument wherein Hobbes treats religion as a tool of the state and looks to the sovereign, however arbitrary, as the only alternative to social chaos and collapse. But as we further explore Hobbes's notion of idolatry and the contrasting possibility of "worshipful reading," we see that such a "dead-end" in politics and philosophy (i.e., sovereignty as a necessary evil) is only inevitable when we in fact capitulate to idolatry itself. In other words, if we see no choice but the lies of the church or the lies of the state, then it might seem that the lies of the state are preferable since they are more clearly lies. But this hardly rescues us from the kingdom of darkness since for Hobbes the practice of demonology is not restricted to religious leaders. Demonology resides in its replacement of the unrepresentable things of this world with clear and "obvious" truths, a practice of the state as well as any church. There is indeed no reason that the sovereign itself might not be demonological (in fact, as I will argue further, by Hobbes's own arguments we may consider it the epitome of demonology).

Idolatry and Worship

If demonology is everywhere, how can it be identified and resisted? In arguing against demonology, Hobbes is not claiming that there is an obvious and demonstrable reality that the demonologists obscure, a "truth" we can reveal to banish demonological fantasies. In fact, for Hobbes, we are prone to demonology exactly because we cannot know anything with certainty, even as our senses appear to give us a knowable, objective world. Hobbes's answer to this dilemma of imperfect perception is not to give up on truth but to ponder the ways in which truth can be evoked (i.e., represented).

Such a turn to representation may seem perilously close to the kinds of demonological practices Hobbes condemns; after all, demonology also deals with things that are not (symbols, simulacra, etc.) standing in for things that are. However, Hobbes himself makes a distinction between idolatry and worship:

> To worship an Image, is voluntarily to doe those externall acts, which are signes of honoring either the matter of the Image, which is Wood, Stone, Metall, or some other visible creature; or the Phantasme of the brain, for the resemblance, or representation whereof, the matter was formed and figured. . . . To be uncovered, before a man of Power and Authority, or before the Throne of a Prince, or in such other places as hee ordaineth to that purpose in his absence, is to Worship that man, or Prince with Civill Worship; as being a signe, not of honoring the stoole, or place, but the Person; and is not Idolatry. But if hee that doth it, should suppose the Soule of the Prince to be in the Stool, or should present a Petition to the Stool, it were Divine Worship and Idolatry. (4.45, p. 449)

The distinction between idolatry (the demonological practice) and worship is a subtle one; in fact, since all representation deals with resemblance to that which is being sought after, the one form easily slips into the other. The outward actions of worship and idolatry are roughly identical (unless the idolator reveals his or her self, in this case by some blunder like "present[ing] a Petition to the Stool"). In practice, then, this distinction is not so much one of action as it is of intent. For Hobbes, worship is an internal state of mind, a style of reading rather than anything intrinsic to an act or an object.

As we have seen, the internal state of mind, the proper style of reading, amounts to a difference between taking the representation as a literal truth and taking it as a representation. The idolator forgets or obliterates the "truth," which is that the figure is of our own invention. Hobbes tells us, "Figure is a quantity every way determined" (he might have added "by us"); by definition, it is only what it is (p. 448). As we have already seen for Hobbes, the more representation "fails" to tell us what it represents, the more accurately it fulfills its function of serving as a sign. All signs "fail" in this way, but it is our direct acknowledgment of this failure that is crucial for

Hobbes. If we are to avoid being seduced by demonological delusions, we must learn to read the signs correctly.

The Brazen Serpent and the Golden Calf

To elaborate both the distinction between idolatry and worship and the ease with which this crucial distinction is erased, Hobbes offers us two moments of representation from the first kingdom of God. Despite the second commandment, there are times when God did demand (via Moses) to be worshipped indirectly via figures (p. 446).

Why is this not simply a violation of the second commandment, with God being inconsistent to (God's own) divine law? How is this worship and not idolatry? Hobbes's explanation comes in his reading of the second commandment: "*Thou shalt not make to thy selfe any graven image.*" Hobbes tells us:

> God commanded Moses to set up the Brazen Serpent; hee did not make it to himselfe; it was not therefore against the Commandement. But the making of the Golden Calfe by Aaron, and the People, as being done without authority from God, was Idolatry; not onely because they held it for God, but also because they made it for a Religious use, without warrant either from God their Soveraign, or from Moses, that was his Lieutenant. (pp. 450–51)

"*[T]hy selfe*" is the operative phrase in the previous passage. Here we get a better sense of the distinction between the Brazen Serpent and the Golden Calf. In making the Golden Calf, Aaron and the Israelites "held it for God." This idol, rather than stand in for God, took the place of God altogether. The Israelites make this mistake, Hobbes suggests, because of the second, and possibly even more crucial error—they made this idol "without warrant" from God or Moses. While this could be read as a parable for the need for people to obey their superiors, whoever they may be, it is crucial to note that in this case their sovereign is actually God. God as sovereign is different than any other sovereign, in no small part because God is infinite and unknowable. Just as importantly, *God is the only sovereign that is not arbitrary.* This is why Hobbes tells us that the kingdom of God can only exist when God is in fact king. For Aaron and the Israelites to make graven images *for themselves*, means that they hold themselves as being capable of making God accessible to them, essentially turning God into a finite, portrayable, and knowable being.

When God is king, the distinction between idolatry and worship is clear, because God's authority (as interpreted by Moses) cannot be questioned. In subsequent times, as God's sovereignty passes from the world, the distinction becomes increasingly tenuous and confusing. No future sovereign can demand, as God does, to be worshipped via images without evoking the danger of demonology.

Ultimately, even the Brazen Serpent itself became an object of Idolatry in the aftermath of Moses's reign: "Wee read (2 Kings 18.4) that Hezekiah brake in pieces the Brazen serpent which Moses had set up, because the People burnt incense to it" (p. 453) Although the Jews worshipped the Brazen Serpent as Moses commanded them, at some point it was decided that "they should doe so no more" (p. 453). Here we get a sense of how even the very same object can turn from sanctioned object of worship into an idol. Idolatry resides not in objects or in set eternal laws but in the representational relationships that are set up by our readings of those images.

The change in status of the Brazen Serpent from worshipful object to idol does not imply that Moses's authority waned after his death but rather indicates the shifting grounds of worship and idolatry in a post-Mosaic world. In our kingdomless time, worship is not defined by our sovereign, but by our own decision. It is ultimately up to us to work this problem out for ourselves, hence the need for "discretion."

IDOLS IN THE CHURCH (AND STATE)

The full implications of Hobbes's understanding of—and resistance to—idolatry emerge when we examine the political and religious debates of his time about imagery, and specifically consider how these debates concerned the second commandment and its relationship to questions of reading and interpretation. As I noted in the previous chapter, Hobbes's formal position on this matter is largely in keeping with mainstream Anglican doctrines of his day. In the bitter controversies that raged over the interpretation and application of the second commandment, Anglicans, as already noted, tended to seek a middle ground between what they saw as the clear idolatry of the Catholic Church and the over-the-top iconoclasm of the Puritans. But even among Anglicans, there was much debate.

Starting with the Renaissance and the Reformation, this question of how to interpret the second commandment (or whether there was even a second commandment at all) dominated a great deal of religious and political discourse.[2] Margaret Aston catalogs the careful work many defenders of imagery employed at that time, distinguishing "idols" from "images," and *latria* (honor due exclusively to God) from *dulia* (honor due to God but that can also be given to other images). These distinctions, she points out, are based on earlier Greek mistranslations of the single Hebrew word *pesel* (the word used in the "second" commandment itself), which in fact covers both concepts. For the Hebrews, there is in fact no difference between an idol and an image: all images are potentially idolatrous.[3]

Among those who sought some accommodation with imagery, as we have already seen in chapter 3, a great deal of attention was focused on the location and context of images. Aston writes:

> An image—the very same image—viewed respectively in a domestic or an ecclesiastical setting could provoke different responses. Some churches inspired greater veneration than others. Even inside a church there were significant differences of place, which affected degrees of reverence. A carving of a saint placed in a niche on a church wall or in a screen was one thing. An image on the altar was another. Set there, in the holiest part of the entire consecrated building, on the spot dedicated to celebrating the mystery of the mass, the holy image was inescapably linked with the highest spiritual worship.[4]

Context, meaning, and association distinguished (or was claimed to distinguish) licit from illicit imagery. The more the image seemed to evoke "reality," the more it suggested a sensible divine presence, the more it was dangerous, and idolatrous. This helps explains the preference for paintings over statues and text over paintings; when image is clearly image and not the thing it stands in for, the viewer is the less likely to misread what she or he is seeing (a sentiment we have seen Hobbes strongly reflect). Aston cites James Calfhill's complaint that statues were too dangerous to have in churches, including the figure of Jesus on the cross, even just the cross itself. Calfhill argues: "You will answer, (I dare say), that ye know well enough the Cross is nothing but a piece of metal; and that he that hangeth in the Rood-loft is not Christ indeed, but a sign of Him. So did the Heathen know." "But," Aston adds, again citing Calfhill, "they too forgot because 'the livelier the counterfeit is, the greater error is engendered.'"[5]

The fear that we might forget that the image is only an image lies at the heart of this controversy. Julie Spraggon tells us it was widely held during the reign of Elizabeth and the Stuart monarchs that there was a "natural proneness of mankind towards idolatry."[6] She cites the nonconformist theologians John Dod and Richard Cleaver as warning against the "highly infectious nature of the disease [of idolatry]."[7]

What is at stake is not just the correct depiction of objects and images but also internal states of understanding (and reading) when confronted with those objects and images. In the early decades of the reign of Queen Elizabeth I, making the sign of the cross in the air was considered a worse violation of the second commandment than having a crucifix, because for more radical Reformers, such a gesture did not simply produce an external image that could be destroyed, but also created in the "mind's eye" an internal image, indicating that idolatry had permeated into the heart and mind of the person in question.[8] Such claims evoke Hobbes's own concerns about demonology; when we forget that the image is an image, we give the image a life of its own; it becomes more real than what our own senses and memory tell us.

"Civill Worship": The Prince's Stool

This question of imagery and the second commandment also had political implications. As I have already argued, for Hobbes, when God demanded to be worshipped via images, that by definition was not a violation of the second commandment. When it comes to contemporary (arbitrary) sovereigns, however, a more critical set of rules apply. Hobbes allows for "Civill Worship," a nonidolatrous style of obeisance to terrestrial rulers, yet recognizes that even such a limited form of worship can become an instance of idolatry, depending on how it is practiced and understood by individual citizens. An analysis of this argument helps us understand Hobbes's practice of worship and how it could be distinguished from idolatry.

Such concerns were certainly not unique to Hobbes. In "The Iconography of Nothing," Peter Goodrich gives an example of the long-running debate over proper civil worship involving imagery associated with the sovereign's power. An argument took place (some twenty years after *Leviathan* came out) between Anglican Bishop Edward Stillingfleet and Thomas Godden, a Catholic, in which Godden accused Stillingfleet of being inconsistent in his strict refusal of any "Catholic-style" use of religious imagery while allowing, in contrast, that it was right to arrest a peasant for not taking off his hat while passing by the throne of the king. If Stillingfleet was consistent, Godden argued, the symbols of state should be as anathema as the symbols of the church.[9]

Stillingfleet's answer, Goodrich explains, was a legal one; he distinguished between divine law and civil law and said that in the case of the throne or chair of the king, we are only dealing with a matter of custom, of whether it is the "will of the Prince, to have men uncovered."[10]

It is worth returning to Hobbes's own answer in an earlier version of this same controversy, which was as vital at the time that Hobbes wrote *Leviathan* as it would be two decades later. Hobbes seems to duplicate the argument that Stillingfleet will make some twenty years later:

> To be uncovered, before a man of Power and Authority, or before the Throne of a Prince, or in such other places as hee ordaineth to that purpose in his absence, is to Worship that man, or Prince with Civill Worship; as being a signe, not of honoring the stoole, or place, but the Person; and is not Idolatry. But if hee that doth it, should suppose the Soule of the Prince to be in the Stool, or should present a Petition to the Stool, it were Divine Worship and Idolatry.[11]

Although Hobbes appears to anticipate Stillingfleet's (Anglican) argument more or less, his argument is actually quite different. He is concerned less with law and custom than he is with the internal intent (or reading) of the person in question. If the image is used in a civil sense—as when one takes one's hat off for the prince's throne or stool—one is not necessarily treating the chair like an idol, but merely (in one' own interpretation, which matters the most for Hobbes) paying obeisance to the king in the manner of the nation's custom; this is civil worship. If on the other hand, one were to actually believe that the king's stool possessed a magical spirit, *that* same gesture of taking off one's hat would become an idolatrous act.

What for Stillingfleet is seemingly a matter of national policy (so that taking off one's hat, regardless of what one thinks, is always expected and can never be "wrong") is for Hobbes a matter of correct reading. For Hobbes, the distinction between idolatry and worship (including "civill worship") once again all depends on how we interpret a situation, on a method and practice of reading. No one act or gesture is "safe from idolatry" because everything depends on how we read (or misread). And no sovereign mandate can either protect us from or force us into idolatry; the choice remains entirely up to each individual person.

Discretion Revisited

Such an insight can help us better understand Hobbes's concept of "discretion" as well as the degree to which Hobbes offers a nonsubjective (or differently subjective) method of reading. For Stillingfleet, discretion plays no part in the question of civil worship. For Hobbes, we must indeed practice discretion, but not in a way that is entirely up to us (that is to say, not in a way that is entirely at our discretion). "Discretion" in this context amounts to correct reading, a recognition of the rhetorical and representational nature of the construction of meaning. It is hence also a recognition of a collective and externalized process, and not some purely subjective feeling or aesthetic preference. Although the distinction between idolatry and proper worship is internal, it is not arbitrary, not subjective in the sense of being utterly "private" after all. It remains subjective only in the sense that the choice of how to read remains one's own decision. But we do have external guidelines by which we can make our judgment, involving the recognition and exposition of signs qua signs. It is crucial to note that such guidelines have nothing to do with sovereign authority, but instead are entirely rooted in the question of good and proper reading, in the recognition of the rhetorical as opposed to "real" nature of the signs to which we are paying homage.

Hobbes's methodology is, once again, extremely similar to Benjamin's. The distinction between idolatry and worship for Hobbes, and symbol and the allegory for Benjamin, share a concern with a means of discernment that does not rely wholly upon our subjective judgments. Such a distinction rather depends upon the actual encounter with the sign as a "material object" in order to save us from delusion. To the extent that we can be aware of our own projections and decisions, we come closer to something that might be called "nonsubjective subjectivity" (or what Benjamin himself boldly calls "truth").[12]

THE METAPHYSICS OF DEMONOLOGY:
THE ERROR OF SEPARATED ESSENCES

What, exactly, is at stake for Hobbes in distinguishing between proper, or worshipful, reading and idolatry? The answer is, everything. For Hobbes, the breadth and depth of demonology can be astonishing. He writes that among the tenets of "Vain Philosophy" (the teachings of demonology), the most odious perhaps is metaphysics.[13] So total is the reach of metaphysics that it determines the

> Definitions of Body, Time, Place, Matter, Forme, Essence, Subject, Substance, Accident, Power, Act, Finite, Infinite, Quantity, Quality, Motion, Action, Passion, and divers others, necessary to the explaining of a mans Conceptions concerning the Nature and Generation of Bodies. (4.46, p. 463)

Through metaphysics, the demonologist may totalize and indeed replace the world just as he or she totalizes and replaces God. Metaphysicians (i.e., demonologists) turn being itself into an idolatrous thing. For Hobbes, metaphysics does not discover being, it (falsely) produces it, chiefly by treating the representations of beings as if they had an existence of their own, as if the term *being* were itself not simply a figure (of speech) but was in fact "being" itself. As we have seen before, when hypostatization is not recognized for what it is, it is seen as constituting reality rather than rhetorically representing it.

Hobbes tells us that the various words for existence, "*Is*, or *Bee*, or *Are*, and the like," are implicit in language: "And if it were so, that were a Language without any Verb answerable to *Est*, or *Is*, or *Bee;* yet the men that used it would bee not a jot the lesse capable of Inferring, Concluding, and of all kind of Reasoning, than were the Greeks, and Latines" (p. 464). Such words, Hobbes tells us, are "no Names of Things; but Signes" (p. 465) The word "is," and a host of other words such as *"to bee a Body, to Walke, to bee Speaking, to Live, to See . . .*and the like, that signifie just the same," are what Hobbes calls "the names of *Nothing"* (p. 465).

Although he calls these signs *"Nothing,"* Hobbes does not mean that what they convey is utterly meaningless. For him, being is implicit even when it is physically absent in the text. In language very reminiscent of Heidegger, Hobbes argues that rather than depend on its sign, being is the ground, the very basis of linguistic signs.[14] The word *being* presupposes but doesn't constitute being itself. The term *being,* like *God,* is the hypostatization of something unknowable; by its failure to represent (as a "name . . . of *Nothing"*) we have the potential to "honor" or speak of being (albeit in a purely negative, absent sense).

For the idolator, on the other hand, "being" becomes something that they define and that belongs to them. Such a stance is precisely what Arendt dislikes about "self-making" in the first place; she lumps Hobbes in with the idolators because she fails to see Hobbes's own distinction between self-making as an arbitrary phantasm and self-making as a practice of correct reading, rooted in the "truth" of representation.

Hobbes calls the idolatrous readings that results from metaphysics the "Error of *Separated Essences,"* as we saw in earlier chapters.[15] The idolator who commits this error misreads the world, producing strange inventions and "phantasms." These are representational forms that become in effect "separated essences," ghostly forms that take on a life of their own and supersede what they purportedly represent. For Hobbes, the belief in witchcraft, in ghosts and possessions, the practice of the Enthusiasts, and other fallacies all follow from this one error (3.34, p. 275).

An example that Hobbes furnishes of such an invention is the idea that our souls are separate from our bodies. The figure for the being of a person has been separated from the body and given its own identity and name, the soul. For Hobbes, the soul is in fact a pure figure, a representation for a person, as when we say "there wasn't a soul [a person] in sight." Once it becomes a "separated essence," this figure actually comes to supplant the body it once represented, becoming, as Hobbes complains, immortal and far more essential than the body itself:

And in particular, of the Essence of a Man, which (they say) is his Soule, they affirm it, to be All of it in his little Finger, and All of it in every other Part (how small soever) of his Body; and yet no more Soule in the Whole Body, than in any of those Parts. . . . And yet all this is necessary to beleeve, to those that will beleeve the Existence of an Incorporeall Soule, Separated from the Body. (4.46, p. 466)

This is just one of many misperceptions that reveal the demonologist for what they are—one could argue that they are as much the slaves of their fallacies as the masters, since the symbols and idols they fetishize take on their own ghostly existence. Hobbes often uses terms like *spirit, haunted,* and *ghost* in speaking of demonological creations, as when he calls the papacy "the *Ghost* of the deceased *Romane Empire*" (4.47, p. 480). These ghosts are the disembodied reflection of the separated essence of being that they have turned into an idol—they occur when we misread a metaphor, failing to recognize it for what it really is.

WORSHIPFUL READING

As I will explain further in chapter 6, Hobbes would oppose the ghosts and phantoms of demonology (and of demonological reading in particular) with a "ghost" of his own, the Holy Spirit. This is not as an actual ghost (to say that would be to replicate the error of separated essences itself), but rather a pure metafigure, a figure of figurativeness. Recall part of a passage already cited in chapter 2, where Hobbes writes that

the safest way is to beleeve, that by the Descending of the Dove upon the Apostles; and by Christs Breathing on them, when hee gave them the Holy Ghost; and by the giving of it by the Imposition of Hands, are understood the signes which God hath been pleased to use, or ordain to bee used, of his promise to assist those persons in their study to Preach his Kingdome, and in their Conversation, that it might not be Scandalous, but Edifying to others. (4.45, p. 451)

The Holy Spirit is depicted as allowing for a careful, and indeed worshipful, reading by countering the ghosts of demonology with a "holy" ghost, a spirit that resists demonological misreading. As we will see further in chapter 6, the blankness of the sign of the Holy Spirit, because it offers us nothing at all to misread, facilitates our worshipful stance towards reading, not just in terms of the figure of the Holy Spirit itself, but by extension all other figures as well.

Hobbes's notion of worshipful reading has important implications for how we read the *Leviathan* itself. When done worshipfully, which means in a way that remains explicitly aware of its rhetorical construction, it seems as if Hobbes completely reverses himself and his apparent textual claims: even though one would think, based on a quick perusal of parts 3 and 4 of *Leviathan*, that the dweller in rhetoric, metaphor, and representation is a demonologist and the dweller in truth and reality is the one who helped deliver us from the kingdom of darkness, in fact the exact reverse may be true. The casual acceptance of material reality as "real" may in fact be the ultimate demonology, a misreading of the world as being much less complex than it actually is. The one who dwells in metaphor and rhetoric may just be the only kind of "truth teller" there is. The realization that a metaphor is in fact only a metaphor is what saves us from the kingdom of darkness, or what reveals that kingdom as an idolatrous (even while still rhetorical) practice.

This may help explain Hobbes's preference for a *ruminant* (to use Nietzsche's term) reading of his own works. The resistance to the obvious and the immediate, the slow realization of doubt, the exposition of rhetoric qua rhetoric, are Hobbes's weapons against demonology and the kingdom of darkness. The demonologist must fear a slow and careful reading because the exposure of their ruse is the end of their power and ill-gotten authority. As we have already seen, in welcoming careful reading, Hobbes may be signaling that our own reading of his text may change.

(RE)READING THE SOVEREIGN

With this in mind, let us endeavor to "reread" *Leviathan* in a worshipful style. With my argument about Hobbes's theory of reading laid out, and having considered how he reads Scripture as a model for our own reading, we are in a position to explore the consequences of this reading for the main arguments of *Leviathan*. We can be much more explicit about the relationship between the rhetorical and religious forms of representation that we have been discussing and politics itself.

First is the all-important question of the sovereign. It is crucial to recognize that for Hobbes the sovereign is a kind of image, thus subject to the complicated questions of reading and representation we have been considering (as when Hobbes tells us that "an earthly Soveraign may be called the Image of God") (4.45, p. 448). To argue that the sovereign is an image does not automatically imply that it's also an idol, since Hobbes rejects the iconoclastic approach to this question. Still, Hobbes allows that it *is* possible to treat the sovereign as an idol. Shortly after the passage just cited, and immediately after he considers the question of whether it is proper to remove one's hat before the king's throne or stool, Hobbes opines:

> To pray to a King for such things, as hee is able to doe for us, though we prostrate our selves before him, is but Civill Worship; because we acknowledge no other power in him, but humane: But voluntarily to pray unto him for fair weather, or for any thing which God onely can doe for us, is Divine Worship, and Idolatry. (p. 449)

We move from a consideration of the "prince's (or king's) stool" to the king, queen, or other human ruler's own person and how we treat (or read) them. To raise the question of the sovereign as an idol is to submit it to the kind of scrutiny about reading that we have been discussing over the last three chapters. It is to suggest that the sovereign who is to "read" all "Man-kind" is also of necessity to be read by its subjects—and perhaps by Hobbes in particular. Since the question of idolatry depends on our practice of interpretation, our reading of the sovereign determines whether we perform "Civill Worship" or idolatry, essentially leaving the "meaning" and, by extension, authority of the sovereign up to us. Indeed, the deeply ambivalent frontispiece of the cover, where the sovereign simultaneously appears to be a godlike figure looming over the landscape (a notion reinforced by Hobbes's calling the sovereign a *"Mortall God"*; 2.17, p. 120) and at the same time appears to be made up of individual persons, suggests the double-edged nature of representation: Is this the king being depicted as God? Is the sovereign simply the product of our various interpretations of it? Is this a divinely sanctioned image, or an idol? When we think about the question of reading and idolatry in terms of both the frontispiece itself and Hobbes's treatment (and imagery) of the sovereign in general, we see that even to pose such questions (however obliquely) is potentially subversive.

What if we read this "image" the way that Hobbes instructs us to read other images? If it is revealed as "empty," what significance do we give to the sovereign? What does "civill worship" mean in this context, when, as Hobbes has repeatedly informed us, we must not worship the image at all, but only what it stands for, people that the sovereign supposedly "represents"? What do we make of the sovereign's authority when it is in fact reduced to or exposed as a symbol—or, if not so reduced, then are we not indeed engaging in an idolatrous misreading of the sovereign after all?

Hanna Pitkin and Hobbes's Concept of Representation

To explore these issues, we must get a clearer sense of how Hobbes's concept of political representation connects to his notions of rhetorical (and religious) representation. Thus further questions arise: What do his comments about the latter tell us about the former? Is Hobbes's political theory of representation itself worshipful or is it idolatrous (i.e., is it consistent to his own theory of reading)? And what does this say in the end about the question of authority and reading, about private and public acts of representation? An important reader of Hobbes, Hanna Pitkin, can help provide some answers.

In her chapter on Hobbes in *The Concept of Representation*, Pitkin argues that Hobbes's concept is not what it seems to be. At first glance, his argument seems irrefutable.[16] Yet as Pitkin shows, when we consider not only his formal description of representation but the examples he furnishes, we come to question the very mode of representation that Hobbes ostensibly promotes (in this way, although she does not say this overtly, Pitkin too is reading according to the "Scope" and "Designe" of the text).

Pitkin considers Hobbes's treatment of political representation in *Leviathan*'s chapter 16, where he writes that "when the Actor maketh a Convenant by Authority, he bindeth thereby the Author, no lesse than if he had made it himselfe."[17] For Pitkin this statement describes a commonwealth in which people have neither any real power, nor any right to complain about

what the sovereign does. In her view, Hobbes's theory of political representation as articulated in this passage neatly accomplishes the submission of
the subjects since they are the "authors" of their own subjection and so have
consented to everything the sovereign does. She writes:

> Calling the sovereign a representative arouses other expectations in the reader
> which the Hobbesian system does not fulfill. When we look at the Hobbes-
> ian political structure as a whole we are most aware of how partial, formal,
> and empty of substance his concept of representation is.[18]

If this is the case, Pitkin asks, why even use the terminology of representation at all, since it brings with it certain (political) expectations? She
continues:

> A Sovereign given complete power in perpetuity, with no obligation to con-
> sult the wishes of his subjects and no duties toward them which they can
> claim—surely nothing could be further from what we ordinarily think of as
> representation or representative government! We read the *Leviathan* and feel
> that somehow we have been tricked.[19]

It seems like a "trick" because by thinking that we are being represented
when we aren't, we become passively acquiescent in our complete loss of
power. Calling us "authors" in this very same chapter (as we have already
seen) seems a cruel joke or at best an attempt to cover over the fact that we
have de facto signed away our authority to someone else.

Pitkin considers a position that is widespread among scholars (especially liberal ones) of Hobbes: that Hobbes did think and wish the sovereign
would "take good care of" its subjects, bound as it is, if not by the covenant,
then by the laws of nature. But for Pitkin herself, this is not really representation, either—at least not what we often ascribe to or wish for in such
a term. To hope or wish that the sovereign does what we would like is not
really representation but a request for good luck in the political leaders that
are foisted upon us.

For Pitkin, Hobbes's definition of (political) representation is "not so
much false as incomplete."[20] It is "incomplete" insofar as it does not address
the fuller implications of representation that chapter 16 itself sets forth.
As Pitkin herself astutely points out, the examples of representation that

Hobbes offers often give us a sense of representation that is different from the one Hobbes formally defines in the text. Thus she cites various "counterexamples" that Hobbes uses in the text to illustrate representation. For example, he cites the case of Cicero, who tells us that as a lawyer "I beare three Persons; my own, my Adversaries, and the Judges," representing each in turn as a way to prepare for trial.[21] Hobbes also describes the guardians of "Children, Fooles and Mad-men," cases in which subjects cannot authorize their own representation, lacking the rationality to do so.[22] Finally, and most important for Pitkin's argument, is the example of a stage actor who similarly complicates the question of representation. In each of these cases, we see examples of representation in which the representer in question must to some extent actually consider the interests of a client, ward, or character, depending on the example (in a way the sovereign doesn't have to). This is particularly true in the case of actors; so total is their attention to their subject that they claim not to be authorized by the playwright or character they are performing, but to be the character itself, i.e., not to be representative at all (and if they are talented, they can sometimes pull this off).[23]

Pitkin is arguing that if Hobbes really meant to fool us, he would only offer examples that suited the argument he was making. By giving a plethora of examples that bring in other ideas about representation, Pitkin seems to suggest that Hobbes is allowing us to see past this ruse, not only allowing for expectations of other forms of representation to occur, but even furnishing examples of what those other forms might look like. Her own claim is that Hobbes is not trying to fool us but was in his own life overly concerned with peace at all costs and so, without denying the fuller implications of representation (indeed evoking them in his counterexamples), he focuses on an aspect of representation that serves his cause. Hence his account of representation is "incomplete."

Another counterexample of representation that Pitkin doesn't mention, but that is vital for the purposes of this book, comes directly after Hobbes's discussion of representing those without reason of their own; this is the case of the personation of an idol. Hobbes writes:

An Idol, or meer Figment of the brain, may be Personated: as were the Gods of the Heathen; which by such Officers as the State appointed, were Personated, and held Possessions, and other Goods, and Rights, which men from time to time dedicated, and consecrated unto them. But Idols cannot be Authors: for an Idol is nothing. The Authority proceeded from the State: and therefore before introduction of Civill Government, the Gods of the Heathen could not be Personated.[24]

In this particular instance, the authority of "heathen" kingdoms stems not, as its citizens might believe, from the idolatrous Gods they worship but rather from the state itself. Naturally, in this case, Hobbes is talking about a country that is idolatrous almost by definition. Seemingly no Christian sovereign could fit this description. Yet if in this instance such an activity can be labeled "Heathen" or idolatrous, even the possibility that this critique could be applied to a Christian sovereign is a radical divergence from the text's pose of orthodoxy.

Such arguments serve to remind us that once again, the crux of authority lies in our reading of it: if a given style of representation is idolatrous, is a misreading, it has no basis for authority other than its own act of symbolization.[25] Even if the comparisons of the sovereign to a stage actor and an idol are intended to work by contrast and distinction, we see the possibility of catching the sovereign at its own pose of authority, much as we might catch an actor trying too hard to convince us of her or his authenticity as a character. The complication of the question of sovereignty implicit in these examples may undermine the very definition they supposedly serve. If the sovereign's power rests on a trick, then Hobbes may have shown us how it is a trick by dramatizing the emptiness of his concept of representation via the contrast between his formal definitions and the examples he offers. And by including the example of an idol, among his other counterexamples, Hobbes may be indicating that his formal definition of sovereignty is not merely empty—since for Hobbes that in and of itself is not a bad thing, as we have seen—but also idolatrous, bringing his consideration of religious representation directly to bear on questions of political representation.

The Demonological Sovereign

If we continue to consider the sovereign through the lens of Hobbes's understanding of (proper) religious forms of representation, we can find further evidence that, by his own argument, the sovereign may be a demonological construct, a product of misreading. For example, Hobbes claims that the sovereign is a *"Mortall God."* We might interpret this, as is often done, as suggesting that the sovereign's rule is established by God and that it rules on earth in God's name (that is indeed the sense of the sentence, which reads more fully "to which wee owe under the *Immortall God*, our peace and defence").[26] But if the sovereign is set up as representative of God, then what theory of representation is operative here? If the sovereign "represents" God the way Hobbes tells us that it represents the rest of us (as laid down in chapter 16 and elsewhere)—that is to say if the sovereign only pretends to represent God, as it pretends to represent the rest of us—then the sovereign is, by Hobbes's own argument, an idol, a concept that the term *Mortall God* can easily evoke.

However, Christopher Pye for one has argued that demonology does not work at cross-purposes with sovereignty itself. In his article on "The Sovereign, the Theater, and the Kingdome of Darknesse," Pye considers the value of demonology as a kind of theatrical performance of sovereign power. For Pye, demonology solves the paradox whereby the sovereign becomes not only the effect but also the source of its own empowerment.[27] He cites Hobbes as discussing an event in ancient Greece wherein an entire community went into a "Fever" after seeing a production of *Andromeda* on a very hot day. The entire community became "imprinted" with what they saw on stage so that they only spoke of and enacted lines from the play itself.[28] In other words the audience's reality became a reflection of the theatrical spectacle that they had witnessed. The "representation" on stage became the epistemological basis of reality for those subjects who witnessed it. For Pye, such a self-generating source of power comes very close to what Hobbes describes as demonology. For Pye, both political and demonological spectacle functions the same way: take something that belongs to people (in the first case authority, in the second case, their sense perceptions) and give it

back to them in an altered and alienated form (as sovereign authority in the
first instance, as ghostly phantoms in the latter).

Pye's claim is that rather than being disabling, such a maneuver is the
basis for the success of sovereign authority:

> Conceiving the sovereign as a daemonic presence does not resolve the prob-
> lem of political origins in Hobbes—it makes it the basis of the monarch's
> undeniable force. As a daemonic moment, the beginnings of the common-
> wealth become irresolvably circular: the terror which enables the sovereign to
> 'forme the will' of the subject is the terror the subject experiences knowing he
> has authored this form. In a sense, the subject's fear would be quite literally
> groundless. But the subject's awareness of the groundlessness of his response
> may be reason enough for genuine terror and idolatrous awe.[29]

If we can see the promulgation of sovereign authority as being analogous
to the production of demonological hallucinations, we are not far from seeing Hobbes as more critical of sovereign authority than he initially lets on.
While Pye himself sees the sovereign's nature as demonological spectacle
and the basis for its power, it is not too far a stretch to read Hobbes as exposing and condemning, rather than stealthily fomenting, sovereign authority over the rest of us, which would amount to using the very techniques he
most bitterly, and repeatedly, condemns. In Pye's argument, the fomenting
of sovereignty relies on the citizenry being unable to recognize the ways
they are being imprinted (because they see the imprint as "reality" itself).
But if, as I have argued, Hobbes's method of reading (and, by extension,
seeing) serves to make us aware of precisely the images and representations
that we receive, then the kind of illusion that Pye describes as the basis of
political authority could not long sustain itself.

Pye offers a useful metaphor that may help to support or illuminate my
own argument. He cites Hobbes's statement that "the decay of Sense" works
"as the light of the Sun obscureth the light of the Starres." While we are
constantly receiving sensory data, a predominant image or effect will eclipse
all the others, despite the fact that they, like the stars "do no less exercise
their vertue."[30] In a similar vein, Pye argues, the spectacle of sovereign authority overwrites all of our other impressions, not that they go away but

that they are simply rendered invisible to us. The act of seeing, like our own considerations of reading earlier in this book, becomes determined by the one overriding image that is to be seen, the image of the sovereign itself. But note that this is not saying that the other sorts of authorities and sensory impressions of people are lost forever. Indeed, the exposure or knowledge of the sovereign image as being idolatrous may indeed allow us to "see" what we have been in fact experiencing, but not recognizing all along: the "exercise [of our own] virtue" in the face of (and despite) sovereign authority. Even as we are being "imprinted" with demonological power, we remain capable of seeing, and reading otherwise.

The "Soule" of the Commonwealth

If alternative ways of seeing, or reading, continue to exist even under conditions of sovereignty, then Hobbes's notion of worshipful reading becomes less a literary conceit and more of a powerful or subversive weapon against sovereignty itself. If, as Pye suggests, our "seeing" (or reading) is overwritten and determined by sovereign imagery, then to learn how to see or read that imagery anew is a direct challenge to sovereign authority. Here I am reading Hobbes in a more subversive fashion than Pye himself does, but to do so I am merely pushing a bit on Pye's own arguments.

To give just one example (albeit a central one) of how we might learn to read images of sovereignty in *Leviathan* anew, let us consider one of the most famous metaphors that Hobbes uses to speak of sovereignty, namely his claim that the sovereign is the "soule" of the body politic:

> The Soveraignty is the Soule of the Common-wealth; which once departed from the Body; the members doe no more receive their motion from it. . . . And though Soveraignty, in the intention of them that make it, be immortall; yet is it in its own nature, not only subject to violent death by forreign war; but also through the ignorance, and passions of men, it hath in it, from the very institution, many seeds of a naturall mortality, by Intestine Discord.[31]

Hobbes's readings of religious doctrine are once again brought directly to bear on his political theory, marking the ongoing synergy between his religious, political, and rhetorical understandings of representation. This passage is typically read by contemporary scholars as a compliment, a pro-sovereign statement; the soul of the commonwealth means the most vital part, the foundation or basis of it. But if we recall that for Hobbes the soul and the belief in its immortality are a prime, indeed perhaps the prime example of the "Error of *Separated Essences*" itself, we can see that sovereignty is depicted here as being idolatrous, as taking over the life of people that it supposedly merely represents.

Although Hobbes appears formally to bemoan the mortality of sovereignty and to blame the "ignorance, and passions of men" for its demise, we can also see him here asserting the true frailty of sovereignty itself; like the soul, sovereignty is a renegade metaphor, and similarly, by exposing it "for what it is," the soul can be shown to "die" just like the body that it has superseded.

Representation, Personation, and the True God

This example of rereading might by itself convince us that Hobbes's notion of sovereignty is not what it appears to be, but in fact in chapter 16, Hobbes offers us another notion of representation that is just as crucial. In addition to his various counterexamples already considered, Hobbes also describes how God has been "personated" (that is to say represented) on earth. Immediately following the paragraph that considers idols as an example, or counterexample of representation, Hobbes states,

> The true God may be Personated. As he was; first, by *Moses;* who governed the Israelites, (that were not his, but Gods people,) not in his own name, with *Hoc dicit Moses;* but in Gods Name, with *Hoc dicit Dominus.* Secondly, by the Son of man, his own Son, our Blessed Saviour *Jesus Christ*, that came to reduce the Jewes, and induce all Nations into the Kingdome of his Father; not as himself, but as sent from his Father. And thirdly, by the Holy Ghost, or Comforter, speaking, and working in the Apostles: which Holy Ghost, was a Comforter that came not of himselfe; but was sent, and proceeded from them both on the day of Pentecost.[32]

This foreshadows much of part 3 of *Leviathan* and anticipates a great deal of the analysis to follow in this book. It describes three personations of God already mentioned (actually, and this is an important distinction, as we will see, only Moses and Jesus are persons; the Holy Spirit is a figure), that is to say the three representations of God that are incarnate (in some form or other) on earth, representations that are nonidolatrous by definition.

As we've already seen with Moses, all three "persons" (or "figures") miraculously deliver us from the kind of abyss that Hobbes's own skepticism threatens to open up. Although, for fairly obvious reasons, Hobbes himself uses the language of messianism only with Jesus himself, it seems clear that for Hobbes, Moses (as we have already seen) and the Holy Spirit (as we will soon see) too are moments of messianic intrusion into the world of human beings. In this sense, we might turn to Arendt's own definition of miracles, which, whether by a human or divine agent, "always must be . . . interruptions of some natural series of events, of some automatic process, in whose context they constitute the wholly unexpected."[33]

Moses and Jesus (the subjects of my next chapter) and the Holy Spirit (the subject of my penultimate chapter) are all miraculous persons and figures, insofar as without telling us anything further about God, they nonetheless infuse the world with newness, with meaning and possibility. Each of them, we will see, ushers something into the world that was not there before; each leaves in its wake (or in its anticipation) a community organized by the reception and interpretation of these events.

This then is not merely a "counterexample" but a completely alternative notion of representation set amid the discussion of terrestrial sovereignty. This does not tell "the true" story of *Leviathan* but simply an alternative story—one, however, with far-reaching and subversive implications. The persons of Moses and Jesus and the figure of the Holy Spirit can be said to spell out what, for lack of a better word, we might call Hobbes's "positive" theory of representation: those aspects of his theory that do not simply undermine or challenge idolatry (although they do that, too, particularly with the Holy Spirit), but offer, through their messianic irruption of the fabric of representation, instances of creativity, of meaningfulness whereby human actors can represent themselves into political life without resorting to ruses,

tyrants, or other manipulations. When we consider these persons and figures, the three strands of representation considered in this book—rhetorical, religious, and political—come most clearly into alignment (particularly
in the case of the figure of the Holy Spirit). We will explore this in more
detail beginning with the two "persons" of God that are connected with
God's actual kingdom—Moses and Jesus—and the kinds of political bonds,
promises, and obligations that are constituted by and through them.

5

The True Covenant

HAVING ESTABLISHED HOBBES'S theory of reading, we can look directly at its political, social, and religious implications, both in terms of how to interpret *Leviathan* and how we can envision a politics that exists independently of the sovereign principle. This chapter will focus especially on the question of obligations, promises, and covenants, those political arrangements that we make with one another both within and without sovereign authority. For Hobbes, these promises and covenants are the lasting basis for an alternative politics to sovereignty; the "horizontal" relationships that people form with one another serve as a font of authority that is different from, and potentially opposed to, the "vertical" relationship between people and the sovereign.

Although much contemporary scholarship focuses on how the sovereign is critical to making our promises to one another meaningful, I will show that for Hobbes, the promises we make to one another are actually made possible by a different sovereign: God. Unlike our contemporary sovereigns, God takes part in promising with people. These promises give us the ability to make our own promises to one another even though God is no longer (or not yet) king; we therefore have a basis to resist the nonpromising, nonreciprocal kind of power represented by contemporary sovereignty.

We will revisit the "political" language of parts 1 and 2 of *Leviathan*—in particular chapter 14, which treats the question of promising, contracts, and covenants directly—from the perspective of the theories of representation that Hobbes elucidates largely (but not entirely) in the second half of his book. More specifically, the question of political obligation will be revisited with Hobbes's notion of two (out of three) "persons" of God, namely Moses and Jesus, and the kinds of bonds and obligations that are fostered through them. If, as we have already begun to see, Moses sets the foundations of political authority for Hobbes, Jesus, as we will soon see, sets the meaning and power of promising and a sense of the future. Together, these persons (or more accurately the rhetorical figures Hobbes associates with these persons—"God the Father" and "God the Son," respectively) offer a particular society a sense of its past and its future, giving an eschatological framework to an otherwise ahistorical understanding of Hobbes's politics.

When we read Hobbes's treatment of the covenants that human beings make with one another against the covenants that they make with God (as instantiated by Moses and Jesus), our ordinary political covenants become potentially infused with the same kind of aporia that God represents in general for Hobbes. Rather than being fixed, or having one meaning (which the sovereign interprets for us), our covenants remain in play, creating an intergenerational bond, a series of obligations that serve to contain and preserve, but not restrict, a community's own self-development. Here again, our understanding of promising becomes a matter of correct reading. When we treat our promises as idolatrous "things," they supersede our own utterance of them, binding us absolutely. Such a reading issues us into the timeless world Hobbes describes in part 2 in which generations of people are bound by promises they never even made. What potentially saves us from this fate is the notion that a hypostatized God makes promises to human beings and keeps these promises regardless of what we do in response. I will argue that such a reading keeps our promises at least potentially open-ended and contingent.

Toward the end of this chapter, I will consider what for lack of a better word might be called Hobbes's voluntarism, the degree to which Hobbes offers a viable model of politics that does not depend upon the kind of external threats and prompts that are associated with sovereignty itself. As I will argue, Hobbes's eschatological understanding of promises and covenants forms the basis of his voluntarism, creating a viable alternative to the sovereign politics *Leviathan* is usually understood as espousing. I will engage with two authors to make this point. First, I will examine the work of Gregory S. Kavka, who also identifies a powerful voluntarist streak in Hobbes. Yet, in the end, Kavka determines that Hobbes requires sovereignty after all to make his system both moral and effective and to "complete" his theory of obligation. I will claim that the sovereign is the antithesis of rather than the solution to Hobbes's voluntarism insofar as it is excluded from the activity of promising; it is unrelated to the future in any way. The reason Kavka does not draw this conclusion himself may have something to do with the fact that he excludes the discussion of God and religious covenants from consideration and thus leaves out the crucial role of the messianic figures and persons that, as I read it, complete Hobbes's theory of obligation.

Following this discussion, I will reconsider how Hannah Arendt's own notions of promising, obligation, and the future relate to Hobbes's understanding. I will compare Arendt's own interest in a politics of "contracts and treaties," a politics of promising, to Hobbes's interest in such questions.[1] I will relate Hobbes's discussion of idolatry to Arendt's concern with what she calls "the absolute," a similarly opaque and future-denying style of antipolitics (something she connects explicitly to sovereignty itself). I will try to show that in his own version of religion, Hobbes is not succumbing to the absolute but is rather demonstrating how the absolute might possibly be banished from political life. I suggest that a turn to a more rhetorical sensibility such as Hobbes himself demonstrates may serve as a balm, if not a solution to the tragic modern politics that Arendt depicts in her own writings.

THE PERSONS OF GOD AND THE PROMISE

To begin this discussion, we must engage in a more detailed description of the "persons" of God who play such a prominent role in Hobbes's eschatology. It is these persons, and more accurately, as we will see, the rhetorical figures that Hobbes associates with these persons, that determine the context for Hobbes's understanding of politics. Here, I must ask the reader's forbearance as we unpack these complex notions.

Consistent with his treatment of other representative figures, the value of these persons of God for Hobbes lies in what effects they convey. This is particularly true of promises and covenants. By establishing a "before" (with Moses) and an "after" (with Jesus), these figures lay out the eschatological framework within which the faculty of promising operates. Without this eschatology, as we will see, promising loses its historical character and becomes inert and timeless (the condition of sovereignty).

For Hobbes, the question of God's personations is not a question of God literally incarnating into flesh (although the case of Jesus is complicated by his dual nature). Instead, these personations constitute yet another way that God can be "read" by human subjects; in this case too, Hobbes is displaying his rhetorical sensibilities. Here, this "reading" takes a peculiar form; unlike words, metaphors, or (potentially) miraculous events, which we have already examined, the personations of God constitute actual human beings. For Hobbes, such persons (at least in the case of Moses and Jesus) did and will rule on earth in God's name, establishing actual kingdoms with real, political consequences.

As we have already seen, Hobbes tells us that there are three instances whereby God has been so "Personated."[2] Moses was God's person in the Old Testament, Jesus was God's person in the New Testament, while the Christian church (and, more specifically, the Apostles) is/are God's person in the "Office of Preaching and Teaching," which has "Represented [God] ever since."[3] Later, after the publication of *Leviathan*, Hobbes retracted his claim that Moses was God's person, calling him instead a "minister" of God. Yet, in so doing, he did not fundamentally alter the critical representational function of Moses in his eschatology. For the sake of convenience, and in keeping with what is written in *Leviathan* itself, I will continue to speak of Moses as God's "person."[4]

To understand this concept of personation, recall Hobbes's definition in chapter 16 of *Leviathan*: "A PERSON, is he *whose words or actions are considered, either as his own, or as representing the words or actions of an other man.*"[5] Thus by labeling these beings as "personations," Hobbes is explicitly considering the representational aspect of Moses, Jesus, and the church and Apostles.

Considering these persons in terms of the Trinity, Hobbes tells us,

> In this Trinity on Earth, the Unity is not of the thing; for the Spirit, the Water, and the Bloud, are not the same substance, though they give the same testimony: But in the Trinity of Heaven, the Persons are the persons of one and the same God, though Represented in three different times and occasions. (3.42, p. 340)

In other words, as themselves, as three separate bodies, these persons do not perfectly reflect the oneness of God ("the Unity is not of the thing"). Hobbes calls Moses God's "lieutenant" (or place holder) and yet, as a physical being, Moses has his own identity; he is not a pure or perfect sign for God. Accordingly, Hobbes tells us that each of these persons also corresponds to a rhetorical figure. Keeping with the language of the Trinity, Moses is figured as "God the Father," Jesus as "the Son," and the church and Apostles are "the Holy Spirit" (pp. 339–40). Of these figurations, Hobbes writes:

> From whence we may gather the reason why those names, *Father, Son,* and *Holy Spirit* in the signification of the Godhead, are never used in the Old Testament: For they are Persons, that is, they have their names from Representing; which could not be, till divers men had Represented Gods Person in ruling, or in directing under him. (p. 341)

Here, as is the case with miracles, the literal event or thing is part of the equation; the actual flesh-and-blood person prefigures the rhetorical name ("Representing . . . could not be, till divers men had Represented Gods Person. . . ."). Hence, Hobbes tells us that we call God the "Father" "from [the time of Moses] forward, but not before" (3.41, p. 338). Similarly God could not be called the "Sonne" till Jesus (p. 338).

But it is once again the rhetorical figure itself that is Hobbes's prime interest. The notion of three separate things sharing one substance can only be expressed by a set of figures that have no substance of their own (i.e., by those signs qua signs that "have their names from Representing"). Only in this way can "there bee a plurality of Persons, though of one and the same Substance" (p. 338). In each case, in their blankness, the rhetorical figure of these personations (as opposed to the persons themselves) allow us to see the "unity" of the trinity as well as "profess[ing the] inconstancy" of the persons (thus preserving our reading of them from idolatry). The figures inform but also affect the persons that they are associated with. Thus Jesus is a man but as "the Son" he is something else as well.

The Promise

For Hobbes, these persons of God and their corresponding figures are iterations of the covenant made between God and Abraham. Hobbes argues that, had they not eaten of the apple of knowledge, Adam and Eve would have lived eternally here on earth, with God as their king (3.38, p. 308). The covenant, as Hobbes sees it, is God's way of redeeming humanity after the fall; it constitutes a promise never to abandon the human race but offer a permanent source of hope for human salvation. Despite God's being frequently abandoned and betrayed by human beings, this promise to humanity is periodically renewed and (re)instantiated through the persons of God and their corresponding figures.

Tracing the history of God's promise to human beings, Hobbes describes the covenant God makes with Abraham wherein God "speak[s] . . . these words, *I will establish my Covenant between me, and thee, and thy seed after thee in their generations, for an everlasting Covenant, to be a God to thee, and to thy seed after thee*" (3.35, pp. 280–81). In this covenant "*Abraham promiseth for himselfe and his posterity to obey as God, the Lord that spake to him: and God on his part promiseth to Abraham the land of Canaan for an everlasting possession*" (p. 281). The mutual promising that constitutes the covenant is utterly unlike the covenant that our contemporary sovereigns preside over, as already mentioned, insofar as the terrestrial sovereign makes no such promises in return. Accordingly, unlike the secular covenant described in parts 1 and 2 (i.e., the social contract), this covenant never ends; it cannot be abrogated by any human action.[6]

For Hobbes, the establishment of the kingdom of God is a "renewing of the same Covenant [as Abraham] by Moses, at Mount Sinai" (p. 281). The coming kingdom of Jesus is similarly a reiteration of this promise. Hobbes tells us that "the Prophets did foretell [God's] restitution [as king]" (p. 283). Even during our own time, after the Israelites rejected God as their king (and before the reestablishment of that kingdom by Christ on earth), the promise remains in effect. The Bible says, "*I will bring you into the bond of the Covenant*" (Ezekiel 20:37), which Hobbes interprets as meaning, "I will reign over you, and make you to stand to that Covenant which you made with me by Moses, and brake in your rebellion against me in the days of Samuel, and in your election of another King" (p. 283). Thus, although human actors have broken the covenant, once it is instantiated we remain bound and obliged by it nonetheless.

The Performance of the Promise

Ever focused on the specifically rhetorical character of promising, Hobbes tells us that God's utterance of the promise is in some sense more important, more material than the very fabric of the world itself. Hobbes cites the passage from Matthew (24:35), "*heaven and earth shall pass away, but my Words shal not pass away*" (3.36, p. 289), and interprets this as meaning "there is nothing that [God has] promised or foretold, that shall not come to passe" (p. 289). Here we see Hobbes's nominalism at its most explicit. As an utterance, the promise, once given by God (or, more accurately, read by us as having been given by God) is prior to—and survives—its various manifestations.

Accordingly, for Hobbes the manifestations of the promise are distinct from the promise itself. Interpreting the biblical passage wherein it is said of Christ that his name is "*the Word of God*" (Revelation 19:13), Hobbes writes that this "is to be understood, as if he had said his name had been, *He that was come according to the purpose of God from the beginning, and according to his Word and promises delivered by the Prophets*" (p. 289). Of this, Hobbes further writes: "There is nothing here of the Incarnation of a Word, but of the Incarnation of God the Son, therefore called *the Word*, because his Incarnation was the Performance of the Promise; In like manner as the Holy Ghost is called *the Promise*" (pp. 289–90). We cannot call this the "Incarnation of the Word" because to suggest that would mean God's Word was actually present and known in the world (an idolatrous notion). Instead of an incarnation of the Word itself, we have only an incarnation of the empty rhetorical figure of "God the Son." This is a "Performance of the Promise," an instance where God's promise is read and understood as having had an effect in the world without itself becoming either manifest or explicit.

As for the physical beings (or "persons") themselves, in the case of Jesus, Hobbes tells us that "*the Word was made Flesh;* that is to say, the Word, or Promise that Christ should come into the world" (3.36, p. 289). Jesus is the manifestation of "the Word, or Promise," not the word or promise itself.

Hobbes interprets the biblical interpretation of Christ as being he "*who in the beginning was with God*" as meaning that it "was in the purpose of God the Father" to send his Son into the world. Thus, in a sense, Christ existed as a promise (or word) before he existed as a person (p. 289). But Hobbes tells us that until Christ's birth "[the promise of Christ's coming] was not till then put in execution, and actually incarnate" (p. 289). Here again, Hobbes is careful not to call Jesus a literal incarnation of God but rather, via his rhetorical figuration as "God the Son," a reflection and performance of God's promise to the world.

Thus Hobbes says "so that our Saviour is there [in the Bible] called *the Word*, not because he was the promise, but the thing promised" (p. 289). As with miracles, the promise, the divine word, is conveyed by the "thing," (in this case, the person of Jesus) but the promise is not exhausted in the thing.[7]

As a pure hypostatization of God's will, the promise is reflected in human history, particularly in terms of the eschatology presented in Scripture, even as it remains in a sense intact and impervious to events on earth. The promise provides continuity for an otherwise random, disparate series of human events without in any way determining the content of those events. It is, as we will see further, what saves us from idolatry, from the randomness and arbitrariness of sovereign pronouncement, and it is what makes our own mutual promising possible and meaningful. Although as far as we are concerned, God's promise is conveyed to us solely via a series of rhetorical constructions (albeit ones that are applied to what Hobbes considered to be real historical—and future—persons), the promise is nonetheless for Hobbes the basic fabric of our world.

THE KINGDOM(S) OF GOD

The political significance of this eschatological history becomes clearer when we follow Hobbes's interest in the question of God's promise and its relationship to the political realms that it ushers into the world, namely the forementioned "kingdom(s) of God." Recall that for Hobbes the term *kingdom of God* refers to a real, earthly kingdom, one of the past (ancient Israel, led by Moses) and one of the future (the kingdom of Christ, led by Jesus).

Thus these personations do more than simply announce or represent God, they also rule and produce authority in God's name.

The astute reader may have noticed that there are three personations of God on earth and three corresponding figures, but only two kingdoms. We have a kingdom of the Father (Israel) and of the Son (the reign of Christ), but what about the third person of God (which after all would constitute the "kingdom" of Hobbes's as well as our own time)? Recall Hobbes's insistence that any church that proclaims the "kingdom of God" to be here is idolatrous. Here, the "third" person of God (the church itself) is explicitly being deprived of any relationship to a "kingdom." This absence, which is structured as an *anacoluthon*, a rhetorical figure wherein the presence of something is inferred from its omission, may be one of the most telling things about Hobbes's narrative. To fail to label our own period a "kingdom of God" in its own right is to call into question precisely the nature of the kingdoms we *do* have, to look critically at the practice of sovereignty itself.

As I will be arguing further in the next chapter, this nonkingdom, contrasted with the "Kingdome of Darknesse" that we have in its stead, is critical for Hobbes insofar as it is the marker of his (as well as our own) contemporary politics. As we will see in the next chapter, it is less the "person" of God (the church) than the figure of "God the Holy Spirit" that is essential for combating the false kingdom of our time. As is so often the case with Hobbes, the exposure of the Holy Spirit as "nothing," as having no kingdom and no (sovereign) power, leads not to a sense of its meaningless, but on the contrary, to precisely its source of power.

We will get to this question in the next chapter. In the meantime, let us examine the kingdoms that did or will exist, those kingdoms that contain our own time between their iterations. To focus on these two kingdoms reminds us of the eschatological history that many readers of Hobbes (with important exceptions) downplay or ignore. There are several questions to ponder in Hobbes's treatment of these two kingdoms. How are these actual kingdoms, and the authority that they did or will produce related to, and expressions of, God's promise? How does the figurative representation of God's covenant with the Jews and then, by extension, the Christians, sit with actual questions of political authority and obligation in our own "kingdomless" time? How does a consideration of those religious covenants affect the secular and political covenants and promises that we make with one another?

Ancient Israel

Hobbes tells us, "By the Kingdome of Heaven, is meant the Kingdome of the King that dwelleth in Heaven; and his Kingdome was the people of Israel." In other words, although God is omnipotent and universal, God's kingdom, to exist at all, exists only on Earth (3.38, p. 309). He calls this "a Civill Kingdome; which consisted, first in the obligation of the people of Israel to those Laws, which Moses should bring unto them from Mount Sinai" (3.35, p. 284) In considering the nature of this "obligation," Hobbes describes what God "tells" Moses on Mount Sinai: "*If you will obey my voice indeed, and keep my Covenant, then yee shall be a peculiar people to me, for all the Earth is mine; And yee shall be unto me a Sacerdotall Kingdome, and a holy Nation*" (p. 281). Hobbes reads the juxtaposition in this passage between "all the earth is mine" on the one hand and "yee shall be a peculiar people to me" on the other as meaning that "they [other people] are all mine, by reason of my Power; but you [Moses and the Israelites] shall be mine, by your own Consent, and Covenant; which is an addition to his ordinary title, to all nations" (p. 282). The difference between these two kinds of rule is crucial to Hobbes. The (absolute) power that God already has over all humanity and the earth is for Hobbes explicitly not a political matter. Political authority, and with it the mutual obligations that follow, can only come into being through the covenant (re)established via Moses, the "first" person of God.

The covenant Hobbes refers to here is, as we have seen, an iteration of the original covenant with Abraham, but in this case it can be said to have "incarnated" something unprecedented in the world, namely God's sovereignty and, along with it, law. The covenant of Abraham does not establish but anticipates the political authority of the first kingdom.

For Hobbes, the instantiation of the kingdom of God ushers in the world of politics and law as we know it. In a superb and rhetorically minded interpretation of the Ten Commandments, Hobbes tells us that "before that time [of Moses's reception of the Ten Commandments], there was no written Law of God, who as yet having not chosen any people to bee his peculiar Kingdome, had given no Law to men, but the Law of Nature, that is to say, the Precepts of Naturall Reason, written in every mans own heart" (3.42, p. 356). Although "written in every mans . . . heart," crucially, the law is not yet written anywhere else. It is the act of representation once again, the inscribing of law into texts (as accomplished by Moses with the two tablets) that conveys and transforms unknowable divine truths into tangible human law.[8] In their promise to *"obey* [God's] *voice indeed, and keep* [God's] *Covenant,"* the Jews represented God's law into the world, binding themselves to one another in the process.

Hobbes tells us that of the two tablets on which the commandments are written, "the first containeth the law of Soveraignty."[9] The first commandment, to have no gods before God, means for Hobbes that "they were forbidden to obey, or honor, as their King and Governour, any other God." The all-important commandment against graven images means "they were not to choose to themselves, neither in heaven, nor in earth, any Representative of their own fancying, but obey Moses and Aaron, whom he had appointed to that office" (pp. 356–57). To make an image of God would be to "represent" God falsely when God is already represented by the person of God. Hobbes interprets "not tak[ing] the Name of God in vain" as meaning that "they should not speak rashly of their King" (p. 357). For Hobbes, these commandments in particular establish God's kingdom on earth. By "ratifying" Moses's representation of the Ten Commandments and reestablishing the covenant in a new, explicitly political guise, the Jews make God their king.

Hobbes tells us that the second tablet contains "the Duty of one man towards another, as *To honor Parents; Not to kill; Not to Commit Adultery; Not to steale"* (p. 357). In considering the relationship of the second tablet to the first (and of the commandments in general to the prior and nonrepresented law of nature itself), Hobbes further tells us:

> Some of them [the laws of the Ten Commandments] were indeed the Laws of Nature, as all the Second Table; and therefore to be acknowledged for Gods Laws; not to the Israelites alone, but to all people. . . . Those that were peculiar to the Israelites, [were] those of the first Table. (p. 357)

The second tablet, then, is the one that expresses the "natural" law that seemingly predates Moses's personation of God. But even here, Hobbes stresses that in the transcribing of these laws, they are changed and made into something new. *Only* as written law (i.e., only as a representation) does natural law too become a political question; only then does it become in a sense "law" as a human contrivance.

Even if it were exactly coincident to the eternal "Natural Law" itself (something that we can never know one way or the other), the second tablet *is* what natural law will be as far as we are concerned. This is not in an idolatrous way (as in replacing natural law with a false representational idol), but rather in the sense that it serves as a basis for our own interpretations of law. But it is once again the first tablet that Hobbes is really interested in because it is not coincident with anything eternal but is the birth of something absolutely new. Unlike the second tablet, which aims to represent something that already is, the first tablet is pure representation, born from its own act of being read and authorized.

The End of God's (First) Kingdom

Thus far, it might appear that for Hobbes this establishment of political and sovereign authority does indeed set up a chain of command stemming from God to future, secular sovereigns, through this covenant. It seems to create an eternal bond of obligation that human beings, once they have promised themselves to God (and read themselves as having been promised in return), cannot wriggle their way out of. Hobbes reinforces this view by calling the kingdom of God a "Civill Kingdome" (3.35, p. 284). He writes,

> It was therefore onely Moses then, and after him the High Priest, whom (by Moses) God declared should administer this his peculiar Kingdome, that had on Earth, the power to make this short Scripture of the Decalogue to bee Law in the Common-wealth of Israel. But Moses, and Aaron, and the succeeding High Priests were the Civill Soveraigns. Therefore hitherto, the Canonizing, or making of the Scripture Law, belonged to the Civill Soveraigne. (3.42, p. 357)

The "Civill Kingdome" of God seemingly becomes the model for all law and all future sovereignty (future civil kingdoms) as well. Hobbes tells us that these tenets "became Lawes, by vertue of the same promise of obedience to Moses," seemingly extending the very basis of the kingdom of God to our own time (p. 357).

Yet to conclude this is once to again to neglect Hobbes's own arguments about the uniqueness, not only of Moses's personation, but also of God's sovereignty, which it ushered into the world. If we focus more specifically on the question of political sovereignty, we see here too, and by Hobbes's own arguments, that the unique nature of God's sovereignty in ancient Israel cannot, by definition, be seen as extending to our present time.

According to Hobbes's own genealogy, God's sovereignty is utterly unlike the terrestrial sovereignty that we have in our own "kingdomless" time. For Hobbes, the unbroken sovereignty of God as king of Israel effectively ends with the rule of the prophet Samuel and the subsequent election of Saul as King of the Israelites:

> The people of Israel refused any more to have God to be their King, in other manner than he was King of other people; and therefore cryed out to *Samuel,* to choose them a King after the manner of the Nations. So that Justice fayling, Faith also fayled: Insomuch, as they deposed their God, from reigning over them. (1.12, p. 85)

At this point God's rule is no longer political. God's kingship reverts to being "in the manner . . . of other people," that is, a king in fact ("by reason of [God's] Power") but not by law ("by your own Consent, and Covenant"). Thus God is no longer a king in any way that Hobbes himself recognizes as political. Here ends the (first) kingdom of God and with it the more or less unbroken line of sovereignty descending from Moses.

In the absence of God's rule, we get a more "ordinary" form of rule (i.e., a rule that we might find in other nations), terrestrial sovereignty. Hobbes's sharp rebuke to the Israelites who sought to choose a king "after the manner of the Nations" forms a parable about the nature of representation, rule, and authority. Here, as is so often the case with Hobbes, rhetorical, religious, and political models of representation are overlaid upon one another. The

Jews' election of Saul is an idolatrous act in which "Justice fayling, Faith also fayled." Here, by Hobbes's own argument, people have actually broken the second commandment in that they have failed to "obey Moses and Aaron, whom [God] had appointed to that office" (although Moses is long dead at this point, he remains God's "person" via the figure of "God the Father"). As a mortal king, Saul is the Israelites' "person" and not God's. He is thus by Hobbes's own logic a kind of idol, a far more accurate model for future sovereigns than Moses himself. All future sovereigns (with the exception, of course, of Jesus Christ) are similarly "chosen" by people, reiterating this "fayling" of faith and justice.[10] It makes sense, then, that such sovereigns promise nothing to their citizenry; not being themselves iterations of the covenant, they don't practice a form of politics based on promises but rather revert to an "anti" or "nonpolitical" rule by force ("in the manner . . . of other people").

Recall once more that for Hobbes, the central tenet of demonology is the conceit that the kingdom of God already exists in our time. Such an idea is the epitome of idolatry precisely because it fails to recognize the fundamentally different nature of authority and representation that occurred when God actually was king of a human kingdom. Similarly, to conflate the sovereignty of God with the sovereignty of contemporary monarchs can be seen for Hobbes as a serious—and idolatrous—mistake. Following the election of Saul as king, the model of sovereignty in Moses is one that becomes sadly distorted in later iterations of human kingdoms. Although the civil and ecclesiastical powers are united under Moses's command, they become separated in later human reproductions of this unique kingdom. Until the restitution of the kingdom of God, no sovereign ever after can rule with the same sort of absolute authority as Moses did as God's "lieutenant" on earth. While Moses (and those who followed him in his role up until Saul) was indeed a "Civill Soveraigne," his rule is utterly tied up with God's own sovereignty in a way that cannot be duplicated after Saul's election. When God is no longer king, we are stuck with other, lesser kings.

A Sovereign Who Makes Promises

For all this, it would be a mistake to conclude that for Hobbes the covenant that God established with the Jews collapsed with God's deposition as king.

God does not abandon the human race—or, more particularly, those who remain bound by the covenant—even when they have abandoned God. For Hobbes, God remains a presence in the world via the ongoing iterations of the promise.

In considering the unique nature of God's sovereignty compared to future sovereigns, it is crucial to note once again that *God is the only sovereign who makes covenants and promises.* Unrelated to the covenant itself, future sovereigns (with the notable exception of Jesus), as Hobbes makes very plain, are not bound by promises, owe their people nothing (unless moved by charity or self-interest), and are hence excluded from an activity that for Hobbes is in a sense the sine qua non of political life.

Accordingly, the style and meaning of the promises that are facilitated by terrestrial sovereigns (that is to say, the meaning of the social contract itself) is vastly different from that of the covenant made with God. To read the first half of *Leviathan* without reference to God's promise ushers us into a realm that is both hopeless, ahistorical, and even, in some regard, *antipolitical* (to use Arendt's term). Hobbes's depiction of promising in an age when God is no longer king seems devoid of a future; bonds and obligations, as we will see further, are made with no reference to consent, to change. We seem bound by promises that Hobbes seems willing to concede we never actually made; our obedience is demanded regardless of circumstances, at the whim of the sovereign and not only now but forever.

The first kingdom of God for Hobbes is not so much the source of a continual line of sovereign practices as it is a kind of frame within which future iterations of political life will be organized. Rather than bind us absolutely with promises and covenants that were made in the infinite past (so that somehow the promises of Abraham are seen to bind Hobbes's contemporary citizens of England to a particular form of political allegiance), Hobbes's treatment of the first kingdom of God offers us a continuity that has no specific content or character.

In our own "kingdomless" time (whether Hobbes's or our own), it may seem as if a now-lost kingdom of God has very little to do with us. This might indeed be the case unless we remember that for Hobbes we are in fact suspended in time between two kingdoms. God's promise to us, represented by the figure of God the Father, will be represented again through the figure of God the Son. The effect of this representation of a "second" kingdom of God is crucial for the ongoing possibility of promising and it is to this other kingdom that we now turn our attention.

The Kingdom of Christ

The "other" kingdom of God, the kingdom of Christ, is distinguished from the kingdom of Israel by the fact that it does not yet exist. Hobbes tells us that unlike Moses, Christ did not have an actual kingdom on earth in his (first) lifetime. When Jesus tells Pontius Pilate, "*My Kingdome is not of this world*" (John 18:36), Hobbes reads this as meaning not that his kingdom is in fact in heaven but rather as an acknowledgment of the fact that "after the day of Judgement . . . there shall bee a new Heaven, and a new Earth; the Kingdome of Christ is not to begin till the generall Resurrection."[11]

Hobbes tells us that Christ is already king in the sense that he *is* God (i.e., that part of Christ that is not God's "person") and hence, like God (and natural law), he is eternally and universally omnipotent. But in terms of his own kingdom, that which stems not from his identity with God but his personation of God, Hobbes writes: "But then he shall be King, not onely as God, in which sense he is King already, and ever shall be, of all the Earth, in vertue of his omnipotence; but also peculiarly of his own Elect, by vertue of the pact they make with him in their Baptisme."[12] Thus this kingdom, like the kingdom of Israel, will be a "civill" kingdom in the sense that it is produced not by God (or Jesus-as-God's) absolute, apolitical power, but by the "Consent, and Covenant" made between God and the Christian community and hence by another iteration of the original covenant itself. Given his focus on our own "kingdomless" time, Hobbes is particularly interested in the way that Christ is himself not yet king. Whereas the kingdom of Israel ushers in law and sovereignty, the kingdom of Christ ushers in another kind of power, as demonstrated by the "pact [Christians] make with him in their Baptisme," an indication of their consent to be ruled in a future kingdom by Jesus Christ. This pact is itself a reiteration of the promise wherein Christ is "the thing promised." As a pact, the sacrament of baptism ensures that the kingdom of Christ will be, like the kingdom of Israel, a particular kingdom, composed only of those who have so promised themselves.

In considering the earthly power of Christ on earth before his kingdom, Hobbes writes,

> For if the Supreme King [God], have not his Regall Power in this world; by
> what authority can obedience be required to his Officers? ... But our Sav-
> iour was sent to perswade the Jews to return to, and to invite the Gentiles,
> to receive the Kingdome of his Father, and not to reign in Majesty, no not,
> as his Fathers Lieutenant, till the day of Judgment.... And [this power of
> persuasion] is compared by our Saviour, to Fishing; that is, to winning men
> to obedience, not by Coercion, and Punishing [i.e., via sovereign law]; but by
> Perswasion: and therefore he said not to his Apostles, hee would make them
> so many.... *Hunters of men; but Fishers of men.*[13]

As opposed to a specifically legal and sovereign power to command (the power of the "first kingdom"), we have with Jesus (the kingdom of God to come) "only" the power to persuade based on the promise that Jesus bears, the promise of everlasting life. Jesus (unlike Moses) will be a full-fledged sovereign, but in our own time, the "power" of this future kingdom comes not from its manifestation, but only from the future promise it conveys. This kingdom then "exists" in our time purely and only as a representation of God's promise.

"JESUS IS THE CHRIST"

Crucially, although "not yet here," for Hobbes the kingdom of God to come already has an effect in the world, that is to say, an effect in Hobbes's (and our own) time. Hobbes tells us (implicitly along with the notion that "God *is*") that Scripture only really tells us one thing: "that JESUS IS THE CHRIST."[14] He tells us that "there can ... be no contradiction between the Laws of God, and the Laws of a Christian Common-wealth" (3.43, p. 414), this by definition. A Christian queen or king must believe or at least say they believe that Jesus is Christ. Should they "make some superstructions of Hay, or Stubble, and command the teaching of the same," that is, should they embellish the Scriptures, as inevitably happens with all sorts of their own fancy and misinterpretation, "yet ... [they] shal be saved" (p. 413). In other words, it is understandable and indeed inevitable that kings and queens, or other leaders in a "kingdomless" time, will demand a certain kind of embellishment to Scripture. Because Scripture tells us so little, most or indeed all sovereign pronouncements about Scripture (and perhaps, by extension, about other matters as well) are little more than "Hay, or Stubble," arbitrary and solipsistic (without however necessarily jeopardizing their chance for salvation). Hobbes tells us that no sovereign can turn false dogma into absolute truth since they can neither add to nor subtract from the one axiom that Scripture offers us.

Hobbes's notion that there can be no "contradiction" between state and church law does not suggest, as it initially appears, that the sovereign can do no wrong. On the contrary, the sovereign can do (and produce) no right, rendering sovereign judgments essentially irrelevant. Nothing that the sovereign says can contradict the basic foundation of Christian faith (nor can an "infidel" sovereign for that matter). The promise as an ongoing capacity cannot be violated by anything the sovereign does.

In arguing that the only truth in Scripture is that "JESUS IS THE CHRIST," Hobbes may be pointing to the irresistible power of the future sovereign of the world, but he might just as easily be revealing the aporia of God's unknowability that is contained by such a phrase. As with his other assertion that "God is," the phrase "JESUS IS THE CHRIST" tells us nothing about Jesus (or God), but only about our power to produce meanings and political effects with words, even meanings about things we cannot possibly know or understand. "JESUS IS THE CHRIST" is a cipher, a sign boiled down to its barest representational level. As such it reveals the blankness of the figure of "God the Son." Such a figure cannot announce a certain, sovereign, and eternal kingdom in advance of that kingdom's actual arrival. While the future sovereignty that Jesus represents may seem to trump and supersede our own self-making future, as far as we can ourselves know, the kingdom of Christ remains only an instantiation of the idea of the future; it has no content (any content that we might infer would only amount to more "Hay, or Stubble"). If the figure of "God the Father" offers us an epistemological envelope, a method of interpretation that no sovereign can avoid, the figure of "God the Son" offers a radically contingent, unstructured future that no contemporary sovereign can fill or replace with their own false musings. In the meantime, it remains our responsibility (with the "assistance" of the Holy Spirit, as we will see in the next chapter) during our own kingdomless time to prepare for and indeed produce the notion of the kingdom that will be. In this way, God's promise remains effective even or perhaps especially when it has not yet delivered anything, when it remains empty and unfulfilled in our own time.

PROMISING AND SOCIAL COVENANTS: CREATING THE FUTURE

When we consider that our own time is positioned between these two kingdoms of God, we can see that for Hobbes we stand between a rule of absolute sovereignty that we no longer have and a promise of life everlasting that we do not yet have. What is the value of the kingdom(s) of God in our (kingdomless) time? More specifically, how do these iterations of God's promise inform our own time? What obligations do they impose on us? What is the nature of the promise itself when God is not our king and has (seemingly) nothing to offer us at this time except faith, persuasion, or belief?

Were he a more conventional theologian, Hobbes might not need to venture beyond the question of faith and belief with a theory of obligation; we would simply be obliged to act in ways that the Christian faith instructs us. But interested as he is in politics and rhetoric, in the effects of belief rather than their actual truth (which cannot be known), for Hobbes the notion of God's persons and the two kingdoms of God must have a tangible value in our own time to be worth considering at all. In order to ascertain, then, the effect of Hobbes's religious considerations of promising on his political statements about covenants and political obligation, it is necessary to directly compare them.

Hobbes facilitates such a comparison because in both cases we are once again dealing with questions of representation. For Hobbes, promises, in their secular or religious sense, constitute an attempt to represent oneself (or perhaps one's descendants) in one's own future. In his consideration of promising in chapter 14, which concerns natural law and contracts, Hobbes tells us that a promise constitutes "words of the future" (1.14, p. 94). As such, they must reflect a particular relationship to that future in order to be binding:

Words alone, if they be of the time to come, and contain a bare promise, are an insufficient signe of a Free-gift and therefore not obligatory. For if they be of the time to Come, as, *To morrow I will Give*, they are a signe I have not given yet, and consequently that my right is not transferred, but remaineth till I transferre it by some other Act. But if the words be of the time Present, or Past, as, *I have given, or do give to be delivered to morrow*, then is my to morrows Right given away to day; and that by the vertue of the words, though there were no other argument of my will. And there is a great difference in the signification of these words, *Volc hoc tuum esse cras*, and *Cras dabo*; that is, between *I will that this be thine to morrow*, and, *I will give it thee to morrow:* For the word *I will*, in the former manner of speech, signifies an act of the will Present; but in the later, it signifies a promise of an act of the will to Come: and therefore the former words, being of the Present, transferre a future right; the later, that be of the Future, transferre nothing. (pp. 94-95)

We can only promise what is true at a particular moment in time, i.e., at the moment that the promise is uttered. We cannot by "words alone" bind our future will, such that we demand that we will then what we will now. Such a promise is void because for Hobbes, the will does not operate that way; it cannot guarantee its own consistency. Indeed, as is well known, for Hobbes the will isn't a faculty at all, but merely *"the last Appetite in Deliberating"* (1.6, p. 45). To promise a consistent will would be to impose a false representation, to pose as a binding truth that which is anything but. We can only promise that at this point in time we wish to want to do something in the future.

Hobbes follows the passage cited above by arguing that a contract is an extension of the notion of "*I will that this be thine to morrow*," that it consists of words of the present that are oriented toward the future. Hobbes tells us that "all Contract is mutuall translation, or change of Right; and therefore he that promiseth onely, because he hath already received the benefit for which he promiseth, is to be understood as if he intended the Right should passe" (1.14, p. 95). A contract then is a mutual agreement made in the present that is binding in the future because "unlesse he had been content to have his words so understood, the other would not have performed his part first" (p. 95). In this case, we are not binding our future wills by our "words alone," so much as we are binding one another through the fact that each of us agrees to and wants something in the present that we will be allowed to receive in the future. Based on the promises we make in the present, a future performance is demanded, regardless of what we will at that time; a future performance is required as based on a present performance. As ever with Hobbes, it is only when a promise is revealed to be purely representative that it has what he would consider to be a binding force.

In this case of such a contract, Hobbes tells us, "a Promise is equivalent to a Covenant; and therefore obligatory."[15] In terms of the distinction for Hobbes between contracts and covenants, Gregory S. Kavka tells us, "contracts in which one or more parties are called on to perform their parts as some time after the contract is made are *covenants*."[16] In this way, the notion of the covenant in particular introduces the notion of the future into the process of promising. As opposed to empty "words alone" where the future is totally absent (since the future will cannot be anticipated), a covenant is an act of mutual obligation that is expressly oriented toward (a possibly extended) future.

But what kind of obligations in the future? A good way to understand these obligations is to consider how Hobbes deals with covenants that have already been made. After all, we live in the "future" of those covenants and so are presumably bound in some way by them. The best place to look at the nature of such obligations is in Hobbes's famous social contract theory. Kavka notes that as a parable for political obligation, Hobbes's notion of a social contract has some problems. For one thing, not all societies have actually made such a contract; for another, even when a society has so "contracted"(as for example the people of the United States presumably did when they ratified the Constitution), future generations of subjects have not. Why then are they bound and if so, how?[17] Kavka tells us that for Hobbes obligation comes from both hypothetical and tacit consent on the part of the promisers.[18]

Yet such forms of consent do not necessarily solve the problem of obligation. Given Hobbes's strict analysis of what constitutes a valid promise, if the promise is never uttered at all, how does it serve its proper representative function (as described above)? Hobbes's representational theory makes the idea of hypothetical consent much more problematic. Kavka himself attempts to make sense of this by looking at Hobbes's treatment of acquisition by conquest, wherein a people "promise future obedience in return for having [their] life spared and liberty allowed [them]."[19] This obedience is then handed down from one generation to the next so long as the basic premise (the protection of life and limited liberty) are honored by the sovereign. The fact that future generations do not necessarily have their life immediately threatened and so themselves gain nothing from this promise does not seem to bear on this analysis.[20] More to the point, it remains unclear how, representationally speaking, a promise made in the present can be said to bind not only one's own future, but that of one's progeny as well. Such a bond seems like the essence of a separated essence, a false imposition of one's own will onto the unknown future.

At the same time, the sorts of political and social obligations depicted here seem at first glance to be quite similar to Hobbes's discussion of religious covenants between God and human subjects. If anything, religious covenants are far more enduring insofar as nothing can break them whatsoever, as we have already seen. Hobbes makes the intergenerational obligation of the covenant with God explicit:

> The Covenant God made with *Abraham* (in a Supernaturall manner) was thus, *This is the Covenant which thou shalt observe between Me and Thee and thy Seed after thee. Abrahams* Seed had not this revelation, nor were yet in being; yet they are a party to the Covenant, and bound to obey what *Abraham* should declare to them for Gods Law; which they could not be, but in vertue of the obedience they owed to their Parents.[21]

If we are so bound by these intergenerational covenants, is it really true that Hobbes has in effect condemned future generations of subjects to promises that may not have ever actually been made? Is the model of religious covenants being used to similarly make political contracts permanent and inalienable? Kavka's attempt to "explain" Hobbes only seems to worsen the implications; are we really to treat the question of political obligation as either (yet again) another ruse or as a kind of permanent semi-slavery (as the model of political conquest suggests)? Once again, Hobbes seems to offer that we have certain rights and recourses (in this case, the right to have meaningful consent and promises) when we have nothing of the kind. The parable of the social contract seems even more perplexing when we recall that the figure to whom we submit ourselves in perpetuity, the sovereign, never promises us anything (even hypothetically); our promises (even if they never actually occurred) are to one another, but we seem to get very little, if anything, out of them.

Here we seem to be devoid both of past (where we actually made a meaningful covenant) and future (where we might actually have some choice about what the meaning and effects of our promising could be). When we read chapter 14 on its own, we not only have very little sense of political reciprocity but also of time itself. Without the sense of time produced by Hobbes's eschatology, we find ourselves in the context of a completely ahistorical tale. Perhaps it's more accurate to say we are in the context of a strange pseudohistory that details how we move from the state of nature to the social contract. The state of nature might supply a sort of past, but markedly (in what is perhaps yet another *anacoluthon*) there is no sense of a real future in this story, no sense of movement beyond what already is; one generation is bound as much as another in an unchanging line—there is no recognition of development, of differentiation, of time.

It is at this point we must distinguish more clearly between the effects of the social contract itself and the effects of the covenant with God. For, as I will argue further, although it is true that the covenants made with God are never-ending, the obligations they produce do change (something not true of the social contract), allowing for a far more democratic politics than that to be found via sovereignty.

Rereading Covenants

To make this argument, we once again have to disentangle Hobbes's consideration of the messianic first kingdom of God from our own "kingdomless" time when it comes to questions of promising and political obligation. Although Hobbes claims that the religious covenants that we find in his eschatology ground the social contract itself, we will see once again how his religious arguments subvert and deflect his overt political arguments.

When Hobbes considers the covenant made between God and Abraham, he argues that the source of the obligation that follows can be found in Abraham's special revelation. He tells us that when God says to Abraham

"In thee shall all Nations of the earth be blessed: For I know thou wilt command thy children, and thy house after thee to keep the way of the Lord, and to observe Righteousnesse and Judgement," this means that "it is manifest, the obedience of his Family, who had no Revelation, depended on their former obligation to obey their Soveraign [Abraham himself via his 'Sovereign power' over his children]."[22] Here the reason for obligation comes not from some immediate benefit (like saving one's life) but from an enduring and permanent state of *"Righteousnesse,"* a product of special revelation.

Hobbes goes on to argue that such a covenant becomes the basis of future (secular) political obligation as well. In the passage cited above, after considering the obligation to Abraham, followed by the obligation that stems from Moses's own revelation, Hobbes writes:

> By which two places [i.e., in Scripture, the description of the respective duties to Abraham and Moses] it sufficiently appeareth, that in a Common-wealth, a subject that has no certain and assured Revelation particularly to himself concerning the Will of God, is to obey for such, the Command of the Common-wealth: for if men were at liberty, to take for Gods Commandements, their own dreams and fancies . . . scarce two men would agree upon what are Gods Commandements.[23]

Hobbes appears to be arguing that, although bereft of any revelation of their own, future sovereigns must stand in for the role played by Abraham and Moses. Yet if we apply Hobbes's own logic, this connection makes little sense. The obligations to Abraham and to Moses remain in effect to this day because their revelation is enduring. It is not therefore true that we who live in a "kingdomless" time are cast utterly adrift with no sense of the "Will of God." Although the kingdom of God has passed, the revelation from that kingdom endures (that is indeed the whole purpose of the third person of God and the figure of the Holy Spirit). God's will is represented to us by the covenant itself, particularly as it comes to us via the Sinaitic events; such a revelation serves as the basis of our ongoing obligation with or without sovereign governments, even as it remains devoid of content. The distinction between obligation that stems from divine representation and obligation that stems from the social contract is therefore quite stark: divine obligation is based on revelation, terrestrial obligation is based on short-term advantages. As I read it, the enduring obligations that we owe to God are exactly what saves us from being perpetually obliged to earthly rulers. Hobbes's attempt to make it seem as if the one leads naturally to the other is defied by his own insistence on their radical differentiation.[24]

Given this distinction, it can be argued that the obligations that stem from our covenant with God have a different meaning and different relevance than any secular covenant does. More to the point, any kind of lasting, intergenerational obligation can be said to come *only* from those religious covenants; only they can truly bind future generations without resorting to idolatry or false representations (whereby some short-term arrangement like "I won't kill you if you do this and that"becomes a timeless, permanent obligation). Whereas most Hobbes scholars argue that the sovereign is required for a community to be able to promise at all (a subject I will return to in the conclusion), we can see that by the time the social contract comes around, we are already suspended in a web of mutual obligation. Secular covenants, it seems, can bind this or that person to this or that action; they can (and must) anticipate the future; but they cannot bind a community *in toto* and forever.

Representationally speaking, when we suspend the character of our promises in Hobbes's eschatological context, we move from a focus on the contract as "thing" to one in which it is "merely" a representational figure. We move from a view of contract that effectively replaces the decision of the promiser with some disembodied, and sovereign, meaning (thereby rendering the covenant superior to the very individuals that formed it, a "separated essence") to one that preserves the divine aporia, returning the ability to make meaningful promises back to those people who are actually bound by them.

If it does anything at all, Hobbes's pseudohistorical depiction of the state of nature and the social contract depicts what time and promising become in the presence of the kingdom of darkness. It is a timeless tale for a kingdomless world. It reflects the epistemological despair that stems from the kind of extreme skepticism that Hobbes illustrates in the earlier parts of *Leviathan* (although even in these earlier parts of the book, he references the persons of God and the promise). But the redemption of such a vision is in effect already potentially accomplished by the time the social contract is described inasmuch as Hobbes locates our "kingdomless" time between the iterations of God's kingdom(s).

Changing Covenants

With this in mind, we can return to a consideration of the secular treatment of contracts in chapter 14. When we reread chapter 14 in light of the comparison with religious covenants, we can see that some of the logic of religious covenants discussed above is in fact reflected in these secular discussions. Even here, we see that contracts are not as absolutely binding as Hobbes sometimes leads us to believe. Thus, for example, Hobbes tells us:

> And therefore, to promise that which is known to be Impossible, is no Covenant. But if that prove impossible afterwards, which before was thought possible, the Covenant is valid, and bindeth, (*though not to the thing it selfe,*) yet to the value; or, if that also be impossible, to the unfeigned endeavor of performing as much as is possible: for to more no man can be obliged.[25]
>
> (My emphasis)

Thus for Hobbes even secular covenants are (or should be) a fluid medium of self-representation whereby the covenant itself is not bound to any particular or single action (*"the thing it selfe"*). In our attempt to represent ourselves in our own future, Hobbes is reminding us that we must indeed be open to the radical contingency of the future, so as not to falsely (and idolatrously) bind us to a phantasm of the present. Naturally, such an interpretation is limited by the question of what we thought was possible at the time of promising, that is, by the fact that we didn't know something was impossible when we promised to do it. Yet this passage reminds us that promises are enacted in real time, in a changing world, and that we must be able to change with those times for those promises to remain valid and binding.

For Hobbes, our promises then are not absolutely binding but we are obliged by them nonetheless. For Hobbes, as we have already seen, by promising or "covenanting" we are allowing our present selves to anticipate and place ourselves into the stream of the future. In this way, we seek to have our promises serve as familiar "guideposts" that help us navigate (without overwriting) the future.[26] This doesn't mean that we can "do as we please," capriciously changing our minds if circumstances don't quite fit our original intentions; for Hobbes, covenants, including secular ones, are indeed binding in ways that both accord with and even supersede the law itself and in ways that we might not desire. Thus Hobbes gives us this well-known example in chapter 14:

> And even in Common-wealths, if I be forced to redeem my selfe from a Theefe by promising him money, I am bound to pay it, till the Civill Law discharge me. For whatsoever I may lawfully do without Obligation, the same I may lawfully Covenant to do through feare: and what I lawfully Covenant, I cannot lawfully break.[27]

While this does not quite amount to a tolerance on Hobbes's part for crime (since there is the chance that the "Civill Law discharge[s] me"), it does suggest that once again this supposed devotee of an all-powerful sovereign is willing to go to great lengths to ensure that we preserve the meaningfulness of our word (at least to ourselves, if no one else). It seems, even in his treatment of purely secular covenants, that for Hobbes we hold to our word not for any one singular purpose per se (certainly not because we like giving money to thieves) but rather to preserve the possibility of our own futurity, one that is not absolutely bound by promises but is rather enabled by them.

While for Hobbes the three figures of God ensure that promising continues to be a meaningful and political activity even in our "kingdomless" time, in keeping with Hobbes's nominalism these figures qua figures are utterly blank, purely sites for human interpretation. In chapter 14, Hobbes tells us that without some mediator interpreting God's covenants (i.e., the persons of God themselves), "we know not whether our Covenants be accepted, or not."[28] When the persons of God are here on earth, whether Moses or the Apostles or Jesus Christ himself, a great deal of the responsibility for and interpretation of promising falls on them. In our own time, however, with only the various churches of the world, or our contemporary sovereigns, who are unconnected to this eschatological legacy, as (highly fallible) guides, the ultimate responsibility for promising falls back on the human beings who are bound by those promises. The persons and figures of God make promising possible, but we must perform and hold to the actual promising itself.

VOLUNTARISM AND OBLIGATION

Many Hobbes scholars make much of the sovereign's role as an enforcer of promises, but if what they enforce is an idolatrous and overliteralized version of our promises, then what is the value of such enforcement? On the other hand, if neither God, nor the persons of God (at least in our "kingdomless" time), nor the contemporary sovereign (who produces only "Hay, or Stubble") can ultimately ensure the validity of our promises, can we be trusted to keep them ourselves? Hobbes himself offers that "Glory, or Pride in appearing not to need to breake [our promises]" is "too rarely found to be presumed on" (fear being a far more effective instrument).[29] As we have seen in Hobbes's treatment of the types of promises that humans have made to God and to one another, our promises are frequently broken, not by God but by human beings. Even when God *is* sovereign, as we have seen, human promises are broken. Given this, it seems that to rely on collective promising as an alternative to the type of enforced promise keeping that we find with sovereignty suggests that promises are not really binding after all. Are we forced then to choose between seeing the contract as a straitjacket that binds us and cuts us off from our own future, or a form of obligation that seems hopelessly weak? Is there a theory of obligation in Hobbes that goes beyond an appeal to fear or pure self-interest? Is there any force behind our promises, anything that actually binds us to our word?[30]

To argue that Hobbes makes promising and contracts viable without recourse to sovereignty (as I believe he does) is to align him with a school of thought called (I think probably erroneously in his case) "voluntarism," that is to say a politics of promising that does not depend on external coercion to be binding.[31] The rest of this chapter will consider the question of Hobbes's voluntarism through the work of two scholars we have already encountered, Gregory S. Kavka and Hannah Arendt. Both scholars support some notion of voluntarism (although in Arendt's case the term is probably even more problematic than it is with Hobbes). Both Kavka and Arendt see the contradictions (at least potentially in Kavka's case) between voluntarism and what might be called the sovereign principle. I will try to show that Kavka appreciates and nicely delineates Hobbes's voluntarism but ultimately backs away from it in favor of sovereign decisionism because he does not include the role of the figures and persons of God in his account of promising. Arendt, who is utterly opposed to sovereignty herself, is someone whom I would once again seek to reconcile with Hobbes despite her heavy criticism of him (including on this exact subject), in part via Bonnie Honig's reading of her. Here too, I will argue that a recognition of the role of God's covenant, far from being redolent of what Arendt calls the "absolute," may help resolve a dilemma in Arendt's own work insofar as she sees the imposition of sovereign as a tragic inevitability (or near inevitability). Let me treat each thinker in turn.

Gregory S. Kavka

In his well-known book, *Hobbesian Moral and Political Theory*, Kavka mulls over the very questions I pose above when he considers whether Hobbes's voluntarist theory of obligation (i.e., one that depends on individual decision) is successful. To demonstrate Hobbes's voluntarism, Kavka cites him as writing, "There [is] no obligation on any man, which ariseth not from some act of his own."[32] Kavka anticipates that his readers will find such a theory of obligation "outrageous" insofar as it seems to deny that we are in fact obliged at all.[33] By this logic, our promises and contracts are binding unless or until we feel that they aren't any longer (we encountered this same problem earlier in this book when we considered the subjective nature of "discretion"). Yet Kavka takes seriously the notion that Hobbes's voluntarism can be considered as a basis for obligation on its own terms. This is particularly the case when it comes to the question of contracts and promises. As Kavka tells us, for Hobbes "injustice (in the wide sense of violating obligations) is 'somewhat like' absurdity, which involves contradicting what one earlier maintained, for injustice involves voluntarily undoing what one has earlier voluntarily done."[34]

Kavka tells us that for Hobbes, to argue one thing and then later argue something totally different (and contrary) "necessarily leaves one's listeners baffled concerning one's beliefs about the state of the world."[35] This characterization of Hobbes is very much like Arendt's notion that only when we speak and act in public do we really come to know what we "mean" (that is to say, to use her own term, *who* we are as speakers).[36] Kavka is arguing that for Hobbes the expectation that we will make sense is part of what binds us to our political community, part of why we "willingly" observe a kind of self-limiting that is inherent in promising and obligation. Such a conception serves as an acknowledgment of other wills and other listeners (and we have already seen something like this before in chapter 2 when we considered Hobbes's understanding of the effects of the public on our own private "deliberations").

In the passage of *Leviathan* from chapter 14 that Kavka is referencing, Hobbes is making an analogy between the requirement for consistency and keeping one's word in political life to those same requirements among the "disputations of Scholers."[37]Among the scholars, he tells us: "It is there called an Absurdity, to contradict what one maintained in the Beginning: so in the world, it is called Injustice, and Injury, voluntarily to undo that, which from the beginning he had voluntarily done."[38] Thus for Hobbes, even the binding power of justice stems not so much from some external power per se but rather from our requirement for self-consistency. And though in this paragraph Hobbes will go on to argue that "Feare of some evill consequence upon the rupture [of one's promise]" is what really forces us to keep our word, we can see that such an appeal to self-interest and fear does not alter the fundamental requirement that we need to develop a kind of consistency over time in order to be able to make any kind of sense at all.[39] In considering his voluntarism in this way, Kavka shows how Hobbes offers ample reason to keep our promises, and to act in a way deemed to be just by our community. Here it is not "Glory" or "Pride in appearing not to need to breake" our word that is at stake, and not even fear, but commonality itself that is the source of our obligation.

Kavka, however, distances himself from his own insight insofar as he seems to find that Hobbes's voluntarism is insufficiently "ought-like," not quite enough to qualify him as a truly "moral" thinker. In general, in looking at Hobbes's theories of obligation and morality, Kavka seeks to correct what he sees as flaws in Hobbes's theory: he strives to either reveal how Hobbes's theory is already moral or to show ways in which it could be made moral without sacrificing what he sees as its great value.

Kavka tells us that Hobbes's "corrected" theory of obligation is not the unilateral golden rule—wherein we do unto others, regardless of what they do to us—but is rather what he calls the "Copper Rule": "Do unto others as they do unto you."[40] In contemplating the slipperiness and limitations of such a moral system, Kavka considers but rejects the claim that Hobbes is essentially arguing that "might makes right," that the sovereign makes this "Copper Rule" system function more or less coherently insofar as it is exempted from its own (i.e., sovereign) dictates (because the sovereign can do unto its subjects as it pleases but those subjects cannot reciprocate and do what they please in return to the sovereign). For Kavka, what saves Hobbes from being an entirely amoral thinker (a thinker who subscribes to this kind of "might makes right" mentality) is the fact that even though the sovereign remains in a state of nature and is not bound by the law that binds its subjects, natural law applies not only to citizens of the social contract but to the sovereign as well.[41]

Thus for Kavka, we have in Hobbes a hybrid of subjective voluntarism and objective morality. Natural law bolsters the weak (but not absent) moral nature of Hobbesian voluntarism. Given that natural law (as Hobbes interprets it) begins with self-preservation as the highest good, there is a happy coincidence of these two perspectives (voluntaristic and nonvoluntaristic). At the same time, Kavka argues that this confluence should not lead us to collapse the distinction between these two moral codes. We should recognize the genuine bindingness of the lawful "ought," which, unlike other forms of obligation, comes not (merely) from our consent but from natural law itself.

Yet for all his attempts to find true objectivity in natural law, Kavka has a hard time locating it in Hobbes, who, as we have seen, is a supremely antiobjectivist thinker even in his renditions of natural law. In the end, Kavka's solution to this puzzle is to turn to the sovereign after all. This is despite his own concession that if the sovereign's power is the source of moral law, the system cannot actually be moral. By turning to the sovereign's decision, "objectivity" is politically produced as a response to the unknowability of God and even natural law itself. So we are back to a by now familiar argument that Hobbes is relying on a sort of ruse.[42] If there is in fact no de facto difference between the ought and obligation (i.e., if the "objective fact" of natural law is produced by sovereign fiat), then is Hobbes a moral theorist according to Kavka's own criteria? Isn't this "might makes right" after all, albeit disguised as "objectivity" wherein the sovereign's subjective "ought" becomes or substitutes for natural law itself (which by Hobbes's own argument would amount to idolatry)? Does Hobbes simply fall into the expedient of pretending there is an objective moral law, revealing the "happy coincidence" that objective law coincides with what we would probably "want" to do anyway when faced with a sovereign who has all the weapons as well as all the moral authority to speak on behalf of God and natural law?

This is clearly not what Kavka wants to argue. He concedes that it is a legitimate question whether such a "rule-egoistic" morality actually qualifies as a "*moral* system" at all.[43] But Kavka claims that to the degree Hobbes represents a departure from older moral systems, his system might in fact constitute an improvement in many ways.[44] At the same time, in considering the facets and advantages of Hobbes's moral system, Kavka does not seem to be able to get away from the sovereign principle, which continually "rescues" Hobbes's morality, in Kavka's view.

Thus for Kavka, Hobbes doesn't offer a perfect moral theory but does give a good working model. But notice that in order to make this model work, Kavka has, with some fair consistency, explained away or actually excised the basic voluntaristic perspective that Hobbes always operates from: convinced that no moral theory can exist where there is not some form of "objective" certainty, Kavka turns to the sovereign (no matter how arbitrary it actually is) to supply it. We can see in his complicated maneuvers how subversive Hobbes's radical nominalism and skepticism can be even to a sympathetic reader like Kavka.

Kavka's concern that we might find Hobbes's radical voluntarism to be "outrageous" stems from sticking fairly close to the secular story within a story that Hobbes weaves about contracts and obligations. Where God is mentioned, Kavka sees simply an opportunity for sovereign dictation. Yet when this story is re-placed in the eschatological envelope that contains it, we can see that voluntarism becomes something quite different. Rather than being bound simply by our word, we are bound by the multigenerational covenant we have made with God, a bond that cannot be broken and that obliges us regardless of our personal desires. Rather than serve as sites for sovereign interpretation, the persons and figures of God serve to prevent sovereign claims from having the status of truth.

Certainly the perception that the sovereign is central and unavoidable in Hobbes is not unique to Kavka. We have seen this same argument made by many other thinkers. Even for those who appreciate a side of Hobbes that is not entirely bound up with authoritarianism (a group to which Kavka himself certainly belongs), there is a reluctance to let go of sovereignty because there is a sense that there is no alternative; it is said to be the price we must pay for the inability of morality to be truly binding as itself. Richard Flathman, as I argued earlier, is one thinker who is quite troubled by this move, yet even he tries to show how Hobbes's sovereign is not only a necessary evil, but can in fact be seen as a virtue in that it allows for the kind of "individuating" he sees occurring on the social level in liberal political systems.[45] Like Kavka, Flathman recognizes the radical possibilities in Hobbes (including his own focus on the role of God as unknowable), but trumps this insight to some extent with the need for an externality, one "ought" that can and must serve as the last word.

Hannah Arendt

For her own part, Arendt is utterly opposed to a notion of such a conception of the "ought" (what she herself calls the "absolute"). She offers us a far stronger version of "voluntarism" than does Kavka , even without recourse to Hobbes's eschatology. To reconcile her with Hobbes may help illuminate and bolster his own voluntarism (and vice versa).

In her refusal of sovereignty as an organizing principle for political life, Arendt parts company not only with Kavka but even with a thinker like Flathman. For Arendt, as we have seen, sovereignty is based on the principle of "free will" or *liberum arbitrium*, wherein an essentially interior, solipsistic position is projected outward into the world. "Free will" and its sovereign expression offers no sense of the future because it seeks only to perpetuate its own phantasms indefinitely. It is by definition antipolitical insofar as it denies or resists human plurality. Arendt tells us that in order to avoid the "philosophical equation of freedom and free will," in order to make genuine freedom in all its contingent and unpredictable aspects possible, "it is precisely sovereignty [we] must renounce."[46]

Because of this conviction, Arendt's work is marked by an attempt to think about foundings and political authority in ways that do not merely perpetuate sovereignty. For Arendt, true authority is no longer a feature of modern political life. Arendt tells us that authority, particularly as it was practiced by the Romans, is neither a form of violence nor merely a form of persuasion but rather "rest[s] on a foundation in the past."[47]

For Arendt, we moderns, bereft of meaningful political authority, suffer from the practice of sovereignty, which turns to violence and force to establish its rule. Although the dream inherent in sovereignty—of total control over the world—is impossible, for Arendt this does not prevent sovereign governments from inflicting themselves on the human race.

In her desire to resist sovereignty, Arendt particularly opposes what she calls the "absolute": a source of authority that comes from beyond the public or political sphere itself. For Arendt in modern times "the absolute" is usually evoked by reference to God or natural law, something eternal and unchanging.[48] Contemporary founders of new states (generally revolutionaries) usually resort to associating themselves with the absolute because every new beginning opens up a hiatus in what passes for authority in our time. The absolute serves as a means to turn a contingent and potentially chaotic transition into a clear delineation of control. Sovereignty is quickly and effectively established as speaking in the name of the absolute itself (in a sense that is remarkably consistent with Hobbes's definition of demonology). For Arendt, such a recourse is both unnecessary to and poisonous for the genuine freedom that is promised by new political beginnings.

Speaking to this question in terms of the American Revolution, the one modern event that in Arendt's eyes did not swiftly succumb to the absolute, sovereignty, and violence, Arendt comments,

> The men of the American Revolution . . . might have been faintly aware that there exists a solution for the perplexities of beginning which needs no absolute to break the vicious circle in which all first things seem to be caught. What saves the act of beginning from its own arbitrariness is that it carries

its own principle within itself, or, to be more precise, that beginning and principle, *principium* and principle, are not only related to each other, but are coeval. The absolute from which the beginning is to derive its own validity and which must save it, as it were, from its inherent arbitrariness is the principle which, together with it, makes its appearance in the world.[49]

In this case, the act of founding itself saved the Americans from their own indeterminacy. Here we find an articulation of the notion of action that Arendt develops most thoroughly in *The Human Condition*, the idea that our actions serve as a (miraculous) revelation to ourselves. Action for Arendt serves as a kind of redemption for (or from) the will and hence, politically speaking, offers an alternative to sovereignty itself. The will, for Arendt, isn't a self-conscious or reflective entity capable of recognizing its position among plural actors. It is fundamentally at war with itself, paralyzed by its own internal phantasms.[50] Action is what breaks this deadlock for Arendt. The will does not know what it has "willed" until action commits it to a certain course.[51] Only in retrospect then does the will "know" what it really willed, which is to say that the will has, after the fact, achieved the kind of self-knowledge and self-reflection that it unsuccessfully pursued on its own prior to this moment of revelation (and it is in this sense alone that we could decently consider Arendt to be a "voluntarist").

Arendt offers what Kavka does not, a purely self-grounding voluntarism, based on her theory of action. The example of the American Revolution offers Arendt some hope (however slight, since that revolution too was ultimately betrayed in her view) that some modern version of real authority remains a possibility in the world, that the absolute need not always be our automatic recourse in terms of political foundings (and refoundings).

Based on the model of the American Revolution, Arendt seeks to promote a politics of promising, what she herself calls a "bod[y] politic that rel[ies] on contracts and treaties." In this politics authority comes not from the past (as it did for the Romans), but from the kinds of actions, ties, and allegiances that people make together. Here, people become a "public," acting before and toward one another. Their mutual acts of promising convince individuals to supersede their own indeterminant wills in favor of a public; to let action rather than willing itself determine their collective experience.

This system of authority stands in contrast to the more usual modern form of governance based on "rule and sovereignty," wherein we submit to one or several individual wills.[52] Thus the politics of promising offers an alternative form of authority very similar to what I have been arguing we find in *Leviathan*. Echoing similar sentiments that we have found with Hobbes, Arendt tells us,

> [A politics of contracts and treaties] leave[s] the unpredictability of human affairs and the unreliability of men as they are, using them merely as the medium, as it were, into which certain islands of predictability are thrown and in which certain guideposts of reliability are erected.[53]

Promising in this view offers a basis for a new and modern form of authority, a way to make human communities able to face a contingent future without sacrificing some sense of continuity and reliability. As I have been arguing is the case for Hobbes as well, Arendt's version of promising does not construct and dominate the future (as does sovereignty and the *liberum arbitrium*) but it allows each member of a community to have a sense of what they are committing to and who they are entering the future with.

The Pure Performative

Given this possibility, it is noteworthy that Arendt tends to end her discussions of such politics with a great deal of pessimism. The last chapters of both *The Human Condition* and *On Revolution* suggest that the future holds less rather than more hope for the kind of politics Arendt seeks. In her own analysis of Arendt's treatment of political foundations and authority, Bonnie Honig elucidates Arendt's claims about authority and promising in ways that may help explain Arendt's ambiguity and pessimism. For all her lauding of the Roman practice of authority, Honig tells us, Arendt is "ambivalent about the disappearance of authority in modernity."[54] Authority is a crucial grounding for the kind of nonviolent forms of politics that Arendt is looking for. Yet, the same time, the newness and action she seeks seem hampered by traditional notions of authority, which, in her own view, are relentlessly backward-looking. It seems as if Arendt wants two contradictory things out of politics: spontaneity on the one hand and lastingness and continuity on the other.

Arendt's ambiguity, Honig tells us, leads her in a particular direction when she depicts the American Revolution. Enlisting the terminology of Austin (via Derrida,) Honig tells us that Arendt seeks a "nonfoundational" notion of authority based on what might be called a politics of "performative utterances."[55] A performative utterance makes something true in the moment of saying it. This is in contrast to "constative utterances," which are statements that are "already true" (i.e., not instantiated but referenced by the constative utterance). Honig says that for Arendt, constative utterances must be shunned because of their evocation of the absolute.[56] Thus for Arendt the quality of our promising must be informed by this performativity, so that each promise becomes the grounds for its own validity (Honig calls this "the authoritative linguistic practice of promising").[57] According to Honig, however, Arendt encounters an obstacle in her quest for a pure performativity because "if action is . . . contingent . . . promising will not by itself be able to provide the stability Arendt expects it to."[58]

We thus come to the same problem faced by Kavka, namely the limits of voluntarism. Naturally, Arendt won't turn, as Kavka does, to natural law and the sovereign. Instead, Honig offers that Arendt's own solution to the problem of authority is to spin a fable about the American Revolution, to cast it as being purely performative (by claiming the constative elements of that revolution were a mistake or could have been avoided). To illuminate her consideration, Honig looks at Arendt's treatment of the first sentence of the second paragraph of Jefferson's Declaration of Independence ("We hold these truths to be self-evident"). Arendt contends with the fact that in this utterance, Jefferson seems to evoke the absolute in his notion of "self-evidence." Honig writes that in Arendt's overall view of the phrase, "the *We hold*—the performative part of Jefferson's 'incongruous phrase'—won out over the constative part, the reference to self-evident truths," which evokes the absolute.[59] In this way, the "real" (and modern) source of authority is said to have been created by the "*We hold.*" This fable, Honig tells us, is Arendt's way of resisting the constative and hence the absolute, to attempt to reproduce authority in a way that purely bolsters the performative. [60]

Yet it is not clear that this fable is in itself sufficient to produce a lasting political foundation. As we have already seen, it does not seem to have
lasted for Arendt in the case of the American Revolution itself; that disliked
phrase, "self-evidence," does not disappear but eventually perverts Jefferson's
revolution.

For Honig, the limitations to a politics of promising that Arendt encounters stem not so much from the nature of performativity itself but from
the fairly artificial line that Arendt draws between the performative and
the constative. In other words, the fact that Arendt suffers from the decision over whether to favor spontaneity or lastingness in politics comes from
her depiction of these options as mutually exclusive. Honig argues that Arendt's search for a performativity that is perfectly free from the constative
is impossible. Drawing upon Derrida's own reading of the Declaration of
Independence, she tells us that "[Arendt] does not see that her cherished
performative *We hold* is *also* a constative utterance."[61]

Hobbes and Arendt Considered Together

Arendt may refuse this equation because of her concern that the constative
is anathema to new beginnings. Yet, as Derrida shows, and I think Hobbes
does as well, the constative is not necessarily the same thing as the absolute. Despite the eternal time frame that Hobbes operates with, there is
something *both* constative and performative about the incarnations of the
persons of God and their representational figures. Recall how Hobbes tells
us that we call God the "Father" "from [the time of Moses] forward, but
not before."[62] These incarnations do indeed issue something radically new
even as they instantiate a presence which is constative by definition. And,
because of Hobbes's radical nominalism, the constative time frame he deals
with (his eschatological history) is in fact the opposite of the *absolute*, insofar as Arendt understands the latter term. As I have argued, rather than
serve as a basis for sovereign force, God's persons and figures in Hobbes's
account serve to undermine and destabilize the "Hay, or Stubble" that any
terrestrial sovereign might seek to assert.

The key difference between Arendt and Hobbes on this point is that
only Arendt makes a distinction between classical and modern conceptions

of authority and religion. It seems fair to say that Arendt's suspicion of the "constative" (keeping in mind that the terminology is not her own) only applies to the modern context. In the case of the Romans, it seems that it is precisely the constative nature of the Roman religion that she appreciates:

> In contrast to Greece, where piety depended upon the immediate revealed presence of the gods, [in Rome] religion literally meant *re-ligare*: to be tied back, obligated by the enormous, almost superhuman and hence always legendary effort to lay the foundations, to build the cornerstone, to found for eternity. To be religious meant to be tied to the past.[63]

The sketch of the Roman religion Arendt presents here is very similar to what I have been arguing religion accomplishes for Hobbes as well.[64] In both Hobbes's and Arendt's treatments, religion "ties back" a community, creating a bond and a continuity with an original establishing moment (one that produces authority in its wake). Certainly the Roman practice of religion, because it was focused on Rome itself, was not the antithesis of politics but that which made politics possible in the first place.

Thus Arendt is not against religion per se. Her specific complaint with Jefferson is not that he invoked God or religion but that he invoked "self-evident" truths that allow for no argument, no politics. Yet in general, Arendt seems extremely suspicious of religion in her (i.e., our) own time and does not foresee any modern correspondence to the role that religion played in the Roman republic.[65]

If we consider Arendt overall, lessening our focus on the way she bifurcates ancient from modern times, it becomes easier to consider Arendt and Hobbes in tandem. As I read them, both tell us a story wherein a politics based on force and violence is supplanted by a politics based, not on mere persuasion or fancy (to use Hobbes's term), but on a lasting sense of political community, on promising, covenants, and social ties. Arendt's version of this story occurs in ancient Rome while Hobbes's version occurs in ancient Israel. In both narratives, there is a disruption of this original authority and a reversion to preauthoritative forms of coercion and violence (via the imposition of sovereignty). In both narratives, contemporary forms of political sovereignty are associated more with mere force and arbitrary power than the kind of collective self-fashioning (and promising) achieved by *re-ligare*. Finally, both thinkers offer a politics of promising that is not tied up with sovereignty and nationalism (whereby we have "one" people with "one" interest). With Arendt the contracts and treaties established by various colonists in America transferred readily to a larger collective (the United States). In Hobbes's eschatological history, the covenant establishes a bond that leaps from nation (of Israel) to world.

For all these similarities, it is true that in "What is Authority?" Arendt distances herself quite explicitly from Hobbes on this exact question. She tells us that "it was the error of Hobbes . . . to hope that authority and religion could be saved without tradition."[66] Thus, as one of the founders of modernity, Hobbes is charged by Arendt with being part of the reason that modernity has no authority, why it tends to produce unstable and violent (i.e., sovereign) forms of government. As with Kavka, I once again think that Arendt reads Hobbes this way because she too does not take his eschatological history seriously, dwelling as she does exclusively on his ahistorical tale of the social contract. Arendt sees Hobbes as abandoning tradition because of the pseudohistory of the (hypothetical) social contract he tells, but Hobbes also tells us of a (by definition) nonhypothetical founding as well, namely, the founding of the kingdom of God in ancient Israel. And Hobbes's narrative, as we have seen, does something Arendt cannot: he extends this tradition right into the future (without however constricting or determining what that future will be) through his evocation of the return of that kingdom at some unknown future point.

If Arendt frets more about the limitations of promising than Hobbes does, it may be in part that she seems to have abandoned or given up on what *re-ligare* can do for our own time. Without the eschatological framework Hobbes is working with, Arendt's future is far more contingent, maybe even too contingent for her taste. She must choose between spontaneity and lastingness, and possibly fall between two stools in the process, because she is forced to do so by her own genealogy of authority.

Without any recourse to religion, or indeed the constative itself, Arendt may engage (as Honig tells us) in fable telling, but it is not clear that such efforts succeed in averting what Arendt seems to see as the tragic nature of modern politics (or rather the failure of the political in modern times). It could be argued that because the absolute is not banished, but only resisted (in part because it is not distinguished from the constative in this rendition of Arendt's political theory), the end result where sovereignty trumps promising becomes inevitable. Ultimately, the "fable" Arendt tells seems to founder on its own irreality.

It is here that I would argue that Hobbes's approach to authority may be a somewhat more tenable solution than Arendt's turn to fables. Although Arendt claims that modernity cannot produce an authority based on *re-ligare*, I would argue that Hobbes (a modern, if anyone is) does just this. Unlike Arendt, and as already mentioned, Hobbes does not bifurcate the world into modern and classical times when it comes to questions of authority. The kind of authority he argues for survives the kingdom that produced it.[67] Whereas Arendt is ambivalent about authority, about religion and its relationship to politics, and even in a sense about the power of promising itself as a viable alternative to sovereignty in modern times, in Hobbes's system we need not be so ambivalent. In Hobbes's work, the constative and the absolute are clearly separate concepts (with the separation between the two being effected by Hobbes's resistance not to the constative but to idolatry, which is his own version of the absolute). Whereas for Arendt the faculty of promising is faulty because it is a purely human contrivance, for Hobbes our promises are bolstered and even made possible by the persons and figures of God. While, in his nominalism and rhetorical approach to political questions, Hobbes is clearly also labeling our promises as human contrivances, we so contrive through the mechanism of the rhetorical figures which serve indeed as a kind of "nonfoundational foundation," or perhaps more accurately a "nonexternal externality" for the promises that we make.

Yet, even as Hobbes offers much to Arendt, Arendt offers a great deal for our reading of Hobbes. Unlike Hobbes, Arendt openly and clearly considers voluntarism and her articulation of action helps us better imagine what a politics of promising might actually look like. At the same time, an engagement between Hobbes and Arendt may temper somewhat the scope of what a Hobbesian politics of promising may offer. After all, unlike Hobbes, Arendt is a witness to myriad failed revolutions, to the tenacity of rule and sovereignty, and to the fragility of systems based on a politics of promising. Still, it can hardly be said that Hobbes lived in a tranquil moment of history; where Arendt faced totalitarianism and sovereign violence in her time, Hobbes faced civil war and demonology in his. He too was faced with a scourge of unreality and illegitimate force. Despite the "dark times" he himself experienced, Hobbes offers that such a threat can be faced, that legitimate political authority can be produced, and that promising can be a means for a lasting and binding polity. In the end, I don't think either thinker would truly dismiss the possibility of a politics of promising. On her own part, Arendt offers us not so much despair but (as Honig suggests) ambivalence. If we see Arendt and Hobbes as allies rather than as offering two competing views of authority, it may be that in their synergism we begin to get a better sense of what a politics of promising might look like.

In the chapter that follows, it will be my claim that when we consider the Holy Spirit, the figure of the person of God for our own time, we can see more of this alternative notion of politics and authority being developed. This alternative is based on the very nominalistic, antifoundational, and "voluntaristic" notions that I believe are inherent in Hobbes's theory of reading and representation. The alternative I will sketch out is one in which we are not forced to choose between total obedience and chaos. This alternative might serve as the basis of a political order that is based not on command and obedience but indeed, as Arendt herself desires, on our mutual acts of promising, and our collective insertion into political life. The figure of the Holy Spirit is particularly relevant to this discussion because as I see it, it is the means by which Hobbes would challenge sovereignty on its most basic level, that is to say at the level of rhetorical performance, which, as we have seen, is the locus of political authority and the obligations that follow from it.

In general, one can say that for the radicals the Holy Spirit was real and tangible, while for the conservatives it was largely metaphorical or symbolic. Thus Hollinworth writes concerning the question of the "in-dwelling" of the Spirit, "The Spirit by a Metonymy, may be said to dwell in us . . . when we partake of his Gifts and Graces, though these be not the Spirit it self; . . . as when we say the Sun comes into a house, we mean not the *body* of the sun (for that abides in its own Orb) but the *Beams* of it" (p. 49).

For the radicals, the Holy Spirit was no metaphor, or rather the metaphors that are used to describe it, describe something very real. The Holy Spirit was so real for them that it made the church almost peripheral to the experience of the Holy Spirit itself. The radical John Owen writes: "There is no need of Traditions, . . . no need of the Authority of any Churches. . . . A Church may beare up the light, it is not the light. It beares witnesse to it, but kindles not one divine beame to further its discovery" (pp. 43–44).

In practice, most Puritans were somewhere between these two extremes, neither relegating the Holy Spirit to a purely symbolic status (as the Anglicans tended to do) nor believing in the certain and absolute presence of the Holy Spirit, as the Quakers and other radical sects tended to do.

These theological questions obviously had strong political connotations; the more radical sects clearly saw religious matters in ways that also had a strong political (and democratic) valence. The idea of a lay clergy, of "gifted brethren" having their own powers of interpretation, even of preaching, denotes a decentralized notion of authority both at the liturgical and political level (although, as we will see, this position is less decentralized than initially appears) (p. 78).

The political connotations of the Holy Spirit reached a short but important culmination just a couple of years after *Leviathan* was published, with the inauguration of the Nominated Assembly (or Barebones Parliament) in July 1653. This parliament, composed of moderate and radical Puritans, was ideologically dominated by the Fifth Monarchist movement led by Thomas Harrison. The Fifth Monarchists held that Jesus himself should be the true king of England ("fifth" because it was to follow the Assyrian, Persian, Greek, and Roman monarchies) and that Scripture was to be the only source of law.[6] The Fifth Monarchist–dominated Barebones Parliament welcomed the absence of a terrestrial monarch and many among them called for the disenfranchisement of all clergy, the ending of funding of the major universities, an end to tithing, and other radical reorganizations of the nation's ecclesiastical and political structure. Lest we imagine them to be radical anarchists, it should be noted that they sought in effect a theocracy (albeit one led by Jesus Christ himself). In the end, after five contentious months with little to show, Cromwell turned on the radicals. Sensing that they had pushed things too far and were alienating the moderates in parliament, he created the Protectorate, which replaced the Barebones Parliament, turning the tide against Puritan extremism in English political life.

The Anglicans and the Holy Spirit

During Hobbes's lifetime, both before and after the publication of *Leviathan*, the notion of the Holy Spirit was thus a highly charged and evolving concept with vast political and theological consequences. Across a broad spectrum (although particularly in terms of Puritan thought), the figure of the Holy Spirit brought questions of interpretation, authority, and indeed reading itself to the fore of both religious and political concerns. Because the Holy Spirit was understood as an interpretive figure, there were tensions over the nature and meaning of such interpretation as well as the question of the kinds of political communities (the "fellowship of the spirit" that some Puritans referred to, for example) that were produced as an effect of the belief in the Holy Spirit.[7]

Among the Anglicans themselves, the question of the Holy Spirit was at most considered along the lines of the most conservative members of the Puritan sects. In the circle at Great Tew, which included Hobbes and his friend Sidney Godolphin, many Anglican scholars, such as John Hales and William Chillingworth, discussed and debated many tenets of theology, including the question of the Holy Spirit and its role in interpretation. As Paul Johnson tells us, for Hales, whenever Scripture was improperly clear, or overly metaphorical, the Holy Spirit alone was a "competent interpreter."[8] While this sentiment echoed the rhetoric of many conservative and moderate Puritans, in practice Hales's particular take on this question effectively eliminated the Holy Spirit from any actual interpretive impact.

He claimed, not unlike Puritan conservatives that were somewhere just to the "left" of him, that the Holy Spirit was only available via the words of the Apostles themselves.[9] Moreover, whatever the Holy Spirit did impart to those disciples is essentially lost to us. Thus Hales writes "[for contemporary people], for information, otherwise than out of these bookes, the [Holy] spirit speaks not."[10] Johnson tells us that the result of this idea was that for Hales "latter-day men are limited for their direction to those plain places where Scripture clearly reveals its meaning. . . . These plain places must contain all that is necessary for man's salvation."[11] This turn on Hales's part to human reason (and hence away from the Holy Spirit itself) was typical of the Great Tew circle and its Arminian tendencies, and in keeping with the general tendencies of the Anglican Church at that time.[12]

Hobbes and the Holy Spirit

In his own consideration of the Holy Spirit, Hobbes seems to go even further in a conservative—and Anglican—direction even than many of his Great Tew colleagues. He speaks of the Holy Spirit as if it were indeed nothing at all: neither an actual separate force or agency that is (in the more radical Puritan sense) or was (in Hales's or Hollinworth's sense) physically and spiritually active in the world.

True to his own radical nominalism, Hobbes warns us explicitly not to read too much into the figure of the Holy Spirit. Considering the Sinaitic events, he writes:

> To say [Moses] spake by Inspiration , or Infusion of the Holy Spirit, as the Holy Spirit signifieth the Deity, is to make Moses equall with Christ, in whom onely the Godhead . . . dwelleth bodily. . . . To say he spake by the Holy Spirit, as it signifieth the graces, or gifts of the Holy Spirit, is to attribute nothing to him supernaturall.[13]

Thus for Hobbes, to speak of the Holy Spirit as being an actual mouthpiece for God in the world is to resort to idolatry, to commit the error of separated essences. The Holy Spirit cannot convey God's actual authority but only our desire for that authority to be made present among us. He also writes:

The wind, that is there said to fill the house wherein the Apostles were assembled on the day of Pentecost, is not to be understood for the Holy *Spirit*, which is the Deity it selfe; but for an Externall sign of Gods speciall working on their hearts, to effect in them the internall graces, and holy vertues hee thought requisite for the performance of their Apostleship. (3.34, p. 279)

According to Nuttall's four criteria, Hobbes seems aligned on the extreme right when it comes to matters of the Holy Spirit. He doesn't see the Holy Spirit as an actual indwelling, personally experienced entity either now or even during biblical times; as we see, even on the day of Pentecost itself, Hobbes is unwilling to cede the literal presence of the Holy Spirit. Furthermore, for Hobbes, human reason is crucial for interpretation (wherein the "Spirit" itself is reduced to a "bare Word") and obviously the very notion of human infallibility is a total delusion for such a skeptical thinker.

As he does with the term *Spirit of God* and other such religious concepts, Hobbes generally "reduces" the Holy Spirit to a metaphor. And it is not even a metaphor in the sense that the term is understood by a conservative Puritan like Hollinworth. For the latter thinker, recall that the Spirit becomes a *"Beam"* of sunlight; as a metaphor it is infused with what it actually represents. For his own part, Hobbes is far more radically nominalist in his approach to the Holy Spirit. For him, the Holy Spirit is no more a beam than anything else; it is a pure and empty hypostatization.

Holy Spirit or Holy Ghost?

For Hobbes, the exposition of the Holy Spirit as empty begins, like everything else, with its name. Usually Hobbes uses the term *Holy Spirit* interchangeably with the term *Holy Ghost*, often reflecting the language of the biblical passage he is considering. At one point, for example, he writes of the " Holy Spirit . . . which we in our language call the Holy Ghost" (3.36, 295). Yet elsewhere Hobbes insists that the term *Holy Ghost* is a misnomer. When Hobbes considers the biblical passage *"And Jesus full of the Holy Ghost"* (Luke 4:1), he interprets this as meaning only a *"Zeal* to doe the work for which hee was sent by God the Father." He goes on to note, but to interpret [the Holy Spirit as] a Ghost, is to say, that God himselfe (for so our Saviour was,) was filled with God; which is very unproper, and unsignificant. How we came to translate *Spirits*, by the word *Ghosts*, which signifieth nothing, neither in heaven, nor earth, but the Imaginary inhabitants of mans brain, I examine not: but this I say, the word *Spirit* in the text signifieth no such thing. (3.34, p. 273)

Although, as we have seen, Hobbes himself engages in the very practice that he seems to denounce, he tells us that to exchange "Ghost" for "Spirit" is to substitute a fantasy, a separated essence, for a pure metaphor. The term *Ghost* does not "profess [its] inconstancy" in the same way that the empty term *Spirit* does.

In any event, and whatever we choose to call it, exposed as hypostatization the Holy Spirit seems to be merely a marker for our own feelings, attitudes, and desires (our own "spirit"), or possibly a way to vest some decision of ours with holiness, to disguise its profane, fallible origins.

So there seems to be no such thing as the Holy Spirit for Hobbes; it is at best a metaphor for our own religious searching, for our desire to know what cannot be known. Nevertheless, as we have seen before, for all of this reduction of the concept of the Holy Spirit to an empty cipher, Hobbes isn't claiming that the Holy Spirit is a meaningless concept by any means. Although Hobbes formally embraces the conservative position, particularly in terms of the centrality he gives the word of God and the need for a "rational" reading of Scripture, he shares with the Puritans an understanding of the Holy Spirit as a key guide to interpretation of Scripture. Indeed, as I'll argue further, he actually ends up with a position that is far more radical (at least politically speaking) than what even the most radical Puritans and Quakers took.

I will develop this argument, claiming that because of his appreciation for the blankness of the figure of "God the Holy Spirit" (as opposed to the Puritans, who, especially as they become increasingly radical, see the Holy Spirit as being very much filled with content), Hobbes makes it impossible for this figure to merely replace one set of dogmas with another. Although radically opposed to Anglican (not to mention Catholic) doctrines, Puritan doctrine in practice is not as radically decentered as might first appear (certainly not in the political form of Puritanism exemplified by Cromwell) because it is based on an expectation that the Holy Spirit actually has some "truth" to convey. Hobbes's understanding of the Holy Spirit as blank makes it into a far more radically democratic figure than even the most subversive of the Puritans who nominally stood to Hobbes's "far left."

To understand how this is so and to draw out the political connotations of these divergent views of the Holy Spirit, we must more fully explore Hobbes's understanding of this all-important figure. The key question is how a figure that is blank and seemingly meaningless can have any political connotations at all.

THE "KINGDOM" OF THE HOLY SPIRIT

At first glance, for Hobbes the political aspects of the Holy Spirit, such as they are, appear to be suspended between the two kingdoms actually manifest. Hobbes suggests as much when he tells us that "[the Holy Spirit] came not of himselfe; but was sent, and proceeded from [Moses and Christ]" (1.16, p. 114). He also tells us that we live not in the "Reigning, but [in the] Regeneration; that is, a Preparation of men for the second and glorious coming of Christ" (3.42, p. 342). The time of the Holy Spirit seems to be simply one of preparation and anticipation of a future kingdom, with no separate political or interpretive mission of its own. Thus the "powers" of the Holy Spirit (if we can speak of them at all) seem to be the weakest, completely derivative from the powers of sovereignty (that was) and the "pacte of baptisme" (the anticipation and promise of the sovereignty that will be).

Hobbes treats this question at some length in the last two chapters of part 3. Appropriately, this discussion, although the "end" of this section, lies toward the middle of the book. Like the person and figure that it describes, this section is in the "now," sandwiched between the beginning and end of the book itself. The longest (by far) chapter in this section, or indeed in *Leviathan* as a whole, is the penultimate chapter 42 ("*Of* POWER ECCLE-SIASTICALL"), the chapter most devoted to matters of the church, which is the current incarnation of the "third person" of God and, by extension the figure of the Holy Spirit.

Here, let us focus for the moment on the "person" of God incarnate in the church. In this chapter, Hobbes argues extensively that the "powers" of the church are in no way coercive or sovereign. For example, he tells us that baptism does not "constitute over us another authority, by which our externall actions are to bee governed in this life" (p. 347). Instead he speaks of "our promise in Baptisme" and says that it is a promise "to take the doctrine of the Apostles for our direction in the way to life eternall" (p. 347). Similarly Hobbes tells us that excommunication is not a punishment akin to state punishment but is "a Denouncing of punishment, that Christ shall inflict, when he shall be in possession of his Kingdome, at the day of Judgment" (p. 388).

Such remarks were not without controversy in Hobbes's own time. A "different" power also was understood to be a "lesser" power. In chapter 42 in particular, he appears to be raising the power of the civil sovereign at the expense of the church, an argument we have already considered in chapter 4. Hobbes certainly drew the ire of the Anglican clergy by claiming that the church was to be completely subsumed to sovereign authority and that the sovereign was the supreme pastor, including having the right to administer sacraments.[14]

In making such arguments, Hobbes is not saying that there is no such thing as ecclesiastical power (indeed the title of the chapter, "*Of* POWER ECCLESIASTICALL," suggests that there certainly is such a thing). And yet much of the argument of chapter 42 suggests that the powers Hobbes illustrates are no different than the powers already attributed to Jesus himself; they are merely the representation and effects of that power in our own time.

In Hobbes's comments on the church, we can see that the third person of God, unlike the persons of Moses and Jesus, is diffused in many persons (in the more ordinary sense of the word) over time. In its contemporary form as "Doctors" of the church, it seems to contain a much weaker interpretive authority today than it had during the time of the Apostles.[15]

In her own account of the third person of God, Patricia Springborg argues that Hobbes's theory is "fundamentally incoherent,"[16] because Hobbes seeks to "reduc[e] apostolic powers to the vanishing point" in order to promote (as we have already seen) the sacerdotal power of kings over the clergy.[17] She writes that Hobbes attempts, paradoxically, to secure the king's ecclesiastical supremacy as God's lieutenant, after Moses and Christ, when he has already established that the peculiar kingdom of God is in suspension. Christian kings are clearly not lieutenants in the sense in which Moses and Christ were as the mouthpiece of God.[18]

Thus Springborg claims that Hobbes wrecks havoc on the "third person" of God in its contemporary form, namely the church, effectively deauthorizing it from its roots in the covenant.

Springborg has essentially helped make some of my own arguments. She acknowledges the vastly different epistemological contexts between the kingdom of God and our own "kingdomless" time. She also acknowledges that there can be no real transmission of sacerdotal authority from the former to the latter and that sovereigns are in effect wholly unconnected to that transmission of authority. But Springborg insists on interpreting this problem from the position that Hobbes's commitment to sovereignty is a given. Where she sees incoherence, I see subversion, not of church by king but of king by God's person (in this case, in the form of the church). As I read it, this story amounts to severing, not the church's authority (since its authority is not its own to sever) but the king's authority as based on Hobbes's eschatology.

Springborg writes that "to the extent that he succeeds in insulating his doctrine of the ecclesiastical supremacy of the king he is destroying his doctrine of the Trinity, or at least seriously undermining its relevance."[19] However, in my own reading of the "persons" of God, consistent with Hobbes's larger rhetorical theories of representation (including religious representation), the tension between "ecclesiastical powers" and the power of sovereignty might just be working the other way around.

The Assister

Even more crucially, for my purposes, we must inquire as to the relationship between these ecclesiastic powers, the powers that extend from the "third person" of God (the successors to the Apostles) and the figure that Hobbes associates with the church, the Holy Spirit itself. It is striking to note how the figure takes on a more prominent role than was (or will be) the case with "God the Father" or "God the Son." In the diffuseness of the "person" of God in its current form we are left with only (or mainly) the figure. Here again, the figure qua figure is reaffirmed in all its blankness. An apparent problem (the weak authority of the church) becomes the basis of "professing [the] inconstancy" of the rhetorical figure with which it is associated.

Yet, even if this is the case, does this third figure, considered in its own right, truly bring nothing new into the world? Does the Holy Spirit really have neither a kingdom nor a power of its own? As I have already suggested, Hobbes demonstrates the value (or "power") of the Holy Spirit in particular when he specifically evokes this figure as something which protects us against hasty or idolatrous readings of signs. In a passage (considered earlier in different contexts) in chapter 45, Hobbes writes:

> Whereas there be, that pretend Divine Inspiration, to be a supernaturall en-
> tring of the Holy Ghost into a man, and not an acquisition of Gods graces,
> by doctrine, and study; I think they are in a very dangerous Dilemma. For
> if they worship not the men whom they beleeve to be so inspired, they fall
> into Impiety; as not adoring Gods supernaturall Presence. And again, if they
> worship them, they commit Idolatry; for the Apostles would never permit
> themselves to be so worshipped. Therefore the safest way is to beleeve, that
> by the Descending of the Dove upon the Apostles; and by Christs Breathing
> on them, when hee gave them the Holy Ghost; and by the giving of it by Im-
> position of Hands, are understood the signes which God hath been pleased
> to use, or ordain to bee used, of his promise to assist those persons in their
> study to Preach his Kingdome, and in their Conversation, that it might not be
> Scandalous, but Edifying to others.[20]

The figure of the Holy Spirit, consistent with Hobbes's argument, is offered as a pure figure, meant to be read metaphorically only. The divine inspiration (the "Holy Spirit" itself) that Hobbes describes is not a supernatural entering of a "[g]host into a man." It is not a separated essence. Nor is it an actual, real thing. Rather it is (only) a sign of God's grace acquired by "doctrine, and study"; it represents our own limited and fallible attempts to understand and represent God. It is not that the Holy Spirit is meaningless, but rather that this hypostatization, and the hypostatizations associated with it (such as the "Dove" or even the "Holy Ghost"), serve as sites upon which we are permitted to read "signes which God has been pleased to use." In a sense it could be said that the figure of the Holy Spirit is the "hypostatization of hypostatization," the figure of figurativeness. By this figure we are permitted to worship God, to seek to acquire God's grace through the figure of the Holy Spirit itself (assuming we continue to read it in its figurative and metaphorical senses only). If we can see the Holy Spirit as empty we can be "inspired" to read other figures as being empty as well. The worshipful reading we thus engage with is distinguished from that "dangerous Dilemma" wherein a false reading of these hypostatizations—a reading in which we fail to recognize the Holy Spirit as a hypostatization in the first place—forces us to choose between impiety (rejecting the Holy Spirit) and idolatry (supplanting the Holy Spirit with a separated essence). For Hobbes, understanding the Holy Spirit as purely figurative does not distance us from God but rather permits us to see that the idea of God can only be approached through language and figuration.

In this sense, the Holy Spirit can be seen as lying at the heart of Hobbes's theory of worship, of proper reading. In Hobbes's view, there is no discrepancy between "the Spirit" and "the Word"—they are both precisely the same phenomena. True to his nominalism, for Hobbes the "Spirit" is only a "Word" and the "Word" can only be understood as a "Spirit." The Holy Spirit as a self-emptying sign is a crucial figure for allowing us the distance from the name of God that we need in order to cease imagining that by naming God we know what (as opposed to that) God is. This figure of figurativeness completes Hobbes's "negative theology."

With this understanding we get a better sense of how the figure of the Holy Spirit constitutes part of God's promise (recall that Hobbes tells us "In like manner as the Holy Ghost is called *the Promise*"[21]), specifically in this case the "promise to assist those persons in their study to Preach his Kingdome." This is a promise to help us avoid overly hasty and false interpretations, including those of the meaning of the Holy Spirit itself; it is in fact a promise to help us to interpret, to learn to be better (nonidolatrous) readers of texts, of ourselves, of other human beings, and the world around us.

Elsewhere Hobbes writes of the Holy Spirit,

Thus wee see how the Power Ecclesiasticall was left by our Saviour to the Apostles; and how they were (to the end they might the better exercise that Power,) endued with the Holy Spirit, which is therefore called sometime in the New Testament *Paracletus* which signifieth an *Assister,* or one called to for helpe, though it bee commonly translated a *Comforter.*[22]

Here too we see that the Holy Spirit represents God's intention to help us in our own time; it is a "*Comforter*" and an "*Assister.*" This is in fact why the figure of the Holy Spirit is the critical one for our kingdomless time. It is (at least potentially) what saves us from the demonology of the kingdom of darkness.

Weak Words

How exactly does the figure of the Holy Spirit effect this assistance? In a time when there is no truth and only falsehood, this cannot mean that the Holy Spirit can actually tell us something about God. Furthermore, as the above passage indicates, it still seems that for Hobbes the "power" of the Holy Spirit—which seems very much tied up with the power of the church—is a power that, as noted before, issues entirely from the "person" of Christ, an entirely derivative power and indeed a "power" that Hobbes has busily (and in this very same chapter) subsumed to the power of the sovereign itself. Does the figure of the Holy Spirit offer anything besides a kind of internal conviction? Does it produce any tangible, political results?

If we rely on J. G. A. Pocock, the answer to this must be no. For all the credence he gives Hobbes's religious writings, Pocock nonetheless tells us that for Hobbes the Holy Spirit does "little more than to represent the Son in his absence ..."[23] If that were really the case, then why establish, in addition to the symbolic trinity, a corresponding bodily trinity of three persons? Read as an *anacoluthon*, this arrangement, whereby three persons correspond to three figures, suggests this third figure is not entirely subsumable to either of the other two.

If we are going to distinguish the Holy Spirit from Jesus (or his own representational figure of "God the Son"), the obvious place to begin is by considering the Holy Spirit as a nonsovereign figure, therefore distinct from the other two figures in the trinity. Given that the "Power Ecclesiasticall" that Hobbes describes is so redolent of sovereignty to come, despite having no sovereignty of its own, it's worth pondering the powers that already do exist, those powers that are made present by the Holy Spirit itself, as opposed to those powers that were and are to be. Indeed, the notion that the power of the Holy Spirit is the power of Christ without the actual reigning that is to come, the power of persuasion without the actuality of what it persuades us of, points us back to the act of persuading itself, in other words, to rhetoric. Unlike the power of the "God the Son," this "power" has no ties to absolute truths or sovereignty; at most it occurs amid the signs and announcements of such future (and past) power, but does not itself partake of these powers (as Hobbes makes very clear in chapter 42).

If the power of the Holy Spirit is also, in a sense, persuasion, it takes on a form of persuasion that is unconnected to sovereign power; it offers a form of persuasion that is not associated with a kingdom. By indicating its kingdomless status, Hobbes may not be pointing to its weakness but its strength, its distance from the sovereign absolute. Such a power can indeed be considered *weak* in the sense of Walter Benjamin's notion of "*weak* Messian[ism]."[24] Rather than offer us a kind of stoic resistance to power that is entirely interior and hence apolitical, Hobbes's text offers us a kind of resistance that is "weak," in other words not recognized as a power at all by dominant sovereign forces; it is weak but not powerless, not weak in an absolute sense.[25]

If we stay with the idea of a power that is weak (as Hobbes may indicate by denying that the figure of the Holy Spirit has any separate power or kingdom of its own), we get a slightly different perspective on some of Hobbes's more famous pronouncements about power and authority. As he tells us right at the beginning of part 2, persuasion without a sovereign kingdom, and promises without the certainty of fulfillment, amount to "Covenants, without the Sword."[26] He calls such covenants "but Words, and of no strength to secure a man at all."[27] Hence words alone are weak.

We have seen this statement before with Hobbes, with the question for example of promises that are also "[w]ords alone," and hence not binding. We have seen this sentiment expressed too in his paradoxical statements about reading "*thy self*" instead of "*Books.*" We have also seen this sentiment among readers of Hobbes, including Kavka's need to move from a linguistically based notion of morality (where injustice is seen as a kind of absurdity) to an "objective" one based in natural law (as proclaimed by the sovereign). Words (and, by extension, books) are weak, hence the need for the sovereign to hold us to, and dictate the meaning of, our word. It is the weakness of words that tells the entire, formal story in the text of *Leviathan* (a text, of course, which is itself composed of such "weak" words).

And therein, from their very weakness, we might discern the true power of words: it is the power to show that words are "but [w]ords," the power to fail to "secure a man," the power of rhetoric, as represented by the Holy Spirit, to reveal itself and arm us all against its abuses, to fail to mean, to resist sovereign interpretation (even the sovereign interpretation of the author of *Leviathan*). The "kingdomless" Holy Spirit, Hobbes's "weak messiah" in this text, is the awareness of rhetoric's power to resist and undermine the very powers that these words convey—*the power even to resist its own persuasive/coercive power,* that is, to deconstruct itself, to fail to become "truth." With this "*Assister*" we can, as it were, inhabit the realm of rhetoric; we can see the revealed codes of language in play and participate in rather than simply suffer the construction and ongoing dynamics of meaning.

Rhetoric itself, I would thus argue, is the "power" of the Holy Spirit, the manifestation of that absent or missing kingdom, which haunts and complicates the iterations of those kingdoms that have and will exist.[28] The Holy Spirit is, in this sense, our passage to the metafigural level of the text, the completion of Hobbes's allegory of reading. If the reader is truly to "*Read* [her or his] *self*," she or he must do so via an awareness of what reading constitutes. To read with the "Spirit" is to read with an awareness that the text is haunted by an aporia, indeed a spirit, the Holy Spirit itself. If *God* is the name of that aporia, the Holy Spirit is its figure, that which rhetorically conveys its (non)existence in the world.

In this sense, the "kingdom" of the Holy Spirit does not offer us anything new: nothing comes into the world that has not been there before. What *is* new is the ongoing possibility of rhetoric itself to see anew (or read anew), even in the face of the already-is and the yet-to-be; it is the power to not just be what words seem to tell us we already are (or will be). The Holy

Spirit, the spirit of rhetoric, is also what brings texts, including Scripture but also the pages of *Leviathan* itself to life, what makes them *new*, in other words, endlessly interpretable. Consistent with Hobbes's arguments about figures in general, this power is not in the thing but in our reading, in the gap we might perceive between text and figure.

The Politics of the Holy Spirit

Having laid out the purpose and role of the Holy Spirit for Hobbes, we are in a better position to understand the differences between a Hobbesian and a Puritan political model (despite their mutual interest in this figure of interpretation) and to see why I think the implications of Hobbes's interpretation of the figure of the Holy Spirit are far more radical than the Puritans or Quakers when it comes to the question of politics. If, as is often claimed, Puritanism is part of the ideological or cultural basis for contemporary liberalism, I would argue that Hobbes's politics, far from serving as a kind of "proto-liberalism" in its own right, is in fact radically different and even opposed to the form of politics that emerges from a Puritan perspective.[29]

In large part this difference arises from the very ephemeralness inherent in Hobbes's reading of the figure of the Holy Spirit. For Hobbes, as we have seen, the Holy Spirit is not a real presence that visits or doesn't visit particular individuals. Instead it is a sign of resistance to demonology, one that is widely and easily available to one and all. In making this claim, Hobbes avoids a central concern or anxiety about the Holy Spirit that was one of the main bones of contention in Puritan and Quaker thought—the question of whether one really was filled with the spirit or just thought (or pretended) that one was.

For the Puritans, the question of how one knew whether oneself or others really had the spirit was critical, given the centrality of the Holy Spirit to their theology. They spoke of the Holy Spirit as a taste, sight, or more usually, a sound to which they were attuned.[30] In seeking to explain the sense of certainty that the experience of the Spirit (either in oneself or in others) was no delusion, Walter Craddock wrote that "a man that hath the spirit may know the spirit in another by the spirit."[31] Morgan Llwyd wrote along similar lines, "How do you discern the voice of the Holy Spirit from the others? Do you not know that a little lamb can discern its own mother's voice from a hundred others?"[32] These arguments may seem tautological (amounting to a claim that "we know we have the spirit because we have the spirit") but this may miss the point. The experience of an "in-dwelling spirit" was seen as belonging to a different epistemological category than anything available to human reason and so didn't need to appeal to logic or reason itself. Yet the fact that these arguments were made over and over suggests the anxieties and dangers inherent in placing so much importance on something that seems so intangible and so subjective. Such intangibility is exactly what alarmed the more conservative Puritans, not to mention the Anglicans about this understanding of the Holy Spirit in the first place. It is also what clearly exercised Hobbes himself, since, as it will be recalled, he tells us that when it comes to religious prophesies and enthusiasm, "he that pretends to teach men the way of so great felicity, pretends to govern them; that is to say, to rule, and reign over them."[33] In other words, so long as the Holy Spirit was seen as conveying something "real" and so long as that conveyance had powerful political consequences, Puritanism as a whole was always in danger of being "spoken for" by whoever claimed access to those forms of esoteric knowledge (and on "behalf of the community").

For Hobbes, on the other hand, being "empty" and without content, the Holy Spirit is widely available to all of us at all times; there is no question of its "reality" or lack therein, no competing claims to it as a source of authority. In Hobbes's terms the authority that stems from the figure of the Holy Spirit can be seen as radically democratic. His reading of the Holy Spirit does not insist on an alien revelation but rather on our own individual powers of reading as allowed for by this purely figurative "*Assister*."

The differences between a Hobbesian and Puritan or Quaker model of politics can most clearly be demonstrated by a consideration of their respective attentions to the question of reading. Whereas, as we have already seen, in its own concern to avoid idolatry, Puritanism and Quakerism had a new interest in textuality and in interpretation, the effect of their treatment of the Holy Spirit as an actual presence had the effect of diminishing the literal experience of reading as the central motif for questions of authority.

This is particularly true at the more radical extremes of seventeenth-century English Protestantism. The entire question of the "reality" of the Holy Spirit perhaps reached its apotheosis, as already mentioned, with the figure of George Fox and the Quakers. Fox was attributed with what Nuttall calls a "loose claim to infallibility."[34] Fox claimed that although nothing that he preached was different from that written in Scripture, it had all been told to him independently (that is to say by the Holy Spirit itself).[35] With the Quakers then, the power of the Holy Spirit moved from an interpretive power to a direct knowledge of the word of God, in some sense bypassing or at least lessening the centrality of Scripture itself, that is, the centrality of reading as the operative epistemological experience.

But this diminution of reading was in a sense true not only for the Quakers but even for a more mainstream Puritan leader like Oliver Cromwell. It is fascinating to note that Cromwell, when he was chancellor of the University of Oxford, urged and approved that the undergraduates there "instead of studying Books, study their own hearts."[36] His language echoes what Hobbes refers to in his Introduction as a "saying much usurped of late, That *Wisedome* is acquired, not by reading of *Books*, but of *Men*."[37] It is worth noting, however, that Cromwell's claim does not come in the form of a book and so does not have that strange and ironic quality we find so often with Hobbes himself. For even as Hobbes appears to denounce reading, he is demonstrating its power (even its power to call reading itself into question). Reading, as opposed to hearing, seeing, or knowing, allows Hobbes to preserve a sense of separate togetherness—a kind of public/privateness that may be something like what Arendt is trying to achieve through her (Kantian) notion of respect.[38]

Coming at the question of reading from a very different perspective from Hobbes, and despite their formal and evident decentralization, Puritanism and radical English Protestantism in general are marked by a centralizing epistemological tendency. The Quakers, rather than have their members vote separately on a particular question, would attempt to collectively feel the spirit among them. For Quakers and Puritans in general, the Holy Spirit stood for *a* truth that, even if somewhat mysterious (especially as Puritanism converged with Anglicanism), remained the goal of spiritual and hence political life. I would argue that this centralizing of experience by Puritan and Quaker political and religious movements of this period influenced more or less directly the emergence of liberalism itself in all of its sovereign (and pseudo-decentralizing) tendencies.

While I would agree with Michael Walzer that "neither Max Weber nor any of his followers have ever demonstrated that Englishmen who actually became Puritans, who really believed in predestination and lived through the salvation panic, went on to become capitalist businessmen," I would still argue (along with quite a few other scholars) that the kind of democratic notions that were received from the period of the English civil war continued to resonate by the time of the Glorious Revolution and beyond.[39] The models for a democratic (or semidemocratic) politics that Locke contends with are thus based, at least in part, on Puritan models of authority, of interpretation and epistemology.[40] I find it no surprise that it is Locke and Rousseau—both of whom have links to Puritanism and Calvinism (however tenuous in the latter case)—who make people "sovereign," that is to say infused with one spirit, one voice, one thought. Whether in Locke's notion of rationality as a faculty that will lead us to similar conclusions (if properly followed) or Rousseau's "General Will," we see a sovereign unity being stamped onto a community via a particular approach to epistemology. Without Hobbes's radically decentered notion of authority based on the actual experience of reading, we get instead a community striving for purpose, even if the expressions of that purpose appear to take myriad and diffuse forms. If Puritan doctrine leads to John Locke and to liberalism, Hobbes's distinction from this movement is clearly marked. The more radical Puritans were looking for a sovereign community, a united feeling, produced by and through actual presence of the Holy Spirit. Despite his own clear distance from radical Puritanism, Locke preserves a great deal of the character of this epistemology, passing it on to liberalism itself.

But for Hobbes, focused as he is on the experience of reading itself, fellowship is always marked by distance, difference, struggle, and contestation (something that is true for Arendt as well). The Holy Spirit does not take over or determine our reading but rather only permits it. There is no great single will, no possibility of or even a desire for absolute harmony. Even if we read Hobbes the way he is usually read—as supporting an arbitrary sovereign to save our lives—we cannot pretend that he expects anything like harmony, but only (at best) quiescence.

Tolerance and Rights

Stemming in part from a Puritan deemphasis on reading, the political form of Puritan politics led not to a diversity of interpretations but to tolerance, which can also be considered liberalism's value *par excellence*. In tolerance, there may be a great deal of latitude for a diversity of practices, but it is understood that those practices nonetheless veer from some idealized perfection, some standard against which all other measures are being judged. Here again we see that, whereas the Puritans prided themselves on their decentered approach to interpretation, from a Hobbesian perspective their literalization of the Holy Spirit served in some ways to reproduce the centrality they sought to avoid (falling into a trap Hobbes himself delimits very clearly). For all their radicalism, it can be argued that they reproduced political sovereignty in a far more subtle and hence ineradicable form than that practiced by the Stuarts and, in doing so, passed this subtler form on to liberalism itself.

For all its own lauding of individualism, liberalism too sees in "rational subjects" an expectation of a kind of community of thinkers who will largely agree on basic and predetermined principles. The coordination that is produced in both Puritan and liberal forms of thought are based on the expectation of reaching some better (or worse) approximation of one central and centralizing idea or value. Hobbes's system, on the other hand, is based only on avoiding absurdity; myriad interpretations are coordinated only with an eye toward mutual intelligibility. Rather than a ladder of rationality, Hobbes offers something more like a web (or, to anticipate the discussion of Benjamin, a constellation).

The sovereign principle behind tolerance (including in terms of what will become liberal versions of tolerance) may be reflected in the actual political practices of Oliver Cromwell. Cromwell may have been very tolerant in his heart (the hanging of Roman Catholic priests, for example, decreased markedly under his reign) but in fact he was only tolerant (in the same fashion as Milton) of some faiths and absolutely intolerant of others. Catholics, Anglicans, and Quakers (especially the former two) were not officially tolerated, although in practice, each faith was somewhat allowed.[41] The point is that the sovereign decides what to tolerate and what not to tolerate and might change its mind at any moment. Even the de facto toleration of Anglican clergy, which waxed and waned during the Commonwealth, was the sovereign's decision and no one else's.

"Tolerance" is not what Hobbes is advocating in his own alternative. A model of politics based on reading is not a question of tolerance—it does not in effect say "this is the community's true and common interest—as defined by the sovereign; if you are doing something else (i.e., something worse) we will put up with it (until or unless we change our mind)." For Hobbes there is no such privileged and central position to be tolerant from. With him, we get an anarchy of positions, truly more an anticipation of Nietzsche than Locke; instead of tolerance, we have reading and we have authors, an ongoing struggle over, and engagement with, meaning and interpretation.[42]

A related point can be made about that other great liberal value, rights, which could be considered the political manifestation of tolerance and, at least to some extent, another offshoot of a Puritan approach to interpretation. Here, a kind of centralized viewpoint predetermines what our rights will be, making them less of a safeguard than we might think.

Hobbes himself may help us understand how this is so (showing once again his consistent distinction from such positions). In chapter 21 of *Leviathan*, titled "*Of the* LIBERTY *of Subjects*," Hobbes offers his own reading of those kinds of liberties that have come to be known as "rights." He makes an important distinction between liberty and power:[43]

LIBERTY, or FREEDOME, signifieth (properly) the absence of Opposition. . . . For whatsoever is so tyed, or environed, as it cannot move . . . we say it hath not Liberty to go further. . . . But when the impediment of motion, is in the constitution of the thing it selfe, we use not to say, it wants the Liberty; but the Power to move; as when a stone lyeth still, or a man is fastened to his bed by sicknesse.[44]

Hobbes offers that liberty is an extremely narrow concept (an argument he makes clear when he argues that freedom is consistent both with fear and necessity). Liberty is essentially a relationship to the external environment, whereby we are "free" or at liberty so long as no external impediment prevents us from doing what we wish (and are able) to do. Power, on the other hand, is "in the constitution of the thing it selfe," that is to say, power is not determined by externalities so much as it determines the environment in which those externalities are brought to bear. If a stone does not have the power to move on its own, there can be no question of its liberty of movement. Liberty is thus for Hobbes merely an attribute of power rather than the other way around.

Taking this analogy directly to questions of politics, we might argue that liberty constitutes those "rights" or privileges we receive as subjects of the Leviathan (as the title of the chapter implies) and that "power" constitutes the parameters of those privileges. As Hobbes tells us, the sovereign completely determines the extent of our liberty. He tells us that we are free to do whatever the sovereign has "praetermitted," i.e., enjoy those liberties permitted to us by the "Silence of the Law" (2.21, pp. 148, 152). Hobbes acknowledges that the subject is not without what one could call "rights" but that such rights or liberties are not the same as "powers." Power remains the purview of the sovereign, to set the parameters of what a subject can and cannot do. And what one has the liberty to do one day, one might not have the next (save the one "right" that Hobbes will not compromise, the right to seek to remain alive).

With both tolerance and rights, then, we see the consequences of a particular (and Puritan) desire for a unitary or near unitary interpretation. With such a model of interpretation, a concordant (and sovereign) model of authority follows. For all the distinctions between Puritanism and liberalism as it emerges with Locke, we can see a continuity in terms of epistemological attitudes. In distinguishing himself from these interpretive models, as I will argue further in the conclusion, Hobbes also distinguishes himself from the political practices that actually were produced by those models. Rather than being a "proto" liberal, Hobbes offers us a different reading of politics altogether.

A Figure for a Kingdomless Time

Having set out some of the political implications of Hobbes's reading of the Holy Spirit, let us briefly return to a consideration of that figure itself. For Hobbes, in our own kingdomless time the divine is neither a source of direct authority (as it is for the Fifth Monarchists) nor of truth (as with "prophesying"). Rather, for Hobbes, the production of truth and authority remains an entirely human affair; the figure of the Holy Spirit simply affirms and assists us in the production of our own authority.

We know that for Hobbes the figure of the Holy Spirit is part of God's promise to humankind ("In like manner as the Holy Ghost is called *the Promise*") (3.36, p. 290). This figure is one of three messianic instantiations for Hobbes but it holds a privileged position in his discourse as the figure of our own time. This figure brings together more clearly than anything else the "Scope" of *Leviathan* as we have been interpreting it. The Holy Spirit brings the two disparate forms of representation we have been considering (rhetorical and religious) into one figure. In its perfect blankness, the Holy Spirit is both pure sign and messiah. Accordingly, the political implications of our reading of *Leviathan* become more clear and explicit when considering this figure.

If we have a better sense of what the Holy Spirit means for Hobbes, what its powers are and what its relationship to authority is, it remains to consider what the figure of the Holy Spirit actually effects in the world. If the Holy Spirit is to be indeed considered a figure of God (matching a corresponding person), then what kind of actual politics are produced by its instantiation for Hobbes? What does a "kingdomless" form of authority actually look like?

THE ALTERNATIVE PUBLIC:
THE "FELLOWSHIP OF THE HOLY SPIRIT"

Although the "power" of the Holy Spirit may be largely negative or deconstructive, Hobbes offers us glimpses of an alternative political model—in particular, an alternative model of authority (and authorship) that comes when we interpret or read with the "assistance" of the Holy Spirit, in other words, when we repossess the original authority that Hobbes claims is always ours. Although "fellowship of the spirit" was a term used by more radical Puritans and so is not one that Hobbes would use himself, it is helpful to think of this concept insofar as it indicates how for Hobbes a community of worshipful readers is of necessity a political community, no longer isolated and passive. Such a term as applied to Hobbes suggests a community that has become aware of the powers of rhetoric and of the collective, democratic nature of language

Throughout this book, I have been arguing that *Leviathan* offers us something besides the false choice between arbitrary rule by the sovereign, and chaos. If the kind of democratization of meaning that I argue is enabled by the Holy Spirit is to mean anything besides textual chaos, in which each of us reads whatever we want, we must ask two related questions: "What sort of politics do we have without sovereignty?" and "What sort of reading do we make, what are the grounds for authority in texts and in the world, when meaning itself becomes a public, collective, and political activity?" Another way to ask this question is, "What kind of politics do we produce when we read with the assistance of the Holy Spirit?"

We already know that the alternative to sovereignty is not chaos for Hobbes. As Gregory S. Kavka tells us, our private interpretations need to be coordinated with other interpretations in order to avoid "absurdity." Yet the degree to which such coordination takes on a political character remains unclear. Throughout *Leviathan*, Hobbes occasionally considers an alternative view of reading as a political model, especially when he describes a time without sovereigns, or at least a time without Christian sovereigns. In particular, he considers the nature of the early Christian church (a time beloved by many Puritan thinkers as well) when there was no Christian sovereign to "decide" the meaning of things, leaving such decisions to the members of the church themselves. Critically, this was the time of the Apostles, those members of God's third "person" who correspond most directly to the rhetorical figure of "God the Holy Spirit." (Certainly they possess a greater interpretive authority than the "Doctors" of the church who remain the current incarnation of that person; 3.42, p. 340.) Of the Apostles, Hobbes tells us:

> None of [the Apostles] preached that himselfe, or any other Apostle was such
> an Interpreter of the Scripture, as all that became Christians, ought to take
> their Interpretation for Law. For to Interpret the Laws, is part of the Admin-
> istration of a present Kingdome; which the Apostles had not. (p. 355)

This is a vision of interpretation and reading that expressly does not evoke
the notion that the sovereign's reading trumps and defines all other readings. Here, the third "person(s)" of God reinforce the antisovereign power of
the third figure of "God the Holy Spirit." The community of this time does
not "need" the sovereign's answer in order to function, nor to be in possession of authority. As Hobbes tells us, "Every of the Evangelists was Interpreter of his own Gospel; and every Apostle of his own Epistle." Private and
individual interpretations are clearly permitted and not overwritten (and, as
we shall soon see, this is the case not only for Apostles but for every member of the community) (p. 355).

Even Jesus himself does not insist (as we have already seen) on a sovereign reading. As Hobbes points out, this messiah, when he lived on the earth
(the first time), told the Jews, "*Search the Scriptures; for in them yee thinke to
have eternall life, and they are they that testifie of me*" (John 5:39). Hobbes interprets this as meaning, "If hee had not meant they should Interpret them,
hee would not have bidden them take thence the proof of his being the
Christ: he would either have Interpreted them himselfe, or referred them to
the Interpretation of the Priests" (p. 355). The idea that the future sovereign
messiah, in his mortal form (as God's second "person"), allows for and even
demands an explicitly nonsovereign notion of interpretation is in and of
itself a major subversion of Hobbes's own purported schema whereby sovereign interpretation lies in an unbroken line from Moses to Jesus (with all
the earthly kings, at least the Christian ones, strung along in between).

Hobbes follows this passage by telling us that the followers of Jesus and
the Apostles actively participated when it came to questions of interpretation, even in the face of a busily organizing church hierarchy:

> When a difficulty arose, the Apostles and Elders of the Church assembled
> themselves together, and determined what should bee preached, and taught,
> and how they should interpret the Scriptures to the People; *but took not from*

the People the liberty to read, and Interpret them to themselves. The Apostles
sent divers Letters to the Churches, and other Writings for their instruction;
which had been in vain, if they had not allowed them to Interpret, that is, to
consider the meaning of them. And as it was in the Apostles time, so it must
be till such time as there should be Pastors, that could authorize an Interpreter, whose Interpretation should generally be stood to: But that could not
be till Kings were Pastors, or Pastors Kings. (pp. 355–56)

(My emphasis)

Such a view is of course not openly at odds with Hobbes's pronouncements
on contemporary (sovereign) authority since, as he shows, this was a time
when there were no (Christian) kings. The people's interpretations could
be read as simply a substitute for sovereign power, rather than as a challenge to it.

Nevertheless, the idea that the Apostles' own reading "took not from the
People the liberty to read, and interpret them to themselves," suggests a very
different, and, from the position of the politics formally espoused in *Leviathan*, a subversive take on reading and interpretation insofar as this is exactly the liberty that Hobbes depicts the sovereign as taking from us through
much of the earlier parts of *Leviathan*. Unlike sovereign "law," which trumps
all reading, the Apostles' reading coexists with individual reading. It seems
that when the persons of God, whether Christ or his Apostles, are in a position of authority, that authority does not detract from but is in fact directly
based upon the "persuasive" (or rhetorical) power of their followers' reading,
that is to say the authority of people. And when the authority of the third
"person" of God deteriorates, as it does when we move from the Apostles to
the church of contemporary time, we find that the power of (and need for)
people to interpret for themselves is, if anything, increased by the lack of
clear doctrinal authority. Insofar as Hobbes's time (and our own) is constituted by such a state of affairs, we can see that the absence of a clear reading
(which we may or may not agree with) is not an impediment but rather a
spur to our own individual and collective acts of interpretation.

In contrast to this depiction of authority during the early Christian
church, when we consider that the sovereign of our time is, as Hobbes tells
us, arbitrary and without the kind of true authority that comes from the

kingdoms and persons of God, it might be the case that our contemporary sovereigns are in fact not true kings (not "Pastor Kings") at all, not a satisfactory replacement for the kind of publicly informed readings that Hobbes describes during the period of the early Christian church.[45] Certainly the sovereign reading should not preempt and replace people's own readings in this schema, as Hobbes often suggests.

We can further consider this notion of public reading and interpretation in the context of Hobbes's own time in light of the notorious sentiment that he expresses toward the end of *Leviathan:*

> And so we are reduced to the Independency of the Primitive Christians to follow Paul, or Cephas, or Apollos, every man as he liketh best: Which, if it be without contention, and without measuring the Doctrine of Christ, by our affection to the Person of his Minister . . . is perhaps the best.[46]

Hobbes makes a direct link between the period of the early Christian church and his own time. He goes on to explain that that this system is "perhaps the best" because "there ought to be no Power over the Consciences of men, but of the Word it selfe," and also because "it is unreasonable in them, who teach there is such danger in every little Errour, to require of a man endued with Reason of his own, to follow the Reason of any other man."[47] Hobbes is making a claim about interpretation (revealing once again the importance of the Holy Spirit that, while not mentioned here, is the power of interpreting the "Word it selfe" in precisely this individualized way). This sentiment matches earlier statements that Hobbes makes wherein he always protects interior thought against sovereign (or other) intrusions, but in this context the statement is far more radical. In the passage cited above, the sovereign *actually has been deposed,* so that the implicit conflict between sovereign and private readings that this book has hinted at all along has come to the surface, with Hobbes seeming to throw his weight behind the "private" readers and interpreters.

This statement, which was very controversial with Anglicans (and that failed to appear in the Latin edition of *Leviathan*), seems to allow that such moments of "reading" (seen as a collection of private interpretations that then get vocalized, discussed, and debated by the community) might not lead, as Hobbes so often seems to suggest, to chaos and endless relativism, but rather might indeed serve as an alternative—and superior—basis to the kind of sovereign reading that this text both promotes and resists. Such a reading produces not merely the linguistic coordination required for mutual comprehension (to avoid "absurdity") but also a viable, alternative political system.

Thus it's clear that the choice Hobbes presents us with is not so much between private readings and public ones as it is between two models of public reading, one wherein the sovereign determines what the public stance is, and another composed of various individual interpretations that nonetheless adjudicate with one another to form widely held (or at least widely entertained) beliefs, opinions, and authorizations. When the sovereign reading trumps "private" readings it is in fact this alternative public model of interpretation that it is actually trouncing and replacing, rendering each of us private and isolated monads in the face of its unimpeachable "truth."

With this in mind, we can see even more clearly why our choice, according to Hobbes, is not between sovereignty and chaos. Indeed for Hobbes the danger of chaos comes not from the notion that everyone can read what they want, but rather from the notion that everyone thinks that their reading is true (and is therefore willing to fight and kill for it). Chaos comes from idolatry, from bad reading, not from a democratization of reading. The notion of one arbitrary demonologist—that is to say, the sovereign itself—forcing its meaning onto the rest of us is not so much the elimination of chaos, but its preservation; the chaos of solipsism and arbitrary meaning must remain until the sovereign principle that embodies and supplants us is finally eliminated.

To truly banish the "Kingdome of Darknesse," it could be argued that we need to retain (or restore) this model for an alternative public, to embrace the "kingdomlessness" of our own time rather than turning to false kingdoms and idolatrous sovereigns. Not unlike Arendt's own view of the "lost treasure" of the revolution, we might say that the early Christian church for Hobbes provided an alternative model of authority that did not pave the ground for but was in fact overwritten by the sovereign's intervention. Such an overwriting is also suggested in the Introduction to *Leviathan* when Hobbes demonstrates the sovereign trumping of "private reading." It is similarly suggested by the fact that Hobbes's initial celebration of collective reading and interpretation in the first chapters of part 1 also get over-written as the book approaches part 2 (only to be reprised in parts 3 and 4). What was once a viable and indeed far superior method of interpreta-tion and source of authority becomes reduced, once it is trumped by the sovereign, to a "merely private" discourse that applies only to "[the private reader's] acquaintance, which are but few."[48] While such sources of author-ity remain in effect in our time (and as I will argue in the next chapter, actually underlie all forms of authority, whether sovereign or not), they are reduced from an actual and effective form of self-rule to something that appears barely noticeable, certainly not worthy of the title of "political." But Hobbes's treatment of the figure of Holy Spirit reminds us that this is not to say that such a relegation need be a permanent feature of public life, nor that the terrestrial sovereign need always have the final word.

CIVIL HONORING

In looking at that much-neglected space in *Leviathan,* the interaction be-tween citizens—the alternative public itself—we can see that even under conditions of sovereignty we continue to engage and represent ourselves to one another in a style that might be called "civil" honoring or worship. As with many concepts that we have explored, such as reading itself and also the matter of "public reading," there is both a sovereign and a nonsovereign version of civil worship in *Leviathan.* We experienced the sovereign form in chapter 3 of this study when we explored the question of how subjects are to properly worship the king (and the related question of whether we can bow to his throne or footstool without risking idolatry). The alternative notion of civil worship (which might more properly be called civil honoring, for reasons we will see below) has to do with how we worship or honor not the sovereign, but one another.

Hobbes reflects on the latter, interpersonal form of civil honoring in chapter 45 in part 4, his main chapter on idolatry, when he considers how we may commemorate our friends:

> I say not, that to draw a Picture after a fancy, is a Sin; but when it is drawn, to hold it for a Representation of God, is against the second Commande-

ment; and can be of no use, but to worship. And the same may be said of the Images of Angels, and of men dead; unlesse as Monuments of friends, or of men worthy remembrance: For such use of an Image, is not Worship of the Image, but a civill honoring of the Person, not that is, but that was: But when it is done to the Image which we make of a Saint, for no other reason, but that we think he heareth our prayers, and is pleased with the honour wee doe him, when dead, and without sense, wee attribute to him more than humane power; and therefore it is Idolatry.[49]

While Hobbes uses the term *civil worship* when speaking of our relationship to the sovereign, in this case he seems to avoid that phrase, contrasting it with "honoring" ("[it] is not Worship of the Image, but a civil honoring of the Person"). We perform "civill honoring," Hobbes tells us, via the "Monuments of friends," a commemoration or representation of those who matter to us. In searching for a nondemonological (and nonsovereign) politics, we might ask what such a politics of honoring or perhaps honorable friendship would look like.[50]

Hobbes tells us that when recognizing a fellow citizen now dead, we remember the person "not that is, but that was." Because, as we can see in the passage above, even the commemoration of other people can lapse into idolatry, Hobbes sees that the proper honoring of another should be consistent with the ways one honors (or worships) God. We honor our friends by offering them those tributes that we ourselves deem best and also by not turning them into something they were not.

Hobbes himself may be demonstrating something of this notion of civil honoring in an act of friendship he commits to the page. Although *Leviathan* is formally dedicated to Francis Godolphin, it becomes immediately clear in the dedication that, as in the book's conclusion, it is his brother Sidney, a late ("not that is, but that was") dear friend of Hobbes, who is the true subject of this dedication. Hobbes tells us "when he lived [Sidney Godolphin] was pleas'd to think my studies something, and otherwise to oblige me . . . with reall testimonies of his good opinion."[51] Here, Hobbes is recognizing the value of having his own opinions validated by his friend whose own opinions were "great in themselves, and the greater for the worthinesse of his person."[52]

In some sense, Hobbes's testament to his friend serves as a parallel to the "submission" that he makes to the sovereign shortly after this in the introduction. There too he tells us that his reading conforms with or is validated by someone else's reading of him (in that case the reading of the sovereign itself). But in this case, there is no sense of truth or objective authority involved. Godolphin's opinion of Hobbes is entirely and explicitly nonsovereign, part of that web of relationships between mutually covenanted citizens from which the sovereign pointedly is excluded. This is not a truth claim at all but a testament of belief, shored up and reciprocated by Hobbes's own belief in and appreciation of his friend's own great qualities.

Perhaps key among those qualities for Hobbes was the way Sidney Godolphin himself used speech and rhetoric.[53] As Miriam Reik puts it, "Hobbes had earlier found in Thucydides, and later in Sidney Godolphin, examples of people who had merged the various uses of speech successfully—the ability of logic to deliberate with the ability of rhetoric to move."[54] In this way it could be argued that Godolphin serves as an example of the kind of virtuous use of rhetoric that Hobbes would counterpose to the sovereign's misuse, an exemplar of how rhetoric can construct new beliefs even as it resists becoming itself idolatry posing as truth.

Anxious about how *Leviathan* will be received, Hobbes sees his friend as a bastion or anchor of his own ability to put this book forward. Near the beginning of his dedication he tells Francis Godolphin,

> There is not any vertue that disposeth a man, either to the service of God, or to the service of his Country, to Civill Society, or private Friendship, that did not manifestly appear in [your brother's] conversation, not as acquired by necessity, or affected upon occasion, but inhaerent, and shining in a generous constitution of his nature.[55]

In this passage, we see a description of virtue that is inherent in this man's personal qualities. Of course, this vision of Godolphin's virtues is "authored" by Hobbes himself (quite literally in this case); it attests to how, for Hobbes, Godolphin serves as a kind of inspiration (in the same mundane but vital sense as the inspiration we receive from the Holy Spirit) for Hobbes himself.

In "A Review, and Conclusion," at the opposite end of *Leviathan,* Hobbes continues in his remembrance of his friend when he writes,

I have known cleernesse of Judgment, and largenesse of Fancy; strength of Reason, and gracefull Elocution; a Courage for the Warre, and a Feare for the Laws, and all eminently in one man; and that was my most noble and honored friend Mr. *Sidney Godolphin;* who hating no man, nor hated of any, was unfortunately slain in the beginning of the late Civill warre, in the Publique quarrell, by an undiscerned and an undiscerning hand.[56]

The simplicity and devotion that Hobbes displays of friendship toward Sidney Godolphin seems quite unlike (even the direct opposite of) the complex and often perverse submissions that Hobbes offers unto the figure of the sovereign. This is very much in the style of Machiavelli, who also appears to praise the Prince with a convoluted language in his own dedication to *The Prince* and who dedicates his *Discourses* to his own friends in a far different (and perhaps more "republican") style of writing.

In his dedication to Godolphin, Hobbes seems to recognize that our image of others is of necessity our own version of them, a figure that stands in for what we see, and a figure of our own invention at that. This figuration does not necessarily absolutely separate us, but rather serves as the grounds for the beginning of our endeavor toward the other (as opposed to idolatry where the other is completely extinguished by our grasping, by our "already knowing" what the other is and means). In this sense, I see Hobbes as anticipating somewhat Emmanuel Levinas in the way he approaches the other.[57] When we are aware that the other is not equivalent to our fantasies of them, when we see our fantasies *as* fantasies, as representations, we have the birth of ethics for Levinas and the beginnings of civil honoring and friendship for Hobbes. In both cases, the model for such relationships is the absolute aporia of our relationship to God.[58]

It is worth noting that in *Leviathan,* these instances of civil honoring occur only between the living and the dead, both in the abstract and in the concrete example of Hobbes's own posthumous appreciation for his friend. And yet, it may be the case that, when for example Hobbes devotes his book, not to his dead friend but his friend's living brother, we see that civil honoring does not need to refer only to those who are no longer alive: it might apply not only to relationships past, but also to relationships present (and future).[59]

HOBBES AND BENJAMIN

As we have seen in these discussions of the early Christian church and civil honoring, Hobbes tells us very little about the actual practice of political authority that occurs without reference to sovereignty. While his method of reading and the figure of the Holy Spirit make such a politics conceivable, *Leviathan* does not tell us all that much about what such a politics looks like.

As this book begins to turn its attention from a reading of Hobbes himself to an application of such a reading to our own time—the main purpose of the conclusion that follows—it becomes clear that we need some more contemporary thinkers to help us examine this question further. The contemporary thinkers already evoked so far, especially Hannah Arendt, are meant to help us in this regard. At this point, I'd like to focus again on Walter Benjamin, to facilitate this discussion. Benjamin is particularly useful at this juncture because of his own interest in representation as well as his embrace of a style of messianism (which I will argue, accords very well with Hobbes's).

The purpose of such comparisons is not to suggest that these thinkers are identical in every way or that Benjamin is responding to Hobbes the way I have read him in this book (much less Arendt!). Clearly, the enormous passage of time and vastly different political and social contexts of their writings suggests that we should be cautious in making connections between these authors. Yet precisely because of their respective positions at the dawn and the full expression of sovereignty and liberal capitalism, it is fruitful and doubly illuminating to think of these authors as being in dialogue. The cross-temporal associations that result are of the kind that Benjamin in particular would greatly appreciate insofar as they serve to revisit and resist a sense of progress and inevitability in the development of liberalism and even sovereignty itself.

For Benjamin, as well as for Hobbes, the subject of representation and misrepresentation is the paramount political question. Benjamin too is concerned with the notion of the image and the sorts of false readings of imagery that facilitate, in his view, fascism, capitalism, and other political evils. In his own work, Benjamin focuses, very much like Hobbes himself, on how such delusions can be combated, but whereas Hobbes focuses on the power of reading, Benjamin focuses far more (as may be appropriate to his, and our, own times) on visual imagery, on commercial organizations of space, and on modern media such as film. In other words, he seems to privilege "seeing" over "reading" as the organizing trope for political life.[60]

Earlier in this book, when considering *The Origin of German Tragic Drama*, we saw how Benjamin considered allegory as a chief weapon against misrepresentation. In works such as "On Some Motifs in Baudelaire," "The Work of Art in the Age of Mechanical Reproduction," "The Paris of the Second Empire in Baudelaire," and the *Arcades Project*, Benjamin updates and applies this project to his own time. These works are replete with strategies for combating what he calls the "phantasmagoria," the delusions and spectacles of modern life (particularly insofar as it is marked by the domination of commodity fetishism).[61]

As with Hobbes, for Benjamin the power of misrepresentation is such that it produces not only a false present but a false past and false future as well. In short, time itself is perverted and corrupted by the phantasmagoria. He describes modern life as a situation in which we are constantly bombarded by the faux appearance of the new and unprecedented, whereas in fact nothing ever changes.[62] History and time become captured and produced by the endless monotony of fashion and commodification, promising but never delivering the possibility of a true (contingent) future.

In his considerations of the writings of Charles Baudelaire especially, Benjamin examines the power of the artist or critic to resist and respond to phantasmagoria under these circumstances. Writing in Paris toward the end of the nineteenth century, Benjamin tells us, Baudelaire had an "allegorical genius."[63] For Benjamin the Parisians of Baudelaire's day were, as we remain to this day, in a constant state of shock. They were (and we are) literally assaulted at every waking moment by the onslaught of commodity fetishization as well as by the bustle and jostling of modern life. But over time we become inured to and ignorant of the shocks we experience. Allegory serves Benjamin's purposes in part because "it is part of [its] nature to shock."[64] Benjamin further tells us that "[i]t is a shock that brings someone engrossed in reverie up from the depths" (p. 325). In the capable hands of Baudelaire (as read by Benjamin himself), allegory potentially reveals the shocks we receive, turning them into weapons against the very system that shocks us in the first place.

Part of Baudelaire's genius for Benjamin is that he does not merely denote but fully occupies the position of someone succumbing to the shocks he describes. In contrasting the baroque allegorists of the seventeenth century to Baudelaire's own time, Benjamin tells us. "Baroque allegory sees the corpse only from the outside; Baudelaire evokes it from within" (p. 329). It is here that the study of Benjamin may add something to Hobbes's own arguments insofar as the condition of modern persons (as Arendt also attests) is quite a bit more compromised and more problematic than what Hobbes describes in his own time. For Hobbes the "kingdom of darkness" was perhaps as much a danger as a certainty, whereas in our own time, there is no question that it is the "kingdom" we live in. Thus Benjamin's treatment of Baudelaire is useful in that it instructs us in how misrepresentation may be resisted in a (fully) modern context.

Correspondances

Among the weapons Benjamin adds to our arsenal for this purpose is the notion of the *correspondances*. *Correspondances* is what Benjamin calls "the antidote to allegory" (p. 377). Speaking of an "antidote" for a rhetorical figure he holds so dear seems strange at first, but we can see that for Benjamin the use of allegory guarantees neither victory nor even perpetually successful resistance. Benjamin tells us that allegory has an essentially "destructive" character (p. 331). He tells us further that for all his genius, Baudelaire battles "with the impotent rage of someone fighting the rain or the wind."[65] If there is a more positive side to Benjamin's exposition of Baudelaire, it is the idea that one can reoccupy time in such a way as to rebuild some semblance of "reality" from the fragments and pieces of a broken world.[66] *Correspondances* is the name of this activity; the wielder of the *correspondances* (who I argue is for Benjamin personified by the figure of the collector) makes connections and "takes up the struggle against dispersion."[67] He tells us "the allegorist is, as it were, the polar opposite of the collector."[68] But Benjamin goes on to say:

> Nevertheless—and this is more important than all the differences that may exist between them—in every collector hides an allegorist, and in every

allegorist a collector. As far as the collector is concerned, his collection is never complete; for let him discover just a single piece missing, and everything he's collected remains a patchwork, which is what things are for allegory from the beginning. On the other hand, the allegorist . . . can never have enough of things. With him, one thing is so little capable of taking the place of another that no possible reflection suffices to foresee what meaning his profundity might lay claim to for each one of them.[69]

Thus allegory and *correspondances* go hand in hand for Benjamin. And *correspondances* in particular is necessary for resisting the pseudo-time (which is in fact no time at all) of the phantasmagoria. Against the false sense of progress and historical linearity, for Benjamin *correspondances* establishes a kind of connection to all that has been lost (without, however, actually reviving any true past, as we will see). Citing Proust, Benjamin tells us that "time is peculiarly chopped up in Baudelaire,"[70] and that

the important thing is that the *correspondances* record a concept of existence which includes ritual elements. Only by appropriating these elements was Baudelaire able to fathom the full meaning of the breakdown which he, a modern man, was witnessing. . . . What Baudelaire meant by *correspondances* may be described as an experience which seeks to establish itself in crisis-proof form. This is possible only within the realm of ritual.[71]

For Benjamin, the *correspondances* does not (re)establish truth itself. Rather, it "constitute[s] the court of judgment before which the object of art is found to be a faithful reproduction."[72] In other words, *correspondances* is what establishes the resemblance (or re-assemblance) of things in an age marked by the permanent loss of truth; it is the act of ritual reenactment rather than perfect instantiation, and so, like allegory itself, exposes rather than obliterates its purely representative character.

Taking the concepts of allegory and *correspondances* together, we get a better idea of Benjamin's strategies. For Benjamin—reflecting both his association with Jewish mysticism and his anticapitalism—the world is in fragments. Therefore any expression of reality must address itself to and reflect this fragmentation. Allegory serves to expose the fragmentation of the world (against the faux sense of space and time generated by the phantasmagoria) and *correspondances* serves to make meaning and new possibility in such a world without succumbing to phantasm all over again.

Hobbes and Benjamin Considered Together

With Benjamin's approach to representation and time in mind, we may be in a better position to think about some of the implications of the reading of Hobbes I am offering.[73] In a sense, Hobbes too can be read as offering a dual strategy for dealing with misrepresentation. We saw early on how Hobbes employs the strategy of allegory himself insofar as he seeks always to expose false depictions: ideas and words and images which fail to "profess their inconstancy." What may become clearer now is how Hobbes can also be read according to Benjamin's notion of *correspondances*, especially in terms of his own approach to temporal and spatial ordering. For Hobbes, too, time is "chopped up" insofar as the three persons of God and their corresponding figures assert an alternative history of the world, a ritual reenactment of God's aporia. These figures too do not instantiate truth but only serve as (ritualized) iterations of representational absence. In the pages of *Leviathan*, this alternative history is dramatized via its contrast to the pseudohistory of the sovereign itself. Just as with Benjamin's depiction, the pseudo-time Hobbes depicts in part 2 of *Leviathan* appears to be "time" itself, but, when judged from the context of the eschatological history, it shows itself to be timeless, and apolitical. The alternative history supplied and produced by Hobbes's eschatology comes from the persons and figures who follow one another in a kind of temporal ordering and yet can also be seen as simultaneous (the Holy Spirit "proceeded from ... both" the past and future kingdoms).[74] Their instantiations are arrayed in a style that could be considered "a constellation," to use another Benjaminian term, that is to say, they are arrayed according to their own *correspondances* and not the temporal narratives of our time. Speaking of constellations in his "Theses on the Philosophy of History," Benjamin tells us:

> [An event or fact] ... became historical posthumously, as it were, through events that may be separated from it by thousands of years. A historian who takes this as his point of departure stops telling the sequence of events like

the beads of a rosary. Instead he grasps the constellation which his own era has formed with a definite earlier one. Thus he establishes a conception of the present as the "time of the now" which is shot through with chips of Messianic time.[75]

With Hobbes, too, it can be argued that the persons and figures of God via their *correspondances* set up a kind of "time of the now," an ongoing and meaningful relationship across time that sets the bounds of political authority without, however, restoring (or resorting to) "truth," in its perfect, original form. Clearly this eschatology is also "shot through with chips of Messianic time." The "collecting" of ideas and opinions that we see in Hobbes also is permitted (or required) by the divine aporia we see in Benjamin. In the case of both thinkers, it seems as if the messianic figures they evoke are less external saviors and more figures that allow and permit our own self-salvation (as we see with Benjamin's melding of Jewish messianism and revolutionary Marxism). In this sense, too, do I consider Hobbes and Benjamin both particularly political thinkers; they focus not on the "perhaps" or the "yet to come," but indeed on the time of the now (including our "kingdomless" time).

If we live in the "time of the now," what of the (nonsovereign) future? Once again, Benjamin can help illuminate Hobbes's ideas. At the end of the "Theses on the Philosophy of History," Benjamin famously writes:

> We know that the Jews were prohibited from investigating the future. The Torah and the prayers instruct them in remembrance, however. This stripped the future of its magic, to which all those succumb who turn to soothsayers for enlightenment. This does not imply, however, that for the Jews the future turned into homogenous, empty time. For every second of time was the strait gate though which the Messiah might enter.[76]

As with Benjamin's description, for Hobbes as well the future itself is not to be surrendered to "soothsayers" and magic, i.e., not to demonologists who falsely fill it with their own phantasms. In a very real sense, the future is already partially here via our promises and covenants as instantiations of God's promise ("every second of time was the strait gate through which the Messiah might enter").[77] Rather than becoming "homogenous, empty time," a sovereign future of life everlasting (i.e., eternal and antipolitical, the very nightmare of a nonfuture that Arendt resists in her own work), the future becomes a matter of human responsibility and possibility. Stripped of its magical illusions, the future does not become empty but rather a blank reflection of something as yet unmade and unknown, something we strive toward via our promises.

Benjamin's Antisovereignty

Finally, and perhaps most crucially, we must consider the correspondences (or *correspondances*) if any, between Hobbes and Benjamin's respective antisovereignty. A perusal of "Critique of Violence" reveals that Benjamin's explicit comments on sovereignty are quite complex. Intriguingly, at the end of that essay, Benjamin speaks of a "sovereign violence" that is explicitly linked to God (as "divine violence"). In this way, Benjamin's approach may be similar to Hobbes, who, as I have already argued, seems to approve of a kind of divine sovereignty but who is more critical of terrestrial attempts to, as it were, "speak for God."[78] Such a reading is amply supported by Derrida's own interpretation of the end of Benjamin's essay. Considering Benjamin's distinction draws between "mythic" and "divine" violence, Derrida writes,

> To this violence of the Greek *mythos*, Benjamin opposes feature for feature the violence of God. From all points of view, he says, it is its opposite. Instead of founding *droit*, it destroys it; instead of setting limits and boundaries, it annihilates them; instead of leading to error and expiation, it causes to expiate; instead of threatening, it strikes; and above all, this is the essential point, instead of killing with blood, it kills and annihilates *without bloodshed.*[79]

For Derrida, this distinction is crucial because *droit* (or "right," the law in all its mythical connotations) must shed blood to establish its power over life. He writes that for Benjamin "in contrast, purely divine (Judaic) violence is exercised on all life but to the profit or in favor of the living."[80] In this distinction, Benjamin has essentially reversed the very basis of positive law; whereas the human-contrived *mythos* that founds *droit* is usually considered to be concrete, and the law of God is mysterious, for Benjamin it is the other way around. For Derrida, divine violence is not simply an alternative to positive law, but its remedy; it serves to expose and destroy the falsities of *droit.*

If we accept Derrida's interpretation, we can see more clearly how Hobbes's eschatological framework not only conflicts with but potentially overcomes the idolatry of a law that has no true recourse to divinity. Mythic violence founds positive law, a law that serves some particular interest in the name of the universal or absolute. Similar to Hobbes's notion of demonology, mythic violence purports to deliver a truth that it is in fact busily producing. Divine law, on the other hand, is manifest only in its mysterious (but imminent) absence; it produces no "truth" of its own but serves to undermine all pretenders.

Crucially for my own purposes, Benjamin ends his essay by explicitly connecting divine violence to sovereignty. Divine violence "may be called sovereign violence."[81] This claim may help align Benjamin with my reading of Hobbes insofar as the term *sovereignty,* although generally applied to precisely the sort of *droit* that Benjamin decries (and that Hobbes is normally understood as supporting), should, in the case of both thinkers, more properly be applied only to God's own rule. For both authors, it seems, only God practices a form of sovereignty that is beneficial, enacted on behalf of rather than at the expense of humanity. And in the narrative both authors give us, divine sovereignty serves mainly to save us from its earthly (pernicious) iterations. In its manifestation as the Holy Spirit for Hobbes and revolution for Benjamin, sovereign violence serves as a weapon against the false idols that mythic violence promotes. Divine sovereign violence cleans and destroys, possibly allowing humans to reprise their relationship with God's sovereignty, or at the very least giving us respite from earthly rulers.[82]

Treating these thinkers in tandem, we get less a sense of some grand organizational scheme for politics from either of them and more of an openended and contingent notion of political community. In general, as I have tried to make clear, I see Hobbes and Benjamin, as well as Arendt, engaged in projects that can be treated as being in dialogue with one another (in the case of Arendt and Benjamin of course, this was literally true). For all three thinkers, there are "messianic" elements—be it action, speech, and promises for Arendt, *correspondences* and revolution for Benjamin, and the Holy Spirit and the power of rhetoric for Hobbes—which enable us to chart our own course in the future. This is not to argue that for these thinkers we don't have to worry about politics. On the contrary, saying that the messiah is already in some sense here does not mean we are "already redeemed." All three of these thinkers show that the messiah's presence is only a possibility, one that then requires our own responsibility and action, our own reading (and seeing). As with Hobbes, Benjamin shows that the act of rhetorical subversion is hard and ongoing work. Its power usually lies dormant, but it is always there to be taken up should we so choose, should we come to believe in and learn to employ its power sufficiently.

Finally, in terms of the actual presence of an alternative politics in the world, we can make a kind of genealogy beginning with Hobbes's readings of the early Christian community and going on, via Benjamin and Arendt's analysis of revolutions, to various iterations in modern revolutionary moments. In such cases, whether it is the American founding, the early days of the Russian Revolution, or other instances, a nonsovereign (taken in the terrestrial sense) form of politics was not only a theory but a lived reality. In each case, we get only glimpses of an alternative source of politics and authority, yet all three thinkers hold that such authority is not annihilated by sovereign power or mythic violence but only overshadowed by it. The consequences of such overshadowing are grave. We must not forget that for Hobbes, the presence of demonology "*dis-prepare*[s us] *for the Kingdome of God to come.*"[83] In other words, so long as demonology is practiced, our redemption, in whatever form that might take, is being forever put off. To repeat once again Arendt's position, if we are ever to have a radically democratic polity, "it is precisely sovereignty [we] must renounce."[84]

This comparison with Hobbes and Benjamin (and Arendt) may illuminate how our reading of *Leviathan* offers not merely resistance for resistance's sake (although it does offer that), but also the realization of alternative forms of authority that are practiced and produced on a daily basis even under the shadow of sovereign power. Let us recall the metaphor Christopher Pye takes from Hobbes whereby "the light of the Sun obscureth the light of the Starres," even as the stars "do no less exercise their vertue."[85] By analogy, the alternative authority ("the Starres") is always with us, even if we do not see it (because of the sovereign "Sun"). Perhaps we must learn to be better readers in order to see the practices of authority that we engage without even realizing it.

In the case of Hobbes, as we have seen in this chapter, the figure of "God the Holy Spirit" offers us the means to deconstruct and challenge the very "Hay, or Stubble" that forms the basis of law and sovereignty as it is currently (and falsely) practiced. If the promise of the first kingdom is enacted in the original covenant with God as reiterated by Moses, and the promise of the second kingdom is enacted in our "pact of Baptisme," the promise of our kingdomless time is enacted in our ability to keep promising, to ceaselessly struggle against the notion that the promise has been fulfilled and the need for politics is now over. Thus do we remain in the nonkingdom of the Holy Spirit, the figure that conveys the promise of God in our own time.

Politics Without Sovereignty

HAVING MADE VARIOUS arguments about Hobbes's theories of reading, authority, and representation (in all its rhetorical, religious, and political variants), we must still more closely examine the implications of this analysis, for Hobbes's politics and our own. What does a rhetorical reading of *Leviathan* finally tell us? How do we reconcile this reading with the text itself, or with our impression of what Hobbes "meant" when he wrote it? Most importantly, even if we accept the basic premises of such a reading, what is its significance for contemporary considerations of the question of sovereignty, authority, and politics, especially given that Hobbes's writings came, not in response to specific perils of modernity (as Arendt's and Benjamin's work does) but at the dawn of modernity when so much remained unknown and unknowable?

To get a clearer sense of the political implications of this reading of *Leviathan*, after revisiting the question of the "meaning" of *Leviathan* I will focus on whether Hobbes should be considered a "proto-liberal," i.e., a harbinger, if not the architect, of liberalism itself (and in particular, the liberal variant of sovereignty). Given the tendency by many (although by no means all) liberal thinkers to read Hobbes as one of their own, or at least as anticipating what liberalism would become, it is useful to show how this is not the case. I read Hobbes as being less a prophet of what was to come than someone who might have warned us off the path that was in fact followed (in this way connecting him all the closer to Arendt and Benjamin, who respond to the very pitfalls that Hobbes may have however dimly foreseen). As part of this argument, I will attempt to anticipate certain liberal (and one decidedly illiberal) responses to my claims about Hobbes and try to address them. I will end with a brief look at the larger implications of this rhetorical reading of Hobbes: questions of religion, interpretation, and the possibility of imagining a political system that exists without reference to sovereignty.

THE "MEANING" OF *LEVIATHAN*

The overriding question to ask about the "meaning" of *Leviathan* is, What do we make of the overriding preponderance of overt support for sovereignty in the pages of this text? In other words, isn't it perverse to claim that *this*, of all books, is antisovereign? One answer might to be claim that this is no more perverse than reading *The Prince* as being against the prince. The announced subject and even general content of a book (in both of these cases) doesn't necessarily commit the author to a particular meaning. Another way to consider this claim is to consider *Leviathan* as allegorizing the condition of the subject in a sovereign state. Like this subject, the reader of this text finds herself or himself in an already sovereign environment, where sovereignty is naturalized, given, and openly supported. The reader/subject can accept this state of affairs and thereby "read" the text as a sign of their own (already achieved) subjugation. Or they can practice both textual and political resistance by a rhetorically informed reading (with the instructions for such a reading being given by Hobbes himself). As I've argued throughout this book, I see that Hobbes's tendency to expose his own uses of rhetoric to us, the readers, tilts the balance in the favor of the second sort of reading. This doesn't mean that we all will or must read the text that way, just that we could.

In rare moments in *Leviathan*, Hobbes indicates to us how he might expect or hope his book to be read. We have already seen his expressed desire that it be read according to its "Scope" and "Designe," which may constitute a request that the book be read against the grain of his own overt, particular comments. In another passage at the end of part 2, Hobbes tells us:

> I am at the point of believing this my labour, as uselesse, as the Commonwealth of *Plato;* For he also is of opinion that it is impossible for the disorders of State, and change of Governments by Civill Warre, ever to be taken away, till Soveraignes be Philosophers.[1]

Hobbes allows that his schemes may seem utopian, may not protect us as much as he wishes they would. He also attests to the fact that sovereigns of his day may not amount to much (a veiled critique of the Stuarts or their successors?) insofar as they are not good readers of *Leviathan*. After speculating that Plato, among others, has not "put into order" the "Science of Naturall Justice" as he has himself, Hobbes takes heart and writes:[2]

> I recover some hope, that one time or other, this writing of mine, may fall into the hands of a Soveraign, who will consider it himselfe, (for it is short, and I think clear,) without the help of any interested, or envious Interpreter; and by the exercise of entire Soveraignty, in protecting the Publique teaching of it [i.e., of *Leviathan*] convert this Truth of Speculation, into the Utility of Practice.[3]

The question of reading thus comes full circle. It appears as if Hobbes wants to be rescued by a sovereign after all, but one who is a better reader than any sovereign that existed in his—or our—time (i.e., the kind of sovereign that God is). But once again, a close reading of these sentences suggests a complication of this message. This sovereign "who will consider it himselfe . . . without the help of any interested or envious Interpreter" is not actually interpreting the book "himselfe" after all, but is rather reading the book exactly the way Hobbes "meant" it to be read (directly addressing, however obtusely, the question of whether the text "means" anything at all). At the same time, Hobbes insists that such a sovereign protect the public teaching of *Leviathan*, which means that widespread reading (and interpretation) of that text must occur. Even if the content of that reading is meant to be strictly controlled, we know that for Hobbes belief cannot be commanded. By being made public, it becomes more difficult for any one meaning to dominate, insofar as readings are pluralized and endlessly complicated.

Here, as with the very beginning of *Leviathan*, we get a kind of centrifugal notion of interpretation where the sovereign's reading is set off against myriad public readings and, concomitantly, a solitary "true" meaning of the text is set off against a myriad of interpretations. The sovereignty of text and nation is produced and then set against another kind of reading, authority, and interpretation. So which reading is correct? Which predominates? By constantly making the reader aware of their act of reading, by locating this contest of interpretations in the context of a book that is actually being read by one of those myriad individual readers and finally, by collapsing the sovereign reading with his own authority in the text (the authority of a private subject), Hobbes is de facto favoring the more popular and democratic style of reading and interpretation. Rather than resolving the problem of interpretation once and for all, Hobbes seems to be perpetuating the rhetorical challenges to singular and sovereign readings and authority.

In the passage cited above, Hobbes seems, as he often does, to be toying with us. Although he tells us that his text is "short" and "clear," this one passage indicates that it is hardly clear (and to say that *Leviathan* is "short" is similarly baffling). Even the question of who this "future sovereign" will be is quite unclear. Is it Jesus, who as a personation of God will be the rightful future king of the world? Is it somehow Hobbes himself (as figured by his supposedly placing his own face on the sovereign's body in the book's frontispiece)? Is it the "sovereign" reader that each of us could be? Is it God, whose own sovereignty sets a standard that all terrestrial monarchs fail to achieve? After announcing that Plato has not resolved the problem of government, Hobbes nonetheless clearly alludes to Plato, updating and modernizing his notion of the philosopher king by converting it "into the Utility of Practice." This is a typical rhetorical ploy on Hobbes's part of overtly denouncing something in his text, while stealthily redeeming that very thing. But if the nature of that sovereign is so unclear, this does not really resolve Hobbes's anxiety. The tension between text and rhetoric once again makes a clear ("sovereign") answer indeterminate and thus perhaps serves as a kind of "answer" after all.

Thus the answer to the question "What does *Leviathan* mean?" might not be so simple; it might not mean one thing or anything at all; perhaps it is simply a text, whose meaning is radically available. In making this claim, I am to some extent reading Hobbes along the same lines that Victoria Kahn reads Machiavelli, wherein rhetoric can be a weapon for tyrant or republican alike. At the same time, as I have argued earlier, I see both Hobbes and Machiavelli as weighing in more on the "republican" side of this question insofar as the exposure of rhetorical practices (including those that serve to produce political authority) serves as a counterweight to sovereign power, as a source of and tool for resistance. In this sense, rhetoric does indeed serve as a "weapon" in the sense of *ornatus:* not a weapon to make one's point better, but a weapon that calls that point into question, a weapon that politicizes the very question of meaning as well as the conclusions and interpretations that we draw from that question.

It's worth returning (briefly) to Walter Benjamin in this regard by reconsidering Hobbes as an allegorist. It was my claim in chapter 2 that Hobbes offers us an allegory of reading in which the reader is figured as "*read[ing] our] self.*" In the *Origin of German Tragic Drama,* Benjamin says of allegory: "The intention which underlies allegory is so opposed to that which is concerned with the discovery of truth that it reveals more clearly than anything else the identity of pure curiosity which is aimed at mere knowledge with the proud isolation of man."[4] That Benjamin evokes the "intention" behind allegory is strange, given his repeated claim in the same text that truth is marked by a "lack of intentionality," in other words, is rendered utterly mysterious and unknowable.[5] But it speaks to the fact, or even inevitability, that the allegorist is not free of intentionality. However, in this case, unlike with other tropes, the intention of the allegorist is in a sense exposed and subverted by the very medium (allegory) in which that intention is expressed (it might make more sense to speak of the "intention" of the allegory itself). So even if Hobbes "meant something" in *Leviathan,* even if he sought to portray a sovereign power that was conservative and absolute, his own rhetorical device turns on him, revealing "the identity of pure curiosity" on Hobbes's part and pointing out to us, his readers, how to subvert the very text in which we encounter these claims and intentions. Although, as mentioned earlier, any text can be deconstructed, I think Hobbes, like Baudelaire, was possessed of an "allegorical genius" that enabled his text to possibly transcend even his own native conservatism, making *Leviathan* a radical text with or without its author's "intentions."

Taken in this sense, we can say that as an allegorical text *Leviathan* does not simply describe politics but is itself political; it embodies, enacts, and makes possible a type of textual resistance that just might, if the structure of the text is allowed to inform the "bare Words," lead to a riot of reinterpretation, reauthorization, and deauthorization, not just in terms of our reading of this book, but of all "texts" (including the nation that we are citizens of). At the very least, such a reading of Hobbes enables us to remain capable of resistance, of textual disobedience, and to ponder further how our "private" act of reading this book can yet have real political ramifications. In his exposition of rhetoric as a weapon, Hobbes offers us a sword, not unlike the one depicted raising over the sovereign's head in his frontispiece, which could come down on citizen and sovereign alike, depending on who wields it and how.

"WOULD-BE ANARCHISM"

If Hobbes offers us an "anarchic" style of interpretation, does he offer an anarchic politics, too? Although the word "anarchy" has a lot of baggage that has nothing to do with Hobbes, it may be useful to think of Hobbes in such terms. Anarchy often evokes images of people running amuck, the strong terrorizing the weak, etc. Such images serve to keep us convinced that anarchy is not a viable or desirable political option. But Hobbes's "anarchism," if that is what we should call it, is not so much against collective politics as it is against sovereignty as the *sine qua non* of political life. I take the term "anarchist" from Richard Flathman, who suggests that this is what he "would be" if he weren't convinced that sovereignty and sovereign forms of authority are a political necessity.[6] A major goal of this book is to engage in a friendly argument with Flathman, asking that he reconsider his "would-be" anarchism and, at least in terms of Hobbes, reconsider the possibility of anarchy itself, period.

In Hobbes's case, such anarchy can be associated with "kingdomlessness" (which might actually be a better, or more accurate word), the form of politics produced and made possible by the figure of God the Holy Spirit. The *anacoluthonic* structure of Hobbes's eschatology, whereby three figures (and three persons) correspond to only two kingdoms, suggests that kingdomlessness is the preferred form of politics in our time (not just "kingdomless" as in having no king but in having no sovereign at all). This depiction of kingdomlessness is opposed to the false "kingdom of darkness" that we do have in our time. As we have seen, in his depictions of such a kingdomless politics, Hobbes shows not wild chaos (as he does in his faux-historical evocation of the "state of nature") but a community deeply bonded by its covenants and obligations to God and to one another from its inception. This is the community of the early Christian church and in a sense, this is the community he depicts in the early parts of part I of *Leviathan:* a community bound by language, by mutuality, and by the eschatological figures that produce it.

Hobbes is only an "anarchist" if Arendt is one, too; they share, I believe, a similar political vision of a life without rulers, without those who speak or act for people themselves.[7] Whether we call this anarchy, kingdomlessness, radical democracy, or something else, the point is that there is no absence of power or authority, only an absence of sovereignty. Indeed, for Arendt a community only possesses "power" when it is free from sovereignty. The ultimate anti-anarchist bogeyman that so many liberals take from Hobbes—his dour vision of the state of nature—comes not from the lack of sovereignty per se but from a state in which people have no framework to communicate with one another, when in a sense we are all miniature sovereigns, randomly deciding on what to do and paying a heavy price for it. Recall that for Hobbes, in our private deliberations it is "very seldome [that] any man is able to see to the end [the consequences of his actions]."[8] As with Arendt, we need other people to help us make better decisions. Since the sovereign is, by definition, isolated from this decision-making process, it can be counted on to make the worst decisions possible. For Hobbes in particular, we need a collective and political framework to coordinate and make sense of our interpretations, such framework as is made available by the persons and figures of God. With such institutions in place, we have political options available to us beyond those offered by sovereign systems (including liberal ones).

LIBERALISM AND SOVEREIGNTY

A more common interpretation of Hobbes (one that tends to be based mostly, even exclusively on readings of parts 1 and 2 of *Leviathan,* besides other works) sees him as either an authoritarian or a proto-liberal or both. To examine whether Hobbes is a "proto-liberal" and what relationship this question has to do with sovereignty, it's helpful to describe the relationship between liberalism and sovereignty in more general terms. Modern-day liberalism is a vast, complex, and internally variegated construct. As Flathman tells us himself, some argue there may not even be such a thing as liberalism at all (he speaks of "liberalisms").[9] I will eschew any attempt here to systematize liberalism and merely note its peculiarly intense but sometimes stealthy orientation toward sovereignty.

To focus on the connection between liberalism and sovereignty may seem odd, in that generally speaking, liberalism seems to soften and alter the nature of sovereignty to the point where it seems no longer objectionable. In Locke's more clearly liberal hands (vis-à-vis Hobbes, that is), sovereignty becomes, not a monopoly on power by some ruler or rulers, as it is with Hobbes, but instead a quality that adheres to all of "the people" (although Locke certainly is not the first to make this argument).[10] This move is in a sense the hallmark of liberalism itself, the change from an authoritarian structure of sovereignty to a (seemingly) democratic one. In light of this, one could very well ask, speaking in a liberal voice, isn't it the case that liberalism delivers exactly the kind of individual self-structuring that I am claiming Hobbes discovers only outside the confines of sovereignty? If anything, one could further argue, liberalism almost does away with sovereignty altogether. Antiliberal critics such as Carl Schmitt have evoked Hobbes himself to point out how liberalism has failed to recognize or understand the true practice and nature of sovereignty.[11] Is it then even reasonable to speak of a connection between sovereignty and liberalism at all? And, even if there is such a connection, can we really say that liberalism itself is inimical to radical democracy?[12]

Despite the concerns mentioned above, it remains the case that most liberal writers recognize (whether explicitly or implicitly) the central role of sovereignty in making liberalism possible at all.[13] As we have already seen, a conviction that sovereignty and centralized political authority are necessary explains why Flathman himself is a "would-be anarchist." It is to Flathman's enormous credit that, although a self-professed liberal, he appreciates and anticipates exactly the kind of anarchistic tendencies to which liberalism is set in opposition. These are the very anarchist tendencies that I have been ascribing to Hobbes, in no small part thanks to Flathman's own reading of *Leviathan*.

More typically, liberals do not address the need for sovereignty directly. Rather, they presuppose sovereignty in their attempt to ameliorate it (this is essentially what Locke does with sovereignty as he receives it, in part, from Hobbes himself). A relatively recent example of this can be found in

John Rawls's book *The Law of Peoples*, which argues, "We must reformulate the powers of sovereignty in light of a reasonable Law of Peoples and deny to states the traditional rights to war and to unrestricted internal autonomy."[14] Here, Rawls acknowledges problems with the theory of sovereignty, but rather than suggest that we dispense with sovereignty altogether, he appears to agree, without saying so explicitly, that sovereignty cannot be done away with and must be endured. (Otherwise, why bother ameliorating it?) Here the key to enduring sovereignty is to soften its hard edges, to make it accountable to certain, basic principles that it cannot contravene. In some sense, such a stance can be seen as the essence of liberalism, broadly defined.[15]

In making this argument, Rawls echoes a conversation that one finds across the spectrum of liberal thought, stretching back nearly to its origins. Benjamin Constant, in his critiques of Hobbes and Rousseau, assails in particular their claim that sovereign power must be unlimited. For Constant, these two thinkers give us respectively a vision of sovereignty as state power (Hobbes) and as popular power (Rousseau). Yet Constant collapses this distinction insofar as both are subject to the same abuse. He tells us that even when sovereignty is invested with "the people,"

> as soon as the sovereign body has to use the force it possesses, that is to say, as
> soon as it is necessary to establish political authority, since the sovereign body
> cannot exercise this itself, it delegates and all its properties disappear. The ac-
> tion carried out in the name of all, being necessarily willy-nilly in the hands
> of one individual or a few people, it follows that in handing yourself over to
> everyone else, it is certainly not true that you are giving yourself to no one.[16]

Indeed, if anything, Constant believes that when "the people" are sovereign, matters may be even worse since "what no tyrant would dare to do in his own name, [popular sovereignty] legitimate[s] by the unlimited extension of boundless political authority."[17] Constant is useful in this regard; although a liberal himself, he exposes the way in which the move toward popular sovereignty is not in and of itself an amelioration of the authoritarian nature of liberal sovereignty. Constant's own council is, like Rawls, not to overthrow sovereignty (since he argues that the alternative is anarchy—a state he presumes to be unthinkably awful) but once again to limit it.[18]

We see this argument echoed too in John Stuart Mill's *On Liberty*. When, in the beginning of chapter 4 of that book, Mill asks, "What, then, is the rightful limit to the sovereignty of the individual over himself?" he has already presupposed that popular sovereignty will be the appropriate (and liberal) form of government.[19] Yet here, too, the very form of this question suggests the notion that it is quite possible "the people" in their sovereign capacity may violate the freedom of "people" taken as individuals. Mill's solution to this is not so different than Constant's. In answer to his own question, he proposes that "to individuality should belong the part of life in which it is chiefly the individual that is interested; to society, the part which chiefly interests society."[20]

This essentially serves as an articulation of rights over and above sovereign power. Isaiah Berlin famously distinguishes this turn to rights as a "negative liberty." In his "Two Concepts of Liberty," Berlin tells us that, in this view, "no power, but only rights, can be regarded as absolute."[21] There, too, he speaks of the "moral validity—irrespective of the laws—of some absolute barrier to the imposition of one man's will on another."[22] For Berlin, as for Constant, Mill, and Rawls, there is no denouncement of sovereignty per se but only a sense that sovereignty cannot trump rights.

Liberal Ambivalence

If we take these authors as being somewhat representative of liberalism as a whole, we can see that a great degree of ambivalence about sovereignty may be one of its characteristics; it is an ambivalence, however, not a rejection. This ambivalence can also be seen in the way that Hobbes is understood by many liberal authors. Among many such authors (Constant, for example), Hobbes is chided as having offered a vision of sovereignty that is too harsh, too blunt an instrument for liberalism itself. Usually those who see Hobbes as a "proto" liberal are acknowledging by that mediating term ("proto") that Hobbes sets a necessary foundation for liberalism but that liberalism itself does not become "liberalism," as we know it, until Hobbes's sovereign is somehow tamed (chiefly by Locke). Hobbes, as read by liberals, does its dirty work; a "good cop/bad cop" situation is produced in which Hobbes ("bad cop") gives a rationale for sovereignty so that "good cop" liberal authors (with important exceptions like Flathman) don't have to. They can safely "ameliorate" liberalism because its rationale—and absolute authority—is firmly in place.

But can sovereignty really be ameliorated by rights? To recall the discussion of tolerance and rights in the last chapter, what Hobbes effectively says (as Schmitt informs us) is that the ameliorations placed on and above sovereignty are only valid so long as the sovereign allows itself to be so ameliorated (i.e., another iteration of Puritan-derived tolerance). This would be true, of course, whether the sovereignty is vested in the state or with "the people" themselves, for as Constant acknowledges, "the people" cannot actually act with one voice, as sovereignty demands. Inevitably there will be some one voice that speaks on behalf of "the people," someone to "rule, and reign over them."[23]

What Rawls and the other liberals discussed above do not acknowledge is that sovereignty is a limit concept and cannot therefore be limited itself. The fundamental ambivalence of liberals cannot overcome their basic reliance on sovereignty. These authors want sovereignty to be both a foundation for liberalism and not one; they seek an absolute that is not quite absolute. This position constantly threatens to fall apart. To argue that there is a "Law of Peoples" or "absolute rights" that trump and ameliorate sovereign power must mean either that sovereign power does not exist (since it must be ultimate to exist at all) or that such rights are merely wishes in the face of sovereign power. Since liberals insist (albeit in very reluctant ways) that sovereignty is always necessary (the alternative being anarchy), one would imagine that, when forced to choose, liberalism chooses the latter "resolution," the assertion of absolute sovereignty even at the expense of rights. Indeed, this is exactly what any reading of Hobbes tells us; if we are going to choose sovereignty, we are choosing something that is absolute. As I see it, the real question that Hobbes poses to us is not so much "How do we ameliorate sovereignty?" (since we can't, at least not in any absolute or certain way) but "Must we choose sovereignty at all?"

In invoking fundamental rights as they do, the liberals I've referred to are seeking a source of authority that is prior to the authority of sovereignty itself. But they get caught in the circularity of their own argument; the sovereign in their own reading sets and determines the very "natural law" that is used to trump sovereign power. As Hobbes shows us, all authority is rhetorical in nature. By holding to "natural rights," liberals succumb to the very kinds of epistemological vacuums that Hobbes warns us will be filled by false prophets and political pretenders, by sovereignty itself (because someone must decide what those "natural rights" are).

By holding on to sovereignty as they do, liberals are in effect defeating the very freedoms that they seek to produce—insofar as they stick to a language of "rights," they remain circumscribed within the bounds of power, as Hobbes shows in chapter 21. In distinguishing liberty and power as we have seen, Hobbes seems to be implicitly telling us that if we are seeking political change, it is not liberty but power that we must turn to. Sovereignty, a system in which all power is kept for the sovereign itself, is incompatible with any genuinely radical democratic practice, even in its "kinder, gentler," more tolerant variance as liberal sovereignty. Liberty is (or rights are) merely the consolation prize for the power we give up when we submit to sovereignty. It is for this reason that liberalism's promise of individual liberty does not in and of itself make liberalism a radical system of thought; when that liberty is contained by and structured within the power system of sovereignty itself, liberty becomes a concept that is already demarcated and delimited.[24]

LIBERAL (AND NOT SO LIBERAL) RESPONSES

In anticipating possible responses to my claims about Hobbes and alternative authority, I would like to focus on three responses: one truly liberal, one not-so-liberal, and one not liberal at all. In constructing these responses, I seek to characterize liberal and non- or antiliberal thinking in our own time. The first two responses are meant to reflect the chastened and heterogeneous nature of modern liberalism. The last response comes from a more Foucauldian perspective.

A Liberal Response: Shouldn't We Choose Sovereignty Anyway?

As mentioned earlier, a liberal response to the alternative notion of politics and authority I have ascribed to Hobbes might be to argue that such an alternative, however persuasive or attractive, is simply impractical. Given that human beings are on the whole restless and unruly, and thus unlikely to be able to avoid idolatry and misrepresentation, isn't sovereignty still the best and only viable option that we have (according to Hobbes's own arguments)? Given that we can't really trust one another to engage in the kind of worshipful readings Hobbes may be modeling here, isn't it better to resort to an arbitrary but decisive sovereign to protect us from those with whom we disagree (and who are potentially stronger than us)? We need not even say that human beings are untrustworthy by nature (a claim Hobbes is not making) to argue that we cannot in fact trust one another.[25]

Such a strain of reasoning is redolent of a style of liberal thinking, a kind of "best of the worst" argument that cheerfully cedes better forms of government to the utopians but insists that when it comes to "reality" we must play it safe and stick to what we know. This argument is often read into *Leviathan* itself. In this case, even when we know the sovereign is arbitrary, when we know that there are alternatives (at least in theory), and know that the sovereign may not always (or even ever) act in our best interest, we must still choose sovereignty. And of course, the argument then goes on to say, if you are going to choose sovereignty (although in the liberal imagination, it is not so much a choice as it is a necessity), you might as well choose liberalism since otherwise you are going to be having a sovereign who will *really* make you miserable. The question of whether Hobbes is promoting sovereignty, as many have argued, or is in fact exposing the ruse of the sovereign, as I have argued, doesn't seem relevant if we would choose the sovereign in any case.

Against this argument, I would point out that the act of exposing the sovereign as both arbitrary and idolatrous is not neutral in respect to sovereign power, but quite destructive. As we have seen in Honig's analysis of Arendt, there must be, it seems, some constative element to authority if it is to be truly authoritative. For a political system to work, there has to be some way that we do not call everything always into question. In exposing the sovereign, Hobbes has robbed it of any constative powers, transferring that power back to people themselves. In so doing, he has deprived sovereignty of the right to speak and read definitively for others. So exposed, the sovereign can *not* serve as a way to "save us from ourselves" or save us from political turmoil. If Hobbes returns the sovereign to its purely representational form, it becomes something unrecognizable to itself and to us, its authors.

It becomes merely a mirror that we hold up to our myriad faces and in that reflection we see not an "answer" but all of the doubts and questions that we have in the first place. Such a sovereign does not therefore answer the problem of politics for us, but throws us back to ourselves, "redeeming" us (in the Nietzschean sense) by failing to redeem us, demanding we respond ourselves to our own problems.

Yet for all of this, it is true that there are no guarantees that we can "all read worshipfully" or that sovereignty in some form or other won't be an ongoing feature of human life. Here we reach an impasse similar to the one Arendt faced after she too sketched out (in a far clearer and more overt way) an alternative to sovereignty, one based on contracts and promises. At some point, she backtracks, admitting that despite all her criticism, sovereignty can offer "a certain limited reality."[26] This may reflect a realization on Arendt's part that sovereignty is not easily gotten rid of and that, in the modern world especially, the will remains unredeemed and recognizes itself only in sovereignty (the political expression of its own solipsism). Perhaps, then, sovereignty has to be accommodated; because we can't expect a return of a classical-style public, we must reconcile ourselves to something less.

However, the radicalness of Hobbes's critique makes such an accommodation even less likely than with Arendt. For when we "open our eyes" to what the sovereign is, the sovereign is no longer sovereign; we can thus no longer choose it. If my reading of *Leviathan* is persuasive, the sovereign for Hobbes is not simply a limit on freedom (which in Arendt's case can itself be limited in turn by our promises) but is the very replacement for our own powers, a separated essence that *"dis-prepare[s]"* us for anything better. The authority of sovereignty rests on the usurpation of people's authority; once that usurpation is exposed, there is no viable basis for its ongoing power and authority.

A Not-So-Liberal Response: The Perils of Irony

Even if Hobbes has exposed the sovereign, we might ask, even if he has rendered it incredible, ludicrous, an idol, isn't it quite possible to know this and still obey the sovereign anyway? Authors ranging from Wendy Brown to

Slavoj Zizek, Todd Gitlin, and Mark Andrejevic have pointed out that the ironic (or, in Zizek's term, *perverted*) response to the exposure of symbols and metanarratives is not necessarily to be "free" of them, but only to find oneself in the peculiar position of simultaneously recognizing and obeying the binds that compel you.[27] These authors, of course, write in opposition to such a stance, but what they describe may be a very accurate portrayal of a great number of subjects who remain bound by liberalism (and even more accurately, liberal capitalism) even though they "know better" (at the same time, I doubt you would find many people who would openly proclaim this to be their position!). As Brown puts it in *Politics Out of History*, this is akin to the fetishist who says, "I know, [it is just a fetish] but still . . . "[28] Not un-like an "ironic" ad on TV that plays with our knowledge of how we are being manipulated, even as it goes on to manipulate us nonetheless (so that, at the end of the day, we buy whatever they are selling), is it not possible that the symbols of sovereignty, having "taken on a life of their own," will maintain their autonomy even in the face of our recognition of that autonomy? (This would be a question to put to Benjamin as well.)

This argument is another version of the "there is no alternative" approach many liberals tacitly argue for; bereft of any truly viable alternative, liberal-ism triumphs as the least bad possibility. Whereas, for Skinner, irony in the hands of Renaissance humanists and their followers was a deft weapon that establishes multiple meanings, it seems that in our own time, irony (or rather what passes for irony in our time) becomes simply another device to enable liberalism to do what it does. Does Hobbes's "exposition" of the sovereign as a false idol then accomplish anything beyond removing the veil that had enabled us to believe we were obeying by an act of free will? Does it change anything at all, and if so, what?

Hobbes's own stance toward representation is far from denying its power, even including representation that is exposed and known as such. Indeed, if he was arguing that once exposed, representation becomes empty or mean-ingless, he would truly be the absolute skeptic he is often accused of being, in which case our recourse to the sovereign would be reaffirmed (since there is nothing but meaninglessness). What Hobbes offers us, even against the pose of irony, I think, is the notion that representation *qua* representation is not meaningless, that we can indeed still believe in it, be seduced by it, be lured by it, even when we know it for what it is. Such a stance is in fact the essence of his notion of worship—otherwise there could be nothing constructive about Hobbes's theory at all. But crucially, for Hobbes *this* representational power is different from the idolatrous power of separated essences—it is weaker, yes, insofar as it has less claim to "truth," "nature," "reality" and other pseudo-constative terms, but it is, as already noted, not itself totally unconnected to the constative function. A worshipful understanding of representation has, as we have seen, its own messianic sources of authority.

In this way, the ironic stance of "I know, but still . . . " is challenged by the possibility of an alternative after all. Without such an alternative, the fetishist has nowhere to go but to hold on to the fetish itself. Although exposed as empty, the fetish must still be read and interpreted as full of its own meaning, a kind of doublethink that binds the fetishist all the more to the idol she or he worships.

I read Hobbes's notion of worship very much along the lines of Benjamin. As argued in the previous chapter, Benjamin suggests, like Hobbes, a kind of worshipful stance whereby the mechanics of the process are not occluded but are exposed and appreciated as the basis of the images produced, even as the lures and powers of representation remain (as with the concept of *correspondances*). A great deal of Benjamin's admiration for Baudelaire, as already mentioned, comes from the way that Baudelaire is totally immersed in and responds to the seductions of commodity fetishism, yet still, he resists. As with Hobbes's discussion of idolatry, for Benjamin the very same actions, the very same representational acts can turn from an invitation to fascist or capitalist manipulation to becoming the grounds for another kind of "reality." This, not in a pseudo-ironic stance of "I know, but still . . . " but rather in a political sense of fostering the possibility of resistance and struggle, using the same tools of representational power, as it were, against itself. *Leviathan* as a text models and exemplifies the resistance to sovereign power that it describes. It encourages the reader to resist the sovereignty of the text itself, not in an idle and meaningless practice of "savviness" but as a kind of training for battle, an attack on sovereignty itself.

An Illiberal Response: Does Sovereignty Even Exist Anymore?

A final response to my arguments about sovereignty comes from a claim that in the face of ever-expanding international capital, sovereignty is a relic of the past. To make this argument clearly puts us beyond the sphere of liberalism itself. The modern political spectrum is no longer (if it ever really was) dominated by nation states who are sovereign both over their own people and vis-à-vis one another. The rise of multinational corporations and changes in technologies of communication and transportation have given us a world in which holding on to a belief in sovereignty can almost appear to be quaint. An excellent albeit unique articulation of this notion can be found in Michel Foucault's lectures given at the Collège de France in 1975–1976. In those lectures (now collected as a book, *"Society Must Be Defended"*), Foucault describes sovereignty as being originally a medieval institution that pertained to the authority of feudal kings.[29] For Foucault this institution of sovereignty was completely incompatible with a "new mechanism of power" that arose in the seventeenth and eighteenth centuries (that is to say, during the times of Hobbes) (p. 35). This "new mechanism" was in service to biopolitics, which, Foucault tells us, amounts to a change from the old (genuinely sovereign) power to "take life or let live" to a new power that offers "the right to make live and to let die" (p. 241). Biopower, the product of such a biopolitics, seeks to control not merely the fact of human existence but the content of it as well. Through its disciplines and regimes, biopower asserts itself into every facet of human life, proving the lie of liberal hopes for "rights" and "autonomy."

Foucault tells us that although sovereignty should have exited the stage at this point in history, it has survived—in the way that so many discourses do for Foucault—in a partial, reformulated, and strange afterlife that continues to implicate itself into the matrices of power despite having no formal use or existence. As Foucault puts it: "This theory [of sovereignty], and the organization of a juridical code centered upon it, made it possible to superimpose on the mechanism of discipline a system of right that concealed its mechanisms and erased the element of domination" (p. 37). In other words, sovereignty provided a convenient and efficient "cover" for other mechanisms of power to extend themselves onto (and into) the subject bodies of the living. A "democratized" and updated doctrine of sovereignty allowed for disciplinary mechanisms to be endured in the name of a sovereignty that was of and for "the people" themselves. Of this Foucault writes: "A right of sovereignty and a mechanics of discipline. It is, I think, between these two limits that power is exercised" (p. 37)

For Foucault, one of the principal authors of the transformation in sovereignty is none other than Hobbes himself. Foucault rejects the notion that for Hobbes politics is merely a form of domination. Looking in particular at Hobbes's arguments about how sovereignty is formed by acquisition (the same notion examined by Kavka), Foucault writes:

> Because once the defeated have shown a preference for life and obedience, they make their victors their representatives and restore a sovereign to replace the one who was killed in the war. It is therefore not the defeat that leads to the brutal and illegal establishment of a society based on domination, slavery, and servitude; it is what happens during the defeat. . . . It is fear, the renunciation of fear, and the renunciation of the risk of death. It is this that introduces us into the order of sovereignty and into a juridical regime: that of absolute power. (p. 95)

For Foucault, it is in effect Hobbes who teaches us that life is precarious and that we should fear death above all. In this way, and despite his own allegiance to sovereignty, Hobbes has turned us into more pliable subjects of biopolitics. For Foucault, Hobbes is eliminating the idea of conquest as a source of illegitimate right (which could then be legitimately resisted) by showing us that even under such circumstances, we accept our bondage in exchange for our life (turning our life itself into something the state holds for us rather than something that is ours but that the state can take away) Hobbes gives sovereignty its pretext to survive, but eventually it gives way to biopower itself. Thus for Foucault, sovereignty is not what we think it is; it is merely a term for the kinds of power that have little or nothing to do with states or kings. There is an absolute power with which sovereignty is associated, but it is not sovereignty itself that is absolute.

There is a distinction to be made between what Foucault says about sovereignty in general and what he says about Hobbes in particular. In terms of sovereignty in general, we can see that Foucault is not saying that it is meaningless, only that so long as we understand sovereignty purely according to a medieval juridical model, we will never understand the true workings of its power. This is an argument that I tend to agree with. It is in fact Hobbes himself, as I read him, who helps us understand how sovereignty is not so much an actual font of authority, but a rhetorical production. Thus we can see how sovereignty can remain effective even—perhaps especially—as a purely metaphorical notion.

Indeed, as a metaphorical device, sovereignty remains highly effective even in our own time. Whether sovereignty is a tool of biopower, as Foucault writes, or of international capital, as Michael Hardt and Antonio Negri claim in *Empire* (these are not necessarily contradicting claims), it should come as no surprise to us that sovereignty was never about representing "the people."[30] What Foucault, Hardt, and Negri may alert us to is which master it is that sovereignty serves. What my reading of Hobbes's *Leviathan* may alert us to is that, whichever master it serves, sovereignty can never and will never "serve" people in all their diversity. Sovereignty will always replace that diversity with a singular image of will. Regardless of whether sovereignty is located in one or many persons, or even in all of "us," it imposes this singularity and thereby dominates that which it purportedly represents.

In terms of Foucault's reading of Hobbes himself, we will not conduct a long discussion, as we did in the case of Arendt, on whether he is reading Hobbes correctly or not. Foucault (like Arendt) is responding to *a* reading of Hobbes, one that is different from my own. If, however, we read *Leviathan* as I have, as a book advocating an ethos of resistance to sovereign power, there is a way in which Foucault's own ethos of resistance can be reconciled with my reading of Hobbes. *"Society Must Be Defended"* is an effective genealogy of sovereign authority, much along the lines of the way that I read *Leviathan* itself (only the former is clearly more openly subversive than the latter). In terms of his theory more generally, Wendy Brown speaks of Foucault's "formulation of freedom as a practice rather than an achievement or institutional guarantee."[31] If we take this viewpoint as a summation of what Foucault is doing, it seems compatible with what I read in Hobbes's *Leviathan*.

So whether sovereignty has changed or not, whether it is merely a tool of capital or a veneer for biopower (or even if it is what liberals say it is), it remains a powerful and effective idea—consider the events at Guantanamo Bay or Abu Ghraib prison if you need any convincing.[32] Even if sovereignty is indeed merely a tool of capital, it is a powerful and effective tool. To strip away this mask (as Foucault himself attempts to do) is to deprive capital of one of its principal means of organizing and controlling human life.

The point to emphasize here is less the "reality" of sovereignty than it is the costs of believing in it. As I've argued, sovereignty continues to help shape the form that power takes, and similarly, it continues to exert a malign influence on many thinkers, including those who resist and resent some of its more brutal forms and implications. To automatically tie politics to the practice of sovereignty, as so many have done, is to condemn us to the ghostly form that Hobbes so earnestly resists in his attacks on "demonology."

IS THERE AN ALTERNATIVE TO SOVEREIGNTY?

If we return to an engagement with liberalism itself, we can see that the lack of any viable alternative is crucial to its logic. Liberalism can present itself as the "best of the worst" because we seem to have no choice. Generally speaking, and as we have seen, in the liberal imagination the alternatives to liberalism are tyranny or chaos; that is, there are no alternatives at all. Liberal writers can be comfortable with a great deal of skepticism, cynicism, and irony because such stances, as they understand them, tend to reinforce rather than undermine this basic position, of a lack of alternatives.

But we have also seen that not all liberals think this way. In his own musings about liberalism and its pros and cons, Richard Flathman tells us that "all genuine liberals" are "haunted . . . by anarchist, antinomian, and nihilist/skeptical objections."[33] Such a haunting, at least in Flathman's case, seems to be caused by his attraction to precisely those scenarios that the arrival of liberalism effectively ends (i.e., trusting each other, dreams of a "real" or "true" public, etc.). Flathman writes: "Lacking the resolve or courage, perhaps reckless, of the antinomian and the anarchist, liberals perforce accommodate themselves to authority, power, and the fixity, structure, and control that those who possess them incessantly seek to establish."[34] Anarchism is courageous but "reckless" for Flathman because it takes a leap of faith, trusting in human beings to govern themselves when they have never proven themselves to be worthy of such confidence. Problems of policing and education—institutional concerns that he feels anarchism cannot and will not address—necessitate a turn to liberalism despite what is sacrificed by such a move.

Yet Flathman allows himself to be haunted by what liberalism overwrites. This haunting informs and nuances his approach to liberalism. Flathman concedes that one of the reasons he appreciates Hobbes is that he offers us a way to live with the kinds of institutions and authorities that we reluctantly turn to in a way that does not utterly preclude what we are giving up on. He writes:

> The minimal and least objectionable manifestation of institutionalist thinking is the view that institutionalized government can *contribute* to the realization of the ideals of individuality, plurality, and freedom. I have argued elsewhere that this is the view of that "protoliberal" Hobbes, and I maintain here that a stance akin to Hobbes's skepticism concerning institutionalism is the appropriate one for liberalism to take.[35]

In other words, the very skepticism that Hobbes displays toward human virtues also extends to all forms of human government. Hobbes forbids anything to be absolute, including, in some sense, the absolute rule of sovereignty itself.

Here, Flathman doesn't sound that different from Aryeh Botwinick, another writer who considers a more radical interpretation of Hobbes but ultimately casts him in liberal terms. But this rescue by skepticism only takes us so far. At some point the sovereign must answer, or silence, skepticism. At some point, as Flathman himself shows, sovereignty must simply assert itself.

In general, there is a kind of tautology to the liberal position; the notion that 'there is no alternative" is a rhetorical argument, a kind of authoritative (and sovereign) decision that denies or dismisses further inquiry, making itself the basis of its own self-justification. It has been the chief undertaking of this book to consider that there just might be an alternative after all (and not just one but an infinite variety) to be found in the pages of Hobbes's *Leviathan*.

This alternative does not announce that human beings are "trustworthy" after all, or that a perfectly self-making and public-minded society is just around the corner. What it does instead is reveal that the "alternative to the alternative," that is to say sovereignty itself (including its liberal variants), is not the "best of the worst" but just plain "worst." It offers that with sovereignty we are not getting the best form of representation, trust, and mutual promising that we are permitted; actually, we are not getting any of these things at all. The sovereign "solution" to the problems of human beings as fallible political actors is no solution but the undoing of exactly what so many liberal thinkers seek in turning to the liberal order in the first place. In short, the "alternative to the alternative" is no alternative at all.

The radical democratic alternative that we have considered in Hobbes's *Leviathan* is not "theoretical" or "utopian" as opposed to the hard-nosed pragmatic realism of liberal orderings. In fact, the alternative political authority already exists and underwrites sovereignty itself—sovereignty merely steals all the credit for and authority from what is being produced by people (through the device of "representation"). In sovereign systems, people give over their authority to the sovereign (and suffer accordingly) but Hobbes reminds us that we do not relinquish our authority once and for all but only so long as we continue to believe (however mistakenly) that we are getting something for delegating our power. For authority to be retracted from sovereignty, nothing new would have to be inaugurated into the world; as citizens of a commonwealth we already have the real authority; we are exercising it, as Hobbes reminds us, even in the most repressive of regimes. And if and when we decide to authorize differently than we do, we will simply be rearticulating the power that already belongs to us. The authority of the sovereign rests upon (and usurps) a web of authorities, collective decisions concerning meaning, political and social understandings, and above all a network of promises and covenants that have come from people. As Hobbes tells us clearly, we are the source of the sovereign's authority, not the other way around.

In this way, Hobbes is once again similar to Arendt insofar as she makes a distinction between force and power. For Arendt, force occurs in the absence of power; sovereign domination occurs when people fail to actualize their potentiality as a political community. For both thinkers then, "power" is always a possibility; force or sovereignty is never an inevitable outcome (unless we abdicate to it).[36] If he tells us nothing else, Hobbes informs us that each of us is the arbiter of what we hear, see, and read, and accordingly, sovereign is only as powerful as we allow it (or authorize it) to be. Hobbes's nominalism and Arendt's interest in action and speech (as well as Benjamin's notion of *correspondances*) serve as means by which we are able to recognize what is already true: our immersion in political life, for better or for worse.

Hobbes's "Religion Without Religion"

At this point, having made the bulk of my arguments, I would like to consider a few final points. The first concerns the question of Hobbes's religiosity, and not so much the question of whether he is atheist (since that was already considered in chapter 3) but whether we need to be religious ourselves in order to partake in the alternative sources of authority that I have sketched above. Given the crucial role of his reading of Scripture, his Christian eschatology, and his intense rootedness in Western traditions of rhetoric and philosophy, it is worth inquiring if this alternative reading of Hobbes offers anything to those of us who are not Christian, or not rooted in the Western tradition. Who can participate in the kinds of political conversations I see Hobbes as describing? Because of his nominalism and skepticism, Hobbes, I think, models a style of politics that is available not only to those of other faiths and traditions (who may or may not live in the West) but also those who may be a product of the West but reject its religious heritage. After all, the real "miracle" that Hobbes describes on Mount Sinai has nothing to do with a true God. Even if God did not exist, the promise conveyed by the hypostatization of such a God would be no less powerful or influential. Because his focus is on the rhetorical instantiation of meaning, Hobbes's use of the divine never strays far from human contrivances. What Hobbes describes is how a human community has managed to overcome arbitrariness through the device of a divine aporia. Similarly, he has shown how our promises and contracts can be worth something, not because a true God has definitively promised us something but because the idea of a promising God underscores our own ability to believe in ourselves and make meaningful promises. Once again, for Hobbes this kind of trust is neither utopian nor mystical; it has already been achieved. The very fact that we are able to make sense to one another, to engage in politics at all, is an indication that the kinds of bonds that we have with one another are not a product of the "sovereign" but of ourselves.

While for Hobbes religion in all its mystery accomplishes the negotiation between the constative and performative nature of political authority, what really matters is not the religion per se but the mystery itself. One can certainly subscribe to the notion of an aporia without being a Christian, Muslim, Hindu, Buddhist, or Jew. The reading of Hobbes we have considered offers not a belief but a method, an approach to politics as inherently rhetorical and democratic. This is a practice we do not need to learn, as Hobbes shows us, for it already constitutes the fabric of our lives.[37]

Politics Without Sovereignty

A last point to consider revisits the question of how difficult it is to disentangle ourselves from sovereignty, in this case, not just as a practice, but also as a theoretical construct. This, as I see it, is one of the central dramas of Hannah Arendt's work and here I think our study of Hobbes might help us somewhat. If liberals and even many nonliberals see one redeeming virtue in sovereignty, it is that it allows people to form themselves into "a people" in the first place.[38] Sovereignty, it seems, is required to represent people into existence, to bring us from our separateness into one public community. Whatever else sovereignty does, this is the one feature of sovereignty that is perhaps hardest to rid ourselves of. The upshot of this claim might seem to be that there can be no politics without sovereignty and that sovereignty must therefore be redeemed, revisited, or revamped but not jettisoned, lest we throw out the baby (politics) with the bath water (sovereignty). It is precisely this argument that I would like to challenge via my reading of Hobbes. For, as we have seen, Hobbes tells us not one origin story for the birth of political authority but two.

The better-known story, the story of the social contract, is redolent with the paradoxes of sovereignty that can also be seen with Rousseau. This paradox, as Robert Bernasconi tells us, lies in the fact that people cannot of themselves be capable of promising anything or even of knowing what they mean when they proclaim the social contract. For Bernasconi, the sovereign is required as the answer to this paradox. As he puts it, "there is not a natural sense of good and bad independent of political society that can be relied upon. . . . These must be determined by the Sovereign by a kind of performative."[39] The sovereign doesn't just institute and sustain the contract produced by these acts of promising; for Bernasconi it also interprets the meaning and outcome of such contracts.[40] Thus without the sovereign there could be no community, no contract, no politics at all.

This might convince us that we should hesitate before jettisoning sovereignty after all until we consider Hobbes's other origin story. As I have argued in earlier chapters, in this second, alternative story, the sovereignty of God does not produce the unity of the nation of Israel per se. Rather that unity, if we can call it that, is produced out of God's very unknowability. The various people of Israel decided to coalesce as a community in the face of this radical undecipherability. They did so on the basis of a decision to decipher and interpret the aporia of God nonetheless. The idea or hypostatization of God was the catalyst for this self-authoring, but in the end people authored themselves for themselves. Unlike in the first story, when as Bernasconi tells us, the sovereign decides on the meaning of words, on the terms of the contract, in this latter case, God tells us nothing at all. It is true that Moses "spoke" for God, but his speech was meaningless until it was ratified by the Israelites themselves. When God is sovereign, and only when God is sovereign, are people truly safe from domestic practices of sovereignty, from sovereign readings and sovereign interpretations. But even when God is no longer sovereign (as is the case with our own time), the hypostatization of God supplies a radical emptiness that cannot be filled by terrestrial demonology. Although for Hobbes when Saul is elected king instead of God, "justice fayled," we can see that justice remains an ongoing possibility in our world.

Rather than see these two stories as being two options that Hobbes offers to us, I see the second one as radically and utterly undermining the first. The emptiness of God exposes the conceits of terrestrial sovereignty, making its pose of authority damaged or even impossible. In light of the second story, politics becomes impossible *with* (terrestrial) sovereignty, rather than without.

There are several radically democratic implications of Hobbes's method of interpretation. He promotes rather than resolves the struggle over interpretation. He exposes the rhetorical sources of authority without collapsing that authority into meaninglessness. He offers in his notion of worship a means of interpretation that is transparent and yet still effective within a given community. He demonstrates an ethos of resistance and struggle even in the guise of supporting sovereignty (what I earlier called his "conspiracy of readers"). Yet none of these contributions is as important in my opinion as his ability to offer us an insight into the possibility of politics (and interpretation) free from sovereignty. As we have seen, Hannah Arendt has struggled mightily with and against the notion of sovereignty; as a modern, she confronts sovereignty as a fait accompli. But Hobbes comes from a different time, when the edifice of sovereignty was not fully built and when its indispensability to politics was an open question. Hobbes thus affords us a precious glimpse into a nonsovereign politics, one that, even if it fails to overcome sovereignty once and for all, does suggest that sovereignty is neither inevitable nor necessarily the "best" of a set of bad political choices.

The value of reading Hobbes in this way is multifaceted. What happens if the author of liberalism turns out to be (or is read as being) opposed to it after all? Such a reading strikes a blow at liberal assurances. This reading of Hobbes may help to expose the false privileging of liberalism as the unique political system that stands in opposition to all others. In this reading, sovereignty emerges as a particular rhetorical production of authority and liberalism emerges as just one version of political life. When sovereignty is not the only choice but a choice, it becomes far less likely that we would actually choose to submit to such a system, even in its liberal version.

Such a reading also has an allegorical value insofar as it retells the story of modernity to show that the future that actually occurred was not a given, not inevitable. Rereading *Leviathan* allows us to see the future as contingent. Since we live in Hobbes's "future," we are one possible outcome of history but there could have been and could still be others. This is the very same idea so beautifully promoted by Benjamin in his "Theses on the Philosophy of History." The imperial (and teleological) sense of progress that comes with a liberal telling of time—one that announces its own inevitability—is undermined in this case by a disturbance at the roots of its very origin myth.

Benjamin's idea of allegory as the "'antidote' to myth" corresponds well with what I believe Hobbes to be practicing.[41]

If we are, as Hobbes tells us, authors of our own selves and of the political lives that reflect those selves, the ability to imagine a life without sovereignty is a prerequisite for our own authority to become not only a practice that we engage without realizing it, but a self-aware and highly politicized exercise of power. What would such a politics look like? For Hobbes, we do not need to be too mysterious about this; such a politics has already happened, not once but many times. It is the politics of the early Christian church and conceivably the politics of his own time, when sovereignty was destabilized. This same politics could, by extension to Walter Benjamin or (in a different way) Hannah Arendt, be seen as the politics of the myriad political revolutions of the last two hundred years. That such politics has never been sustained is, for Arendt, the tragedy of modernity.

It may be true that we will never be free from new outcroppings of sovereign contentions, false symbols, force, mythic violence, demonology. Even if that is the case, we nonetheless have a Hobbesian style of anarchic or "kingdomless" interpretation as a form of resistance to these demonological practices. But it may be too that the only reason we think that anarchy itself is not a viable, sustainable politics, or that sovereignty will keep cropping up is because, in the famous words of Foucault, we have not yet learned to "cut off the King's head."[42]

To reiterate an earlier claim, I am not saying that my reading of *Leviathan* is right when all others are wrong (although, rhetorically speaking, I have tried to be as persuasive as I can), but rather that this reading, enabled by Hobbes's own instructions, is (also) possible. If so, if we recognize the sources of political authority for what they are, if we can break the link between politics and sovereignty, if we can read the origin story of sovereignty differently, then it remains to be seen what we will find out about the political practices that go unrecognized in the face of the overawing spectacle, the "Sun" of the sovereign itself.

INTRODUCTION

1. The word *Puritan* is somewhat controversial. It was not generally a label that
    "Puritans" applied to themselves. Depending on who is consulted, it covers
    a gamut of religious movements in the sixteenth and seventeenth centu-
    ries (and beyond), some within the confines of the Church of England and
    some without. For some, the Quakers are not Puritans. (For Alan Simpson,
    among others, they are. See his *Puritanism in Old and New England* [Chi-
    cago: University of Chicago Press, 1964], p. 1.) Accordingly *Puritanism* can
    be hard to define, and some writers avoid the term altogether. Nonetheless, a
    great number of writers use the term, including some of the most important
    historians of the period. Patrick Collinson writes that "Puritanism consisted,
    at its heart, of something called 'practical divinity,' a strenuous search for
    salvation according to Calvinist understandings." (See his *The Reformation*
    [London: Weidenfeld and Nicolson, 2003], p. 117.) In this book, I use the
    term *Puritan* to refer broadly to any number of movements agitating for
    greater reformation along the models of Calvinism and other Protestant
    movements from Europe. In the context of Hobbes's own time, the term
    will refer to those Protestant movements that largely broke with the Angli-
    can church. I use the term *Quaker* separately because that seems to be the
    general usage. See William Haller, *The Rise of Puritanism: Or, The Way to the
    New Jerusalem as Set Forth in Pulpit and Press from Thomas Cartwright to John
    Lilburne and John Milton, 1570–1643* (Philadelphia: University of Pennsyl-
    vania Press, 1938), p. 3. See also William Haller's *Liberty and Reformation in
    the Puritan Revolution* (New York: Columbia University Press, 1955). For a
    history of Puritanism that mainly predates Hobbes's career see Patrick Col-
    linson, *The Elizabethan Puritan Movement* (Oxford: Clarendon, 1967).

2. Thomas Hobbes, *Leviathan*, Richard Tuck, ed. (New York: Cambridge University Press, 1996), 3.43, p. 415.

3. Ibid.

4. John Bowle, *Hobbes and His Critics: A Study in Seventeenth Century Constitutionalism* (London: Cape, 1951), p. 163.

5. Miriam Reik, *The Golden Lands of Thomas Hobbes* (Detroit: Wayne State University Press, 1977), p. 130.

6. A. P. Martinich, *The Two Gods of Leviathan: Thomas Hobbes on Religion and Politics* (New York: Cambridge University Press, 1992), p. 23.

7. Bowle, *Hobbes and His Critics*, pp. 160–61. For more on the reception of Hobbes during his own time, see Samuel I. Mintz, *The Hunting of Leviathan: Seventeenth-Century Reactions to the Materialism and Moral Philosophy of Thomas Hobbes* (Cambridge: Cambridge University Press, 1962).

8. Among contemporary readers, Hanna Pitkin for one explicitly sees Machiavelli as arguing for something that Hobbes does not when it comes to the question of sovereignty. See Hanna Fenichel Pitkin, *Fortune Is a Woman: Gender and Politics in the Thought of Niccolò Machiavelli* (Berkeley: University of California Press, 1984), p. 279.

9. Victoria Kahn, *Machiavellian Rhetoric: From the Counter-Reformation to Milton* (Princeton: Princeton University Press, 1994), p. 5.

10. Ibid., p. 4.

11. Thus for example, Kahn tells us that Stephen Gardiner, in his own "Machiavellian" treatise, which is heavily modeled on (and even copies long passages from) *The Prince*, "simultaneously exploits and exposes the appeal to providence as a rhetorical argument in defense of de facto political power." Ibid., p. 98.

12. Bowle, *Hobbes and His Critics*, p. 162.

13. Ibid., p. 138.

14. A. P. Martinich, *Hobbes: A Biography* (New York: Cambridge University Press, 1999), p. 227.

15. Bowle, *Hobbes and His Critics*, p. 57.

16. Martinich, *The Two Gods of Leviathan*, pp. 26–27.

17. Hobbes, *Leviathan*, 4.47, pp. 479–80.

18. In his own response to this claim, Bramhall, although a keen monarchist himself, argued that the sovereign's power was indeed absolute, but that it

was limited by his coronation oath as well as other arrangements. Reik, *The Golden Lands of Thomas Hobbes*, p. 102.

19. Ibid., pp. 129–32.

20. There are certainly contemporary scholars who appreciate Hobbes's rhetoric and see a far more paradoxical author than is usually currently acknowledged. See for example Robert Bernasconi, "Opening the Future: The Paradox of Promising in the Hobbesian Social Contract," *Philosophy Today* (Spring 1997): 77–86, 78.

21. Leo Strauss, *The Political Philosophy of Hobbes: Its Basis and Its Genesis*, translated from the German manuscript by Elsa M. Sinclair (Chicago: University of Chicago Press, 1952), p. 5.

22. Ibid., p. 128.

23. In fact, Strauss's book on Hobbes does not appear to be particularly critical at first blush but certainly Strauss's more conservative followers lump Hobbes as well as Machiavelli into a category of modernizers who have essentially abandoned the entire classical approach to politics and philosophy and are hence deserving of great approbation.

24. Gregory S. Kavka, *Hobbesian Moral and Political Theory* (Princeton: Princeton University Press, 1986), p. 347.

25. I deal with Flathman's treatment of Hobbes at some length in my earlier book, *Love Is a Sweet Chain: Desire, Autonomy, and Friendship in Liberal Political Theory* (New York: Routledge, 2001), pp. 207–8.

26. Richard E. Flathman, *Willful Liberalism: Voluntarism and Individuality in Political Theory and Practice* (Ithaca: Cornell University Press, 1992), p. 20.

27. See Richard E. Flathman, *Reflections of a Would-Be Anarchist: Ideals and Institutions of Liberalism* (Minneapolis: University of Minnesota Press, 1998).

28. Flathman, *Willful Liberalism*, p. 36.

29. For that matter, even Strauss may recognize a kind of subversive or dangerous potential in Hobbes. He opines that "the structure which Hobbes ... began to raise, hid the foundation [of modernity] as long as the structure stood, i.e., as long as its stability was believed in" (suggesting the possibility of subversion if that belief no longer prevailed). Strauss, *The Political Philosophy of Hobbes*, p. 5.

30. For a review that catalogs how Flathman radicalizes liberalism, see Kennan Ferguson, "Liberalism's Threat: Review of *Reflections of a Would-Be Anarchist*," *Theory and Event* 2, no. 3 (1998).

31. See, for example, Victoria Kahn, *Rhetoric, Prudence, and Skepticism in the Renaissance* (Ithaca: Cornell University Press, 1985); and David Johnston, *The Rhetoric of Leviathan: Thomas Hobbes and the Politics of Cultural Transformation* (Princeton: Princeton University Press, 1986).

32. This is where I part company somewhat with Victoria Kahn. She sees Hobbes as subscribing to a secretive style of rhetoric, whereas I see him as being opposed to such a practice of rhetoric. In all other ways, I see Kahn, along with Victoria Silver, as being uniquely helpful in regards to Hobbes; their analysis is crucial for my own. See Victoria Silver, "A Matter of Interpretation," *Critical Inquiry* 20 (Autumn 1993): 160–71.

33. See J. G. A. Pocock, *Politics, Language, and Time: Essays on Political Thought and History* (New York: Atheneum, 1973).

34. Hannah Arendt, *The Human Condition* (Chicago: University of Chicago Press, 1958), p. 244.

35. Jodi Dean addresses something like this question in *Publicity's Secret: How Technoculture Capitalizes on Democracy* (Ithaca: Cornell University Press, 2002).

36. However, a great deal of Hobbes's discussion of the persons and kingdoms of God which I focus on in this book can also be found in *De Cive*. See Thomas Hobbes, *Man and Citizen (De Homine and De Cive)*, Bernard Gert, ed. (Indianapolis: Hackett, 1991). Like *Leviathan*, the latter parts of *De Cive* are dominated by discussions of religion. Hobbes's slightly earlier book, *The Elements of Law*, has a bit less on religion. In his introduction to that book, M. M. Goldsmith writes that "the most evident change in the development of *The Elements of Law* into *Leviathan* is the amount of attention Hobbes devotes to religion. It had occupied a few chapters in *The Elements of Law*. Only two years later in *De Cive* Hobbes wrote more than twice as much. In *Leviathan* the problem swells to half the book." See "New Introduction," in Thomas Hobbes, *The Elements of Law: Natural and Politic*, Ferdinand Tönnies, ed. (London: Frank Cass, 1969), p. ix.

37. Tracy Strong makes a similar claim, though as will be made clear in chapter 2, he means something very different by this than I do. See Tracy Strong, "How to Write Scripture: Words, Authority, and Politics in Thomas Hobbes," *Critical Inquiry* 20 (Autumn 1993): 128–59, 131.

I. HOBBES'S USE OF RHETORIC

1. Thomas Hobbes, *Leviathan,* Richard Tuck, ed. (New York: Cambridge University Press, 1996), 3.43, p. 415.

2. That is indeed the title of a short monograph Sheldon Wolin wrote: *Hobbes and the Epic Tradition of Political Theory* (Los Angeles: William Andrews Clark Memorial Library, 1970). See also Sheldon Wolin, *Politics and Vision: Continuity and Innovation in Western Political Thought,* expanded ed. (Princeton: Princeton University Press, 2004). There Wolin notes that although the sovereign is set up as a "Great Definer," in fact there is no reason that the sovereign would make definitions in accordance with a kind of perfect and pure (i.e., mathematical) model of definition. Ibid., pp. 232–33. For a good account of Hobbes's attempt to understand a "first philosophy" see Yves-Charles Zarka, "First Philosophy and the Foundations of Knowledge," in Tom Sorell, ed., *The Cambridge Companion to Hobbes* (Cambridge: Cambridge University Press, 1996), pp. 62–85.

3. Hobbes, *Leviathan,* 1.9, p. 61.

4. This is for instance the claim of Leo Strauss in *The Political Philosophy of Hobbes: Its Basis and Its Genesis.* See Thomas Hobbes, *Hobbes's Thucydides,* Richard Schlatter, ed. (New Brunswick, N.J.: Rutgers University Press, 1975).

5. See for example Richard Tuck, *Hobbes* (Oxford: Oxford University Press, 1989).

6. See Johnston's *The Rhetoric of Leviathan: Thomas Hobbes and the Politics of Cultural Transformation* (Princeton: Princeton University Press, 1986). Quentin Skinner makes a fairly similar argument in his *Reason and Rhetoric in the Philosophy of Hobbes* (New York: Cambridge University Press, 1996). For a critique of Skinner's book, and an alternative view that stresses logic over rhetoric, see Gabriella Slomp, *Thomas Hobbes and the Political Philosophy of Glory* (New York: St. Martin's, 2000).

7. *Leviathan,* "A Review, and Conclusion," pp. 483–84.

8. Naturally, these three texts are just a representative sample of a very large literature. See Tom Sorell, "Hobbes's Persuasive Civil Science," *Philosophical Quarterly* 40, no. 160 (1990): 342–51, as well as his "Hobbes's UnAristotelian Political Rhetoric," *Philosophy and Rhetoric* 23 (1990): 96–108. See also Jeffrey Barnouw, "Persuasion in Hobbes's *Leviathan,*" *Hobbes Studies* 1 (1988): 3–25; George Shulman, "Metaphor and Modernization in the Political Thought of Thomas Hobbes," *Political Theory* 17, no. 3 (August 1989): 392–416; Jeremy

Rayner, "Hobbes and the Rhetoricians," *Hobbes Studies* 4 (1991): 76–95; William Mathie, "Reason and Rhetoric in Hobbes's *Leviathan*," *Interpretation* 14 (May–September 1986): 281–98.

9. Skinner, *Reason and Rhetoric in the Philosophy of Hobbes*, p. 6.

10. Hobbes, *Leviathan*, 1.1, p. 14.

11. Raia Prokhovnik, *Rhetoric and Philosophy in Hobbes' Leviathan* (New York: Garland, 1991), p. 224.

12. Ibid., p. 195.

13. Ibid., pp. 198–99. Here, Prokhovnik is not that far from Victoria Silver's views. See Victoria Silver, "Hobbes on Rhetoric," in *The Cambridge Companion to Hobbes*, pp. 338–39.

14. Prokhovnik, *Rhetoric and Philosophy*, p. 218.

15. Johnston, *The Rhetoric of Leviathan*, p. 78.

16. Ibid., pp. 119–20. Note that Prokhovnik makes almost the exactly opposite argument.

17. He approvingly cites, for example, the "licence that Naaman had." In Scripture, Naaman was forced to swear obeisance to an idol but remained true to God in his heart. *Leviathan*, 3.43, p. 414.

18. Victoria Silver tells us that the *Rhetoric* was the only work of Aristotle's that Hobbes actually respected. Silver, "Hobbes on Rhetoric," p. 340.

19. Paul de Man, *Allegories of Reading: Figural Language in Rousseau, Nietzsche, Rilke, and Proust* (New Haven: Yale University Press, 1979), p. 131.

2. PUBLIC AND PRIVATE READING

1. *Behemoth* is replete with such attitudes. See Thomas Hobbes, *Behemoth: The History of the causes of the civil wars of England, and of the counsels and artifices by which they were carried on from the year 1640 to the year 1660* (New York: Burt Franklin, 1963), p. 73. He suggests something of this in the English version of *Leviathan* too when he writes about general differences in opinion leading to the civil war. These differences occurred "in Politiques; and after between the Dissenters about the liberty of Religion." *Leviathan* 2.18, p. 127. He claims that the remedy for this will not come "except the vulgar be better taught than they have hetherto been." Ibid.

2. Although he writes, "It is beleeved on all hands, that the first and originall *Author* of [scripture] is God," this is true in a mystical sense only. Ibid., 3.33,

p. 267. In fact, Hobbes points to the human origins of the actual books that we read. Of these authors we know virtually nothing ("the originall writers of the severall Books of Holy Scripture, has not been made evident"). Ibid., 3.33, p. 261. Hence in a sense both the divine and human origins of the Scriptures are unknowable.

3. Ibid., 3.36, p. 297.

4. Hobbes tells us that "seeing therefore Miracles now cease, we have no sign [of God] left . . . farther than is conformable to the Holy Scriptures . . . and from which, by wise and learned interpretation, and carefull ratiocination, all rules and precepts necessary to the knowledge of our duty both to God and man without Enthusiasme, or supernaturall Inspiration, may easily be deduced." Ibid., 3.32, p. 259.

5. Ibid., 3.32, p. 255.

6. Ibid., 3.32, pp. 255–56.

7. Eldon Eisenach writes that for Hobbes "an interpretation of scriptural prophecy which does not contradict natural reason is 'divine politiques.'" Eldon J. Eisenach, *Two Worlds of Liberalism: Religion and Politics in Hobbes, Locke, and Mill* (Chicago: University of Chicago Press, 1981), p. 57.

8. Scholarship which accepts this as Hobbes's basic message has formed the predominant view for many years. See for example C. B. MacPherson, in his introduction to the Penguin edition of *Leviathan* and in his great work *The Political Theory of Possessive Individualism: Hobbes to Locke* (New York: Oxford University Press, 1962). There is, however, a new (and even not so new) interest in Hobbes that does not simply accept this dark view of him. Foremost is Richard Flathman in such books as *Willful Liberalism* and *Thomas Hobbes: Skepticism, Individuality and Chastened Politics* (Newbury Park, Calif.: Sage, 1993). See also Kavka, *Hobbesian Moral and Political Theory*. More specifically, in terms of Hobbes's religious writing, much traditional scholarship has either ignored this dimension or dismissed it. An example of the latter case is Leo Strauss. More recently, there have been a number of attempts to read parts 3 and 4 of *Leviathan* against or in contrast to the meaning of parts 1 and 2. J. G. A. Pocock is, again, perhaps the greatest example of this. See also Patricia Springborg, "*Leviathan* and the Problem of Ecclesiastical Authority," *Political Theory* 3, no. 3 (1975): 289–303; Eldon J. Eisenach, *Two Worlds of Liberalism*; F. C. Hood, *The Divine Politics of Thomas Hobbes: An Interpretation of Leviathan* (Oxford: Clarendon, 1964), particularly pp. 226–32;

Martinich, *The Two Gods of Leviathan: Thomas Hobbes on Religion and Politics* (New York: Cambridge University Press, 1992).

9. Hobbes, Introduction, *Leviathan*, p. 10.

10. Ibid., p. 11.

11. It is true that these two passages are distinguished by the fact that in the first instance, a person "know[s], what are the thoughts, and Passions of all other men . . ." when they consider their own internal thoughts, and in the second passage, the person reads "another by his actions," which suggests a more externalized kind of reading. Nevertheless, the contrast between the subject having access to the thoughts and passions of "all other men" is remarkably contrasted with the subject knowing "onely . . . his acquaintance[s]." The rhetorical contrast between "all others" and "only acquaintances" suggests a kind of retraction of the subject's reading ability in the face of the sovereign reader who is being introduced. For his own treatment of this question, see Flathman, *Thomas Hobbes*, p. 112.

12. *Leviathan*, 2.29, p. 226.

13. Ibid., 3.33, p. 267.

14. Ibid., 4.46, p. 471. Although Hobbes states this in *Leviathan*, Miriam Reik, among others, disputes that Hobbes finds the sovereign arbitrary. Reik, *The Golden Lands of Thomas Hobbes* (Detroit: Wayne State University Press, 1977), p. 99.

15. *Leviathan*, 3.40, p. 326. Hood says there is a case for a kind of "private reading" of Scripture that cannot interfere with civil law, which is the encoding of Scripture as the basis for society itself. Hood, *The Divine Politics of Thomas Hobbes*, p. 243.

16. *Leviathan*, Dedication, p. 3.

17. Martinich, *Hobbes: A Biography*, pp. 214–15.

18. See Hood, *The Divine Politics of Thomas Hobbes*, p. 236; Reik, *The Golden Lands of Thomas Hobbes*, pp. 100–4.

19. *Leviathan*, Introduction, p. 11.

20. Victoria Kahn, *Rhetoric, Prudence, and Skepticism in the Renaissance*, (Ithaca: Cornell University Press, 1985), p. 177.

21. Ibid., p. 178.

22. Ibid., p. 177.

23. Tracy Strong, "How to Write Scripture: Words, Authority, and Politics in Thomas Hobbes," *Critical Inquiry* 20 (Autumn, 1993): 128–59, 159.

24. Ibid., p. 136, n. 20. Strong tells us, "This is what William Tyndale in 1525 called 'the literal sense' of the Scripture, the sense of confidence that the meaning of the Scripture stands in front of us and that 'interpretation' is a way of avoiding that directness." Ibid., p. 137.

25. Ibid., p. 149.

26. Here Strong argues for a Protestant aesthetic of literalism. Ibid., p. 145.

27. Ibid., p. 157.

28. Ibid., p. 130. Here it seems instead that Hobbes may be employing the rhetorical figure of *paralipsis*, the act of drawing attention to something in the guise of ignoring it, a form of irony. (It is as if, when the Wizard of Oz says "pay no attention to the man behind the curtain," he does so as a way to draw attention to himself.)

29. Victoria Silver writes that for Hobbes, "to the extent that meaningfulness devolves to each person, natural or textual, to decide what authority or canon of judgment they will recognize, it resists a collective existence, much less a collective force." Victoria Silver, "A Matter of Interpretation," *Critical Inquiry* 20 (Autumn 1993): 160–71, 163.

30. Ibid., p. 164. Here she makes a similar argument to Pocock, who also argues that for Hobbes we can't reason our way to God.

31. Ibid., p.165.

32. Strong, "How to Write Scripture," p. 143.

33. Kahn has a radically different reading than Strong when it comes to Hobbes's view of Scripture. She writes that "Hobbes may seem to be appealing to the authority of Scripture [as a basis for shoring up the sovereign's power], but his aim is precisely to undermine that authority, to subordinate belief in Scripture to belief in the state." Kahn, *Rhetoric, Prudence, and Skepticism in the Renaissance*, p. 172.

34. Ibid., p.158.

35. Ibid., p. 178.

36. *Leviathan*, 4.45, p. 451.

37. Raia Prokhovnik writes: "what Hobbes is perhaps concerned with primarily, in his discussion of language, is the rhetorical effect of speech in civil society." Prokhovnik, *Rhetoric and Philosophy in Hobbes' Leviathan* (New York: Garland, 1991), pp. 114–15.

38. *Leviathan*, 1.6, p. 46.

39. Ibid., 1.8, p. 52. For a superb rendition of Hobbes's theories about how we think and act, one which reconciles Hobbes's mechanism with some version of self-determination, see the forthcoming book by Samantha Frost, *Lessons from a Materialist Thinker: Hobbesian Reflections on Ethics and Politics* (Stanford: Stanford University Press, forthcoming). See also Frost, "Faking It: Hobbes's Thinking-Bodies and the Ethics of Dissimulation," *Political Theory* 29, no. 1 (February 2001): 30–57.

40. *Leviathan*, 2.26, pp. 188–89.

41. Ibid, 1.7, p. 49.

42. Ibid., 1.7, p. 47.

43. Ibid., 3.42, p. 343.

44. See Kenneth Burke, *A Rhetoric of Motives* (Berkeley: University of California Press, 1969).

45. De Man, *Allegories of Reading*, p. 14.

46. Prokhovnik, *Rhetoric and Philosophy in Hobbes' Leviathan*, p. 166.

47. Ibid., p. 93.

48. Ibid., p. 92.

49. Ibid., p. 174.

50. Later in the book we will see a similar sentiment expressed by none other than Oliver Cromwell.

51. Ibid., pp. 174–75.

52. Prokhovnik writes that "there can be no other source of authority than the indivisible sovereign [the members of society] have constructed and form." Ibid., p. 147. At the same time, she offers a more nuanced possibility: "It is also interesting to note that Hobbes' metaphor stresses the profoundly private nature of experience and so of knowledge (though the possibility of a shared or a public knowledge is offered through agreement on the definition of words)." Ibid., p. 174. Here she may be gesturing toward the same kind of decentered sources of knowledge and authority as I.

53. Walter Benjamin, *The Origin of German Tragic Drama (Ursprung des deutschen Trauerspiels)* (London: NLB, 1977), p. 160.

54. Ibid., p. 182.

55. Ibid., p. 183.

56. Ibid., p. 184. The quote goes on to say "such significance as it has, it acquires from the allegorist." Or perhaps better yet, from the allegory; as we have just

seen, the allegory does not necessarily follow the allegorists' "intentions," unless we understand those intentions as coming from the practice of allegory itself.

57. *Leviathan*, 1.16, p. 112.

58. As will be discussed further in chapter 4 Hanna Pitkin describes a similar situation whereby Hobbes seems to promise us meaningful representation and, failing to deliver it, makes us "feel that somehow we have been tricked." Hanna Pitkin, *The Concept of Representation* (Berkeley: University of California Press, 1967), p. 34.

59. *Leviathan*, 1.16, p. 112.

60. Ibid., 3.33, p. 267.

61. Ibid., 1.16, p. 113.

62. Ibid.

63. Like Kahn and Silver, Botwinick concerns himself with the political implications of authority, reading, and interpretation. See Aryeh Botwinick, *Skepticism, Belief, and the Modern: Maimonides to Nietzsche* (Ithaca: Cornell University Press, 1997).

64. Botwinick certainly did not invent the term *negative theology*, but he is helpful in clearly relating that term to Hobbes's own philosophy and religion. Botwinick makes no historical claim that Hobbes read Maimonides (although he argues it is plausible, given the availability in Hobbes's day of translations of the twelfth-century Jewish scholar), but he argues that Hobbes "duplicat[es] . . . Maimonidean patterns of argument." Ibid., p. 6.

65. *Leviathan*, 3.40, p. 324.

66. Botwinick, *Skepticism, Belief, and the Modern*, p. 139.

67. Ibid.

68. *Leviathan*, 3.40, p. 325.

69. Ibid., 3.36, p. 296.

70. Ibid., 3.36, p. 297.

71. Ibid., 3.40, p. 326.

72. In her own writing on this subject, as we will see a bit more clearly in chapter 6, Patricia Springborg claims that Hobbes undermines his own assertion that there is an unbroken line of authority from Moses to contemporary times. See Springborg, "Hobbes on Religion," in Tom Sorell, ed., *The Cambridge Companion to Hobbes* (New York: Cambridge University Press, 1996), pp. 346–80.

73. Botwinick, *Skepticism, Belief, and the Modern*, p. 145.

74. Ibid., p. 7.

3. A SKEPTICAL THEOLOGY?

1. Hobbes, *Leviathan*, 1.7, p. 47.

2. See Hobbes's objection to Descartes' *Meditations*. René Descartes, *Meditations and Other Metaphysical Writings* (New York: Penguin, 1998), p. 87. For more on this see Richard Tuck, "Hobbes and Descartes," in G. A. J. Rogers and Alan Ryan, eds., *Perspectives on Thomas Hobbes* (Oxford: Clarendon, 1988), pp. 11–42.

3. A. P. Martinich, says that in this discussion, Hobbes and Descartes are "talking-past-one-another." Martinich, *Hobbes: A Biography* (New York: Cambridge University Press, 1999), p. 164.

4. Hobbes, *Leviathan*, 4.46, p. 466.

5. Ibid., 1.7, p. 48. Actually he says this is "Rhetorically said" of the conscience. For a brilliant discussion of this question see Karen S. Feldman, *Binding Words: Conscience and Rhetoric in Hobbes, Hegel, and Heidegger* (Evanston, Ill.: Northwestern University Press, 2006). This book describes how Hobbes rhetorically produces and enacts our interiority, the zone of our conscience.

6. Martinich writes that while Hobbes might not have been a skeptic per se (at least in the classical sense of the term), he was at least "sanguine about skepticism." Martinich, *Hobbes: A Biography*, p. 165.

7. Hobbes, *Leviathan*, 3.32, p. 256.

8. Prokhovnik, *Rhetoric and Philosophy in Hobbes' Leviathan* (New York: Garland, 1991), p. 92.

9. Hobbes, *Leviathan*, 3.34, p. 270.

10. Ibid.

11. We see this argument put forth by Aryeh Botwinick himself in *Hobbes and Modernity: Five Exercises in Political Philosophical Exegesis* (Lanham, Md.: University Press of America, 1983), p. 32. We see a slightly different and less absolute understanding of Hobbes's skepticism with David Johnston. With his arguments in *The Rhetoric of Leviathan: Thomas Hobbes and the Politics of Cultural Transformation* (Princeton: Princeton University Press, 1986), Johnston is directly addressing Dorothea Krook, who offers a more metaphysical and radically nominalistic view of Hobbes. See Krook, "Thomas Hobbes's

Doctrine of Meaning and Truth," *Philosophy* 31 (1956): 3–22. See also Reik, *The Golden Lands of Thomas Hobbes* (Detroit: Wayne State University Press, 1977), pp. 53–66.

12. Hobbes, *Leviathan*, 1.7, p. 47.

13. Ibid., 1.4, p. 26.

14. As I see it, Hannah Arendt effectively solves the riddle of Hobbes's empiricism by arguing that in fact none of the British empiricists were actually believers in the absolute truth given to them by their senses. She writes: "Empiricism is only seemingly a vindication of the senses; actually it rests on the assumption that only common-sense arguing can give them meaning, and it always starts with a declaration of non-confidence in the truth- or reality-revealing capacity of the senses. Puritanism and empiricism, in fact, are only two sides of the same coin." Hannah Arendt, "The Concept of History," in *Between Past and Future: Eight Exercises in Political Thought* (New York: Penguin, 1954), p. 56.

15. Hobbes, *Leviathan*, 3.34, p. 271. This is the very passage Botwinick turns to to make his claim that Hobbes has a "negative theology."

16. As with Levinas's notion of the "God Who hides His face," for Hobbes God allows us a relationship to radical alterity exactly in the way God is not present to us in any way and yet insistently *is*. See Emmanuel Levinas, *Difficult Freedom: Essays on Judaism* (Baltimore: Johns Hopkins, 1990), p. 144.

17. As Victoria Silver puts it, "We are obliged by our mortality to create God for ourselves over and over and over again." Silver, "A Matter of Interpretation," *Critical Inquiry* 20 (Autumn 1993): 160–71, 168.

18. Even as early as the fourteenth century, England experienced a wave of anti-imagism known as Lollardy. See John Phillips, *The Reformation of Images: Destruction of Art in England, 1535–1660* (Berkeley: University of California Press, 1973), pp. 30–35.

19. Margaret Aston, *England's Iconoclasts*, vol 1, *Laws Against Images* (Oxford: Clarendon, 1988), p. 18.

20. Patrick Collinson, *The Reformation* (London: Weidenfeld and Nicolson, 2003), p. 167. Such was the extent of this debate that in the previous century, John Jewel, Bishop of Derry, despaired over the controversy that was sure to erupt from the fact that Elizabeth I had a small silver crucifix in her chapel. Aston, *England's Iconoclasts*, p. 307.

21. Peter Goodrich, "The Iconography of Nothing: Blank Spaces and the Representation of Law in *Edward VI and the Pope*," in Costas Douzinas and

Lynda Nead, eds., *Law and the Image: The Authority of Art and the Aesthetics of Law* (Chicago: University of Chicago Press, 1999), p. 99.

22. Goodrich says it takes place "through the destruction of idols or false images." Ibid., p. 100.

23. Goodrich tells us that for the Reformers, it was noteworthy that God is heard but never seen. Ibid., p. 107.

24. Aston, *England's Iconoclasts,* p. 404.

25. Goodrich, "The Iconography of Nothing," pp. 107–8.

26. Ibid., p. 108.

27. Ibid. This accords with what Prokhovnik says as well.

28. Aston, *England's Iconoclasts,* p. 363.

29. Ibid., p. 368.

30. Ibid., p. 367.

31. Eamon Duffy, *The Stripping of the Altars: Traditional Religion in England c. 1400–1580* (New Haven: Yale University Press, 1992), p. 570.

32. Ibid., p. 586.

33. Ibid., p. 485.

34. Phillips, *The Reformation of Images,* p. 119.

35. As Aston tells us, "Elizabeth was prepared to regard 'comely' biblical inscriptions as both ornament and edification: the word could replace the image as decorative medium as well as divine message." Aston, *England's Iconoclasts,* p. 363.

36. Goodrich, "The Iconography of Nothing," p. 109.

37. Hobbes, *Leviathan,* 1.4, p. 31.

38. Ibid.

39. Ibid., 1.8, p. 52.

40. And, as de Man tells us at the end of *Allegories of Reading,* we need not limit ourselves to a discussion of tropes and figures at this point. He writes: "Irony is no longer a trope but the undoing of the deconstructive allegory of all tropological cognitions, the systemic undoing, in other words, of understanding. As such, far from closing off the tropological system, irony enforces the repetition of its aberration." De Man, *Allegories of Reading: Figural Language in Rousseau, Nietzsche, Rilke, and Proust* (New Haven: Yale University Press, 1979), p. 301.

41. In his book *The First Coming: How the Kingdom of God Became Christianity,* which is very helpful for our present purposes, Thomas Sheehan focuses on

the religious usages of hypostatization. See Sheehan, *The First Coming: How the Kingdom of God Became Christianity* (New York: Random House, 1986), p. 210.

42. Hobbes, *Leviathan*, 3.36, p. 287.

43. Ibid., 3.36, p. 288.

44. Ibid.

45. Ibid.

46. Since, as Hobbes points out, Moses actually dies in the book and is buried in a mysterious place, he couldn't possibly be the author of all of it—or possibly even any of it—directly. Ibid., 3.33, p. 261.

47. For discussions of speech as performance or as action, see J. L. Austin, *How to Do Things with Words* (New York: Oxford University Press, 1965); Judith Butler, *Excitable Speech: A Politics of the Performative* (New York: Routledge, 1997); Hannah Arendt, *The Human Condition* (Chicago: University of Chicago Press, 1958). Hobbes himself uses the language of performativity, as when he writes "the Incarnation of God the Son . . . was the Performance of [God's] Promise," a subject we will be returning to in much greater length in chapter 5. *Leviathan*, 3.36, p. 290. There is a large literature on the connection between Hobbes and performativity. See for example Geraint Parry, "Performative Utterances and Obligation in Hobbes," *Philosophical Quarterly* 17, no. 68 (July 1967): 246–52; Samuel Mintz, "Leviathan as Metaphor," *Hobbes Studies* 1 (1988): 3–9; as well as Martin Bertman, "Hobbes and Performatives," *Critica* 10, no. 30 (December 1978): 41–52.

48. Hobbes, *Leviathan*, 3.34, p. 271.

49. Ibid. 3.34, p. 270. Here David Johnston tells us that one thing "spirit" can't mean is "a substance that has no bodily nature at all." Johnston, *The Rhetoric of Leviathan*, p. 147. Martinich attempts to reconcile Hobbes's radical nominalism with his claim that angels and spirits, if they exist at all, must exist as material bodies, by arguing that Hobbes preserves the *aporia* or mystery of these concepts. What we get from Hobbes, Martinich tells us, is a "candid admission of a problem that remains to be solved." Martinich, *The Two Gods of Leviathan: Thomas Hobbes on Religion and Politics* (New York: Cambridge University Press, 1992), p. 249.

50. Hobbes, *Leviathan*, 3.34, p. 278.

51. Ibid., 3.34, p. 272.

52. Ibid. 3.34, pp. 272–73.

53. Walter Benjamin, *The Origin of German Tragic Drama [Ursprung des deutschen Trauerspiels]* (London: NLB, 1977), p. 175.

54. *Leviathan*, 3.37, p. 301.

55. However, even Johnston acknowledges that "an event is miraculous because it is *perceived* to be strange and inexplicable, not because it really is inexplicable." Johnston., *The Rhetoric of Leviathan*, p. 161.

56. Hobbes, *Leviathan*, 3.37, p. 304.

57. This leads to an important question: is the sign haunted by the divine presence or is the sign itself actually the divine presence? In a way this question is unanswerable for Hobbes, getting to the heart of what he means by "the Holy Spirit," as we will later see. The haunting seems to be exactly the inability to distinguish exactly what is divine and what is our reading of the divine. To see our representation of the divine as not being empty, we need the notion that the divine *is*, but what the divine is, or how it may or may not be different than what we infer to it, we cannot know. For this question and many insights throughout this book, I am greatly indebted to Karen Feldman.

58. Niccolò Machiavelli, *The Prince and The Discourses* (New York: Modern Library, 1950), p. 147. Of course, Machiavelli himself may be subverting this notion insofar as he is letting us in on Numa's tricks.

59. Hobbes, *Leviathan*, 3.43, p. 406.

60. Silver, "A Matter of Interpretation," p. 168.

61. Raia Prokhovnik, for example, as we have already seen, tends simply to disbelieve any claims that Hobbes makes about religion. Prokhovnik, *Rhetoric and Philosophy in Hobbes' Leviathan*, p. 161. An earlier reader of Hobbes, Christopher Hill, makes a somewhat similar case. He writes, "It is quite clear, in fact, that Hobbes does not really believe in Christianity, in any normal sense of the word 'belief,' and merely accepts it as the creed authorized in the state in which he lived." Hill, *Puritanism and Revolution: Studies in Interpretation of the English Revolution of the Seventeenth Century* (London: Secker and Warburg, 1965), p. 286. Raymond Polin argues that Hobbes's religious views should not be seen as explaining or unifying his political theory. See Raymond Polin, *Hobbes, Dieu, et les hommes* (Paris: Presses Universitaires de France, 1981).

62. The term is used by Jacques Derrida. See Derrida, *The Gift of Death* (Chicago: University of Chicago Press, 1995), p. 49.

63. This is something that Victoria Silver implies as well in "A Matter of Interpretation," p. 165.

64. It may be that Arendt does not utterly dislike Hobbes even on her own terms. Her attitude may be more of a mixture of criticism and fascination. For example, while she waits to leave France to escape from Nazism, she is said to "discover and devour [*dévore*]" a copy of *Leviathan*. See Laure Adler, *Dans les pas de Hannah Arendt* (Paris: Gallimard, 2005), p. 177.

65. Hannah Arendt, "The Concept of History," in *Between Past and Future*, p. 76.

66. Hannah Arendt, "What Is Freedom?" in *Between Past and Future*, p. 163.

67. Ibid., p. 164.

68. Hobbes, *Leviathan*, 3.34, p. 271.

69. Arendt, "The Concept of History," p. 74.

4. FALSE IDOLS AND POLITICAL REPRESENTATION

1. *Leviathan*, 1.8, p. 51.

2. Patrick Collinson notes that Lutherans tended to read the second commandment as a "mere gloss" on the first. In Zwinglian Protestantism, which greatly influenced English Puritan conceptions, "the second commandment was free-standing and absolute within itself." Collinson, *The Reformation* (London: Weidenfeld and Nicolson, 2003), p. 161. As Margaret Aston points out, the question of whether what we now know as the "second commandment" is in fact separate from the first commandment has long been a major source of contention in Christian doctrine. One tradition coming from Philo, Josephus, and Origen has "Thou shall not make thyself a graven image" as a separate commandment from "Thou shall have no other Gods before me." The Augustinian tradition folded them into one and made up for this by splitting the commandment against covetousness into two. Aston, *England's Iconoclasts*, Vol. 1, *Laws Against Images* (Oxford: Clarendon, 1988), p. 372.

3. Ibid., pp. 397–99.

4. Ibid., p. 404.

5. Ibid., p. 408.

6. Julie Spraggon, *Puritan Iconoclasm during the English Civil War* (London: Boydell, 2003), p.11.

7. Ibid.

8. Peter Goodrich, "The Iconography of Nothing: Blank Spaces and the Representation of Law in Edward VI and the Pope," in Costas Douzinas and Lynda Nead, eds., *Law and the Image: The Authority of Art and the Aesthetics of Law* (Chicago: University of Chicago Press, 1999), pp. 106–7.

9. Ibid., p. 110.

10. Ibid., p. 111.

11. *Leviathan*, 4.45, p. 449.

12. Walter Benjamin, *The Origin of German Tragic Drama [Ursprung des deutschen Trauerspiels]* (London: NLB, 1977), p. 36. However, this term should probably be taken with a grain of salt. He tells us "[t]ruth is the death of intention," i.e., is divorced from our own conceptions of whatever truth may consist of. Ibid. By the same token, in similar ways Benjamin is a radical nominalist, too. He tells us that in the case of Adam's act of naming the things of the world, "Ideas are displayed, without intention, in the act of naming, and they have to be renewed in philosophical contemplation." Ibid., p. 37.

13. *Leviathan*, 4.46, pp. 462–63.

14. In *The Basic Problems of Phenomenology*, Heidegger describes Hobbes's use of *is* as the "copula," which is to say, the sign of coupling, of uniting two terms (such as "man is an animal"). For Heidegger, there is a limit to Hobbes's nominalism insofar as the copula is not a purely physical thing (as a sound or symbol) for Hobbes. Heidegger, reading from Hobbes's *De Corpore*, argues, "Despite his whole nominalistic attack on the problem, the 'is' means, for Hobbes, too, more than a mere phenomenon of sound or script which is somehow inserted between others. The copula as a coupling of words is the index of the thought of the cause for the identical referability of two names to the same thing. The 'is' means the whatness of the thing about which the assertion is made." Heidegger, *The Basic Problems of Phenomenology* (Bloomington: Indiana University Press, 1988), p. 192. Karen Feldman's book, *Binding Words: Conscience and Rhetoric in Hobbes, Hegel, and Heidegger* (Evanston, Ill.: Northwestern University Press, 2006), provides a superb discussion of the use of *is* in Hobbes and makes connections with Heidegger as well in a separate chapter.

15. *Leviathan*, 4.46, p. 466.

16. Hanna Pitkin, *The Concept of Representation* (Berkeley: University of California Press, 1967), pp. 36–37.

17. *Leviathan*, 1.16, p.112.

18. Pitkin, *The Concept of Representation*, p. 34.

19. Ibid.

20. Ibid., p. 35.

21. *Leviathan*, 1.16, p. 112.

22. Ibid., 1.16, p. 113.

23. Pitkin, *The Concept of Representation.*, p. 26.

24. *Leviathan*, 1.16, pp. 113–14.

25. Pitkin herself echoes something of this view when she writes, "For an author is not only someone with authority, who can authorize; he is also the one who writes or composes or originates something—who controls its development or outcome or final form." Pitkin, *The Concept of Representation*, p. 28.

26. *Leviathan*, 1.17, p. 120.

27. Christopher Pye, "The Sovereign, the Theater, and the Kingdome of Darknesse: Hobbes and the Spectacle of Power," *Representations* 8 (Fall 1984): 85–106, 92.

28. Ibid., p. 93.

29. Ibid., p. 96.

30. Ibid., p. 95.

31. *Leviathan*, 2.21, p. 153.

32. Ibid., 1.16, p. 114. Here Hobbes is perhaps not being consistent with his own distinction.

33. Hannah Arendt, "What Is Freedom?" in *Between Past and Future: Eight Exercises in Political Thought* (New York: Penguin, 1954), p. 168.

5. THE TRUE COVENANT

1. Hannah Arendt, *The Human Condition* (Chicago: University of Chicago Press, 1958), p. 244.

2. *Leviathan*, 3.42, p. 339. For Martinich, this discussion of the persons of God has an explicitly political parallel. A. P. Martinich, *The Two Gods of Leviathan: Thomas Hobbes on Religion and Politics* (New York: Cambridge University Press, 1992), p. 206.

3. *Leviathan*, 3.42.p. 339.

4. In later years, Hobbes responded to criticism from John Bramhall, among others, by arguing that he should have written "ministry of Moses." See Patricia Springborg, "Hobbes on Religion," in Tom Sorell, ed., *The Cambridge Companion to Hobbes* (New York: Cambridge University Press, 1996),

p. 365. Yet I don't see this as a significant retraction on Hobbes's part. Such a move does not for example address the crucial association he makes between Moses as person of God and the rhetorical figure of "God the Father."

5. *Leviathan*, 1.16, p. 111.

6. It does not, however, always have a specifically political character. Hobbes tells us that in that time "the name of *King* be not yet given to God, nor of *Kingdome* to Abraham and his seed." Ibid., 3.35, p. 281.

7. Given that neither figure nor person fully constitutes the promise itself, we might say that the person is that thing which is delivered by the promise and the figure is the site on which the promise is read and understood by human beings.

8. Michael Oakeshott makes a somewhat similar argument in *Hobbes on Civil Association* (Berkeley: University of California Press, 1975), p. 108.

9. *Leviathan*, 3.42, p. 356.

10. In the context of this passage the "failure" of justice specifically refers to the fact that the "sons of *Samuel* . . . received bribes, and judged unjustly, the people of Israel. . . ." Ibid., 1.12, p. 85. But this immediate failure of justice is indicative of a larger failure to obey and hold God as King. The responsibility of this generation to keep their faith in God fails because they prove themselves unwilling to perform the political duties that are a product of that faith.

11. Ibid., 3.41, p. 333.

12. Ibid., 3.41, pp. 335–36.

13. Ibid., 3.42, pp. 341–42.

14. Ibid., 3.43, p. 407. I see this as a radicalized version of the rhetorical figure of omission (i.e., by saying only one thing he is effectively unsaying all other things about Scripture).

15. Ibid., 1.12, p. 85. The entire question of the nature of covenants and even the word *covenant* do not come out of a vacuum. The term was very commonly used in seventeenth century England. In some cases, the use expressly links religious and political terms, as we find with the National Covenant in Scotland (1638). See John F. H. New, *Anglican and Puritan: The Basis of Their Opposition, 1558–1640* (Stanford, Calif.: Stanford University Press, 1964), p. 94. New writes that one of the most contentious questions about covenant with God was whether God could revoke the covenant formed with human beings.

16. Gregory S. Kavka, *Hobbesian Moral and Political Theory* (Princeton: Princeton University Press, 1986), p. 304.

17. Ibid., p. 391.
18. Ibid., pp. 391–92.
19. Ibid., p. 393.
20. As Foucault, however, explains it, Hobbes has made life itself utterly precarious and in this sense we are all in constant danger after all. See Michel Foucault, "*Society Must Be Defended*" (New York: Picador, 2003), p. 95.
21. *Leviathan*, 2.26, p. 198.
22. Ibid., 1.26, p. 199. Hobbes does not include a citation for his biblical passage here.
23. Ibid.
24. See Springborg, "Hobbes on Religion." As I'll argue in the next chapter, Springborg makes more or less this same point in her contribution to the *Cambridge Companion to Hobbes*, albeit with different conclusions than mine.
25. *Leviathan*, 1.14, p. 97.
26. The term is Arendt's. *The Human Condition*, p. 244.
27. *Leviathan*, 1.14, p. 98.
28. Ibid., 1.14, p. 97.
29. Ibid., 1.14, p. 99.
30. One of Karen Feldman's insights is that this bindingness is actually produced rhetorically. See her chapter on Hobbes in *Binding Words: Conscience and Rhetoric in Hobbes, Hegel, and Heidegger* (Evanston, Ill.: Northwestern University Press, 2006), pp. 19–47. There is a huge literature in Hobbes scholarship on the sources of obligation in Hobbes. For a rational choice perspective on Hobbes see David P. Gauthier, *The Logic of Leviathan: The Moral and Political Theory of Thomas Hobbes* (Oxford: Clarendon, 1969). See also Jean Hampton, *Hobbes and the Social Contract Tradition* (Cambridge, U.K.: Cambridge University Press, 1986). For a more deontological account of Hobbes's theory of obligation see Howard Warrender, *The Political Philosophy of Hobbes: His Theory of Obligation* (Oxford: Clarendon, 1957). See also John Plamenatz, "Mr. Warrender's Hobbes" and Howard Warrender's "A Reply to Mr. Plamenatz," both in K. C. Brown, ed., *Hobbes Studies* (Oxford: Blackwell, 1965), pp. 73–87 and 89–100, respectively.
31. Erroneous because, as I will develop further, Hobbes has little interest in the will per se.

32. Kavka, *Hobbesian Moral and Political Theory*, p. 305. For another consideration of Hobbes' voluntarism see Gordon J. Schochet's "Intending (Political) Obligation: Hobbes and the Voluntary Basis of Society," in Mary Dietz, ed., *Thomas Hobbes and Political Theory* (Lawrence: University Press of Kansas, 1990), pp. 55–73.

33. Kavka, *Hobbesian Moral and Political Theory*, p. 306.

34. Ibid.

35. Ibid.

36. Arendt, *The Human Condition*, p. 179.

37. *Leviathan*, 1.14, p. 93.

38. Ibid.

39. Ibid.

40. Kavka, *Hobbesian Moral and Political Theory*, p. 347.

41. Ibid., p. 357.

42. This is not how Kavka would put it, however.

43. Ibid., p. 365.

44. Ibid., p. 369.

45. Flathman, *Thomas Hobbes: Skepticism, Individuality, and Chastened Politics* (Newbury Park, Calif.: Sage, 1993), p. 109.

46. Arendt, "What Is Freedom?" in *Between Past and Future: Eight Exercises in Political Thought* (New York: Penguin, 1954), pp. 164–65. Arendt's use of the term *sovereignty* needs to be parsed somewhat, since at times she seems to be using the term differently in different passages. Hanna Pitkin cautions us that Arendt may in fact be dealing with two notions of sovereignty: one on the individual level and one on the collective level. See Pitkin, *The Attack of the Blob: Hannah Arendt's Concept of the Social* (Chicago: University of Chicago Press, 1998), pp. 199–200. Even in its collective sense, however, it is not clear that *sovereignty* as such escapes the problem of the will for Arendt.

47. Hannah Arendt, "What Is Authority?" in *Between Past and Future*, pp. 93, 95.

48. Hannah Arendt, *On Revolution* (New York: Penguin, 1986), p. 212.

49. Ibid.

50. Arendt, "What Is Freedom?" pp. 158–59.

51. Citing John Duns Scotus, Arendt tells us that although an action may have "happened quite at random," once it happens, it "loses its aspect of contin-

gency and presents itself to us in the guise of necessity." Arendt, *Willing*, in
The Life of the Mind (New York: Harcourt, Brace Jovanovich, 1978), p. 138.

52. Arendt, *The Human Condition*, p. 244.

53. Ibid.

54. B. Honig, "Declarations of Independence: Arendt and Derrida on the Prob-
lem of Founding a Republic," *American Political Science Review* 85, no. 1
(March 1991): 97–113, 97. A fuller account of this appears in Bonnie Honig,
Political Theory and the Displacement of Politics (Ithaca: Cornell University
Press, 1993).

55. Honig, "Declarations of Independence," p. 99.

56. Ibid.

57. Ibid., p.102. This is very much in keeping with what we have already considered in our treatment of Arendt above.

58. Ibid., p. 104.

59. Ibid., p. 100.

60. In "What Is Authority?" Arendt tells us that the American Revolution, unlike other revolutions, managed to remain "relatively nonviolent" in part because the Declaration of Independence and the Constitution "[fell] back
on existing charters and agreements . . . rather than ma[king a body politic]
anew." Arendt, "What Is Authority?" p. 140.

61. Honig, "Declarations of Independence," p. 106.

62. *Leviathan*, 3.41, p. 338.

63. Arendt, "What Is Authority?" p. 121.

64. It is true that Arendt tells us that in Rome, such a bond was very hierarchical
while for Hobbes it seems, as I have been suggesting, more collective, more
egalitarian, but the essential structure and role of religion in both thinkers'
accounts remains essentially similar. Ibid., p. 93.

65. It's also possible that Arendt is not quite as enamored of the pure performative as she sometimes seems to be. Jacques Taminiaux for one argues that
Arendt far prefers the Roman version of performativity, contextualized as it
was in a self-consciously historical setting, to the utter spontaneity favored
by the Greeks. See Taminiaux, "Athens and Rome," in Dana Villa, ed., *The
Cambridge Companion to Hannah Arendt* (New York: Cambridge University
Press, 2000), pp. 165–77. Her admiration for the Romans does suggest the
possibility of a combination of constative and performative elements as a
basis for political authority, but this again does not resolve the problem of

our own time, since for Arendt, the Roman approach to authority can never be reestablished.

66. Arendt, "What Is Authority?" p. 128.

67. Part of this might be an accident of history. As an early modern, Hobbes did not have the same vocabulary or experience as Arendt.

6. "THE FELLOWSHIP OF THE HOLY SPIRIT"

1. *Leviathan,* 3.42, p. 339.

2. Ibid., 1.4, p. 31.

3. Walter Benjamin, "Theses on the Philosophy of History," in *Illuminations: Essays and Reflections* (New York: Schocken, 1968), p. 254.

4. Geoffrey F. Nuttall, *The Holy Spirit in Puritan Faith and Experience* (Oxford: Blackwell, 1947), pp. 3–4. For an account of the Holy Spirit more generally, and historically, see Stanley M. Burgess, *The Holy Spirit: Medieval Roman Catholic and Reformation Traditions (Sixth–Sixteenth Centuries)* (Peabody, Mass.: Hendrickson, 1997).

5. Nuttall, *The Holy Spirit in Puritan Faith and Experience,* p. 155.

6. Ibid., p. 109. This messianic kingdom, to follow four terrestrial kingdoms, is mentioned in Daniel 7:23.

7. Nuttall writes that this term "the fellowship of the spirit" was "[not only] confined to the more enthusiastic type of Puritan." Ibid., p. 142.

8. Paul J. Johnson, "Hobbes's Anglican Doctrine of Salvation," in Ralph Ross, Herbert W. Scheider, and Theodore Waldman, eds., *Thomas Hobbes in His Time* (Minneapolis: University of Minnesota Press, 1974), pp. 102–125, 107.

9. Ibid.

10. Ibid., p. 108.

11. Ibid.

12. For an argument that Anglican Arminianism (and especially Archbishop Laud) radicalized the Puritans, see Nicholas Tyacke, "Puritanism, Arminianism and Counter-Revolution," in Margo Todd, ed., *Reformation to Revolution: Politics and Religion in Early Modern England* (New York: Routledge, 1995), pp. 53–70. For a counter view see Kevin Sharpe, "Archbiship Laud," in the same volume, pp. 71–77.

13. *Leviathan,* 3.36, p. 295.

14. See for example F. C. Hood, *The Divine Politics of Thomas Hobbes: An Inter-pretation of Leviathan* (Oxford: Clarendon, 1964), p. 241.

15. *Leviathan*, 3.42, p. 340.

16. Springborg, "Hobbes on Religion," in Tom Sorell, ed., *The Cambridge Companion to Hobbes* (New York: Cambridge University Press, 1996), p. 365.

17. Ibid., p. 364.

18. Ibid., p. 362.

19. Ibid., pp. 364–65.

20. *Leviathan*, 4.45, p. 451.

21. Ibid., 3.36, p. 290.

22. Ibid., 3.42, p. 341.

23. J. G. A. Pocock, *Politics, Language and Time: Essays on Political Thought in History* (New York: Atheneum, 1973), p. 188.

24. See Benjamin, "Theses on the Philosophy of History," p. 254. For a discussion of a "weak messianic force," see also Jacques Derrida, *Spectres of Marx: The State of the Debt, the Work of Mourning, & the New International*, Peggy Kamuf, trans. (New York: Routledge, 1994), p. 55.

25. Benjamin was able to reconcile Marxist workers' revolution with Jewish messianism by insisting that what we build together *is* the (bringing of) the messiah. See Walter Benjamin, "Critique of Violence," in *Reflections: Essays, Aphorisms, Autobiographical Writings* (New York: Schocken, 1978).

26. *Leviathan*, 2.17, p. 117.

27. Ibid.

28. In terms of what this "weak messiah" might portend for Hobbes's view of the sovereign messiah, i.e., Jesus himself, we do not need to speculate. Hobbes, for all his eschatology, is very much focused on "time of the now," to cite Benjamin once again, and in this time our messiah is not one who will come, but one who is (weakly) already here. Benjamin, "Theses on the Philosophy of History," p. 263.

29. The link between Puritanism, Calvinism, and liberalism has been widely asserted, perhaps most famously by Max Weber (see his *The Protestant Ethic and the Spirit of Capitalism* [New York: Charles Scribner's Sons, 1958]). See also Michael Walzer, *The Revolution of the Saints: A Study in the Origins of Radical Politics* (Cambridge: Harvard University Press, 1965), p. 303. Walzer complicates this connection a bit by noting that liberalism radically changed

and secularized Puritan doctrine. See also Sheldon Wolin, *Politics and Vision: Continuity and Innovation in Western Political Thought*, expanded edition (Princeton: Princeton University Press, 2004), p. 267; Christopher Hill, *The Century of Revolution: 1603–1714* (Edinburgh: Thomas Nelson & Sons, 1961), p. 295. Patrick Collinson calls the connection between Calvinism and Puritanism and future liberalism a case of "elective affinit[ies]." See Collinson, *The Reformation* (London: Weidenfeld and Nicolson, 2003), p. 176. For a discussion of Locke's relationship to Puritanism more specifically, see Richard Ashcraft, *Revolutionary Politics & Locke's Two Treatises of Government* (Princeton: Princeton University Press, 1986) and John Dunn, *Locke: A Very Short Introduction* (Oxford: Oxford University Press, 1984).

30. Nuttall, *The Holy Spirit in Puritan Faith and Experience,* pp. 40–41.

31. Ibid., p. 142.

32. Ibid., p. 144.

33. *Leviathan*, 3.36, p. 297.

34. Nuttall, *The Holy Spirit in Puritan Faith and Experience,* p. 55.

35. Ibid., p. 52.

36. Ibid., p. 85.

37. *Leviathan*, Introduction, p. 10.

38. Arendt, *The Human Condition* (Chicago: University of Chicago Press, 1958), p. 243.

39. Walzer, *The Revolution of the Saints,* p. 306. This claim is made by quite a few scholars of Locke, especially via a connection between Locke and the Levellers. See Jacqueline Stevens, "The Reasonableness of John Locke's Majority," *Political Theory* 24, no. 3 (August 1996): 423–63. Richard Ashcraft discusses this, in *Revolutionary Politics & Locke's Two Treatises of Government,* as does John Dunn in *Locke: A Very Short Introduction.*

40. See Dunn, *Locke: A Very Short Introduction,* p. 2. For example, Dunn sees the Puritan influence as explaining Locke's tendency to want to rein in the excesses of the landed elite, as well as a generally restricted notion of individual (and collective) liberty. See also John Dunn, *The Political Thought of John Locke: A Historical Account of the Argument of the 'Two Treatises of Government'* (Cambridge, U.K.: Cambridge University Press, 1969), pp. 256–57. For the account of the debates at Putney, see A. S. P. Woodhouse, ed., *Puritanism and Liberty: Being the Army Debates (1647–9) from the CLARKE MANUSCRIPTS with Supplementary Documents* (London: J. M. Dent & Sons, 1974).

41. Nuttall, *The Holy Spirit in Puritan Faith and Experience,* p. 128.

42. Richard Tuck argues that Hobbes and Locke had very similar views on tolerance. See Richard Tuck, "Hobbes and Locke on Toleration," in Mary Dietz, ed., *Thomas Hobbes and Political Theory* (Lawrence: University Press of Kansas,1990), pp. 153–71. See also Alan Ryan, "Hobbes, Toleration, and the Inner Life," in David Miller and Larry Siedentop, eds., *The Nature of Political Theory* (Oxford: Clarendon, 1983), pp. 197–218. For a recent and excellent account of liberal tolerance and its many problems, see Wendy Brown, *Regulating Aversion: Tolerance in the Age of Identity and Empire* (Princeton: Princeton University Press, 2006).

43. John Wesley Vavricka pointed this distinction out to me in a graduate seminar.

44. *Leviathan,* 2.21, pp. 145–46.

45. In other words, not kings in which ecclesiastical and political authority are united, which was the case with Moses.

46. Ibid., 4.47, pp. 479–80.

47. Ibid., 4.47, p. 480.

48. Ibid., Introduction, p. 11.

49. Ibid., 4.45, p. 454.

50. In a previous book, *Love is a Sweet Chain,* I argue that Hobbes is engaged in a long-standing "immense rumor" (as Derrida puts it) to counter liberal understandings of friendship and relationality. See Martel, *Love Is a Sweet Chain: Desire, Autonomy, and Friendship in Liberal Political Theory* (New York: Routledge, 2001), p. 5. See also Jacques Derrida, *Politics of Friendship* (New York: Verso, 2000).

51. *Leviathan,* Dedication, p. 3.

52. Ibid.

53. Michael Oakeshott writes that for Hobbes, Godolphin exemplified the positive side of pride, not a selfish competitiveness but a kind of pride commensurate with the *civitas* itself. Oakeshott, *Hobbes on Civil Association* (Berkeley: University of California Press, 1975), p. 124.

54. Miriam Reik, *The Golden Lands of Thomas Hobbes* (Detroit: Wayne State University Press, 1977), p. 149.

55. *Leviathan,* Dedication, p. 3.

56. *Leviathan,* "A Review, and Conclusion," p. 484.

57. As when Emmanuel Levinas writes, "I am at home with myself in the world because it offers itself to or resists possession. . . . Over [the stranger] I have no *power*. He escapes my grasp by an essential dimension, even if I have him at my disposal. He is not wholly in my site." Levinas, *Totality and Infinity: An Essay on Exteriority* (Pittsburgh: Duquesne University Press, 1969), pp. 38–39.

58. For a consideration of Levinas and Hobbes, see Jill Stauffer, "This Weakness Is Needed: An Intervention in Social Contract Theory" (Ph.D. diss., University of California, Berkeley, 2003).

59. There is another explanation for this dedication that is far less flattering. John Bowle cites Clarendon (who was a great critic of Hobbes and therefore perhaps not to be trusted) in relating how Sidney Godolphin had left Hobbes two hundred pounds, and suggests Hobbes dedicated *Leviathan* to Francis to get his money. Bowle, *Hobbes and His Critics: A Study in Seventeenth Century Constitutionalism* (London: Cape, 1951), p. 162. If true, this only partially paid off as a strategy: Bowle tells us Godolphin paid him one hundred pounds and promised him the rest later. He also tells us that Hobbes denied this claim. Ibid., p. 163.

60. It may seem strange to compare a dialectical materialist like Benjamin to a radical nominalist like Hobbes, yet our engagement with these questions shows that Benjamin is no garden-variety materialist. He does not hold to a positivist reality and meaning of imagery—otherwise he would have no fears or concerns about the dangers of propaganda in the first place; the images would just "speak for themselves" (although this is a position Adorno seems to attribute to Benjamin). See Theodore W. Adorno and Walter Benjamin, *The Complete Correspondence 1928–1940* (Cambridge: Harvard University Press, 1999), pp. 280–87.

61. For a well-known account of "the spectacle" more generally, see Guy Debord, *The Society of the Spectacle* (New York: Zone, 1995).

62. Walter Benjamin, *The Arcades Project* (Cambridge: Harvard University Press, 2003), p. 11 ("Exposé of 1935"). For explorations of this book see Susan Buck-Morss, *The Dialectics of Seeing: Walter Benjamin and the Arcades Project* (Cambridge: MIT Press, 1999) and Pierre Missac, *Walter Benjamin's Passages,* Shierry Weber Nicholsen, trans. (Cambridge: MIT Press, 1996). See also Paul de Man, "Allegory and Irony in Baudelaire," in de Man, *Romanticism and Contemporary Criticism: The Gauss Seminar and Other Papers* (Baltimore: Johns Hopkins University Press, 1993), pp. 101–19, on Baudelaire (and *cor-*

respondances) in particular. See also Benjamin's *The Writer of Modern Life: Essays on Charles Baudelaire* (Cambridge, Mass.: Belknap, 2006).

63. Benjamin, *Arcades Project*, p. 10.

64. Ibid., p. 325 ("Konvolute J: Baudelaire"). However, in that same passage, we are informed that this makes allegory "dated."

65. Walter Benjamin "On Some Motifs in Baudelaire," in Benjamin, *Illuminations*, p. 194.

66. I put the term in quotes to distinguish it from actual reality, as will be made clear shortly.

67. Benjamin, *Arcades Project*, p. 211 ("Konvolute H: The Collector"). Relating this dispersal to a question of memory, Benjamin also tells us: "How the scatter of allegorical properties (the patchwork) relates to this creative disorder [of memory] is a question calling for further study." Ibid. See also Michael P. Steinberg, "The Collector as Allegorist: Goods, Gods, and the Objects of History," in Michael P. Steinberg, ed., *Walter Benjamin and the Demands of History* (Ithaca: Cornell University Press, 1996), pp. 88–118. See also "Eduard Fuchs, Collector and Historian," in Howard Eiland and Michael W. Jennings, eds., *Walter Benjamin: Selected Writings. Volume 3, 1935–1938* (Cambridge, Mass.: Belknap, 2002).

68. Benjamin, *Arcades Project*, p. 211 ("Konvolute H: The Collector).

69. Ibid. In "Central Park," Benjamin furthers the connection between allegory and *correspondances* through the figure of *souvenir* (memory). He writes: "The key figure of the later allegory is the '*souvenir*' (*Andenken*). The '*souvenir*' is the schema of the transformation of the commodity into a collector's object. The *correspondances* are the endlessly multiple resonances of each *souvenir* with all the others." Walter Benjamin, "Central Park," Lloyd Spencer, trans., *New German Critique* 34 (Winter 1985): 32–58, 55.

70. Benjamin, "On Some Motifs in Baudelaire," p. 181.

71. Ibid., pp. 181–82.

72. Ibid., p. 199.

73. Rather than say that they are saying exactly the same thing, we might look at the *correspondances* between these thinkers and illuminate Hobbes (and Benjamin) accordingly.

74. *Leviathan*, 1.16, p. 114.

75. Benjamin, "Theses on the Philosophy of History," p. 263.

76. Ibid., p. 264.

77. This is also very much like Arendt's notion of "dispos[ing] of the future as though it were the present." Arendt, *The Human Condition*, p. 245.

78. Walter Benjamin, "Critique of Violence," p. 300. Benjamin also speak of the "Kingdom of God." See his "Theological-Political Fragment," in Eiland and Jennings, eds., *Walter Benjamin: Selected Writings: Volume 3, 1935–1938* (Cambridge, Mass.: Belknap, 2002).

79. Jacques Derrida, "Force of Law: The 'Mystical Foundation of Authority,'" in Drucilla Cornell, Michel Rosenfeld, and David Gray Carlson, eds., *Deconstruction and the Possibility of Justice* (New York: Routledge, 1992), p. 52.

80. Ibid., pp. 52–53.

81. Benjamin, "Critique of Violence," p. 300. Giorgio Agamben writes, "*The Messiah* [in Benjamin] *is, in other words, the figure through which religion confronts the problem of the Law. . . .*" Agamben, "The Messiah and the Sovereign," in Daniel Heller-Roazen, ed., *Potentialities: Collected Essays in Philosophy* (Stanford: Stanford University Press, 1999), p.163. I would add this same insight to Hobbes himself.

82. Technically, it is incorrect to speak either of Hobbes or of Benjamin as "antisovereign" insofar as they seek to replace a false sort of (terrestrial) sovereign with a proper (divine) one.

83. *Leviathan*, 4.44, p. 418.

84. Arendt, "What Is Freedom?" in *Between Past and Future: Eight Exercises in Political Thought* (New York: Penguin, 1954), p. 165.

85. Pye, "The Sovereign, the Theater, and the Kingdome of Darknesse: Hobbes and the Spectacle of Power," *Representations* 8 (Fall 1984): 85–106, 95.

CONCLUSION

1. *Leviathan*, 2.31, p. 254.

2. Ibid.

3. Ibid.

4. Benjamin, *The Origin of German Tragic Drama (Ursprung des deutschen Trauerspiels)* (London: NLB, 1977), p. 229.

5. Ibid., p. 36.

6. Hence the title of his book *Reflections of a Would-Be Anarchist: Ideals and Institutions of Liberalism* (Minneapolis: University of Minnesota Press, 1998).

7. In Arendt's case, this "anarchism" is tempered by her love of all things Roman. Yet, although much has been made of her favoring Rome over Greece, her admiration for the Greek form of self-rule should not be totally discounted.

8. *Leviathan*, 1.6, p. 46.

9. Flathman, *Reflections of a Would-Be Anarchist*, pp. 18, 128. For a good overview of the relationship between liberalism, broadly considered, and sovereignty see Jürgen Habermas, *Theory and Practice* (Boston: Beacon, 1973).

10. F. H. Hinsley writes that such ideas were introduced—at least in their modern variant—by the Protestant *Monarchomachi* in the sixteenth century, including figures like François Hotman and John Knox. F. H. Hinsley, *Sovereignty* (New York: Basic, 1966), p. 132.

11. See, for example, Carl Schmitt, *Political Theology: Four Chapters on the Concept of Sovereignty* (Cambridge: MIT Press, 1985).

12. Sheldon Wolin argues that democratic radicalism and liberalism form "two distinct traditions of political thought" but are often erroneously associated with one another. Wolin, *Politics and Vision: Continuity and Innovation in Western Political Thought*, expanded edition (Princeton: Princeton University Press, 2004), p. 263.

13. In his book *Sovereignty: An Inquiry into the Political Good*, Bertrand de Jouvenel exemplifies a common approach to the question of sovereignty among those liberals who directly treat this question. See de Jouvenel, *Sovereignty: An Inquiry into the Political Good* (Indianapolis: Liberty Fund, 1997).

14. John Rawls, *The Law of Peoples* (Cambridge: Harvard University Press, 1999), pp. 26–27.

15. For other liberal writers who write in opposition to a more "Hobbesian" style interpretation of sovereignty see H. L. A. Hart, *The Concept of Law* (London: Oxford University Press, 1961), as well as Ronald Dworkin, "The Model of Rules I," and "The Model of Rules II" (which otherwise critique Hart), in *Taking Rights Seriously* (Cambridge: Harvard University Press, 1977). Robert Ladenson defends the Hobbesian definition of law (as he defines it). Ladenson, "In Defense of a Hobbesian Conception of Law," in Joseph Raz, ed., *Authority* (New York: New York University Press, 1990), pp. 32–55. Joseph Raz himself contends with Ladenson's arguments in that same volume. See Raz, "Authority and Justification," pp. 115–41.

16. Benjamin Constant, *Principles of Politics Applicable to All Governments* (Indianapolis: Liberty Fund, 2003), p. 16.

17. Ibid., p. 19.

18. Ibid., p. 22.

19. John Stuart Mill, *On Liberty and Utilitarianism* (New York: Bantam, 1993), p. 86.

20. Ibid.

21. Isaiah Berlin, "Two Concepts of Liberty," in *The Proper Study of Mankind: An Anthology of Essays* (New York: Farrar, Straus and Giroux, 1997), p. 236.

22. Ibid., p. 237.

23. *Leviathan*, 3.36, p. 297.

24. To put this in somewhat simpler terms, when Rawls et al. set up a claim of rights over and above sovereignty, they beg the question of who is going to enforce, interpret, or even conceive of these selfsame rights.

25. Although Hobbes himself is typically thought of as having a dim view of human nature, he tells us, right after his infamous description of life in the state of nature as "solitary, poore, nasty, brutish, and short" (*Leviathan*, 1.13, p. 89), that just because we don't trust one another (and thereby "accuse mankind by [our] actions," ibid.), still we do not "accuse mans nature" by such distrust. Ibid.

26. Arendt, *The Human Condition* (Chicago: University of Chicago Press, 1958), p. 245.

27. See Wendy Brown, *Politics Out of History* (Princeton: Princeton University Press, 2001); Slavoj Zizek, *The Ticklish Subject: The Absent Centre of Political Ontology* (New York: Verso, 1999); Todd Gitlin, "Blips, Bites, and Savvy Talk: Television's Impact on American Politics," *Dissent* (Winter 1990): 18–26; Mark Andrejevic, *Reality TV: The Work of Being Watched* (New York: Rowman and Littlefield, 2004).

28. Brown, *Politics Out of History*, p. 4.

29. Michel Foucault, "*Society Must Be Defended*" (New York: Picador, 2003), p. 34.

30. Michael Hardt and Antonio Negri, *Empire* (Cambridge: Harvard University Press, 2000), pp. 85–86.

31. Wendy Brown, "Learning to Love Again: An Interview with Wendy Brown," *Contretemps* 6 (January 2006): 25–42, 27.

32. For a discussion of whether sovereignty is making a "comeback" see Judith Butler's chapter "Indefinite Detention" in *Precarious Life: Powers of Mourning and Violence* (New York: Verso, 2004).

33. Flathman, *Reflections of a Would-Be Anarchist*, p. 135.

34. Ibid., p. 80.

35. Ibid.

36. Indeed, for Hobbes, if we think about the distinction between "power" and "liberty" (the latter term meaning for Hobbes something quite different than it does for Arendt), we can better understand what power is by this link to Arendt. See Arendt, *The Human Condition*, pp. 199–205.

37. If there is one thing that really distinguishes Hobbes and Benjamin, it is that for Hobbes we can really have a "messsianism without a messiah" insofar as the main messianic figure in *Leviathan* is arguably the Holy Spirit, which has absolutely no content of any sort. For Benjamin, on the other hand, an actual messiah seems to be a requirement (unless we argue that for Benjamin revolution *is* in some sense his messianic figure, in which case they may not be so different after all).

38. Even nonliberals like Robert Bernasconi and Jacques Derrida have noted this feature of sovereignty.

39. Robert Bernasconi, "Opening the Future: The Paradox of Promising in the Hobbesian Social Contract," *Philosophy Today* (Spring 1997): 77–86, 82. For another interesting account of origins in Hobbesian theory see Matthew H. Kramer, *Hobbes and the Paradoxes of Political Origins* (New York: St. Martin's, 1997).

40. Bernasconi, "Opening the Future," p. 82.

41. Walter Benjamin, "Central Park," translated by Lloyd Spencer, *New German Critique* 34 (1985): 32–58, 46. And in turn, *correspondance* is the "antidote" to allegory. Benjamin goes on to write "myth was the easy path which Baudelaire forbade himself." Ibid.

42. Michel Foucault, "Truth and Power," in *Power/Knowledge: Selected Interviews and Other Writings, 1972–1977* (New York: Pantheon, 1980), p. 121.

Selected Bibliography

Adler, Laure. *Dans les pas de Hannah Arendt*. Paris: Gallimard, 2005.

Adorno, Theodore W., and Walter Benjamin. *The Complete Correspondence, 1928–1940*. Cambridge: Harvard University Press, 1999.

Agamben, Giorgio. "The Messiah and the Sovereign." In Daniel Heller-Roazen, ed., *Potentialities: Collected Essays in Philosophy*. Stanford: Stanford University Press, 1999.

Andrejevic, Mark. *Reality TV: The Work of Being Watched*. New York: Rowman and Littlefield, 2004.

Arendt, Hannah, "The Concept of History," "What Is Authority," and "What Is Freedom?" In *Between Past and Future: Eight Exercises in Political Thought*. New York: Penguin, 1954.

——. *The Human Condition*. Chicago: University of Chicago Press, 1958.

——. *On Revolution*. New York: Penguin, 1968.

——. *Willing*. In *The Life of the Mind*. New York: Harcourt, Brace Jovanovich, 1978.

Ashcraft, Richard. *Revolutionary Politics and Locke's Two Treatises of Government*. Princeton: Princeton University Press, 1986.

Aston, Margaret. *England's Iconoclasts*. Vol 1. *Laws Against Images*. Oxford: Clarendon, 1988.

Austin, J. L. *How to Do Things with Words*. New York: Oxford University Press, 1965.

Barnouw, Jeffrey. "Persuasion in Hobbes's *Leviathan*." *Hobbes Studies* 1 (1988): 3–25.

Benjamin, Walter. *The Arcades Project*. Cambridge: Harvard University Press, 2003.

——. "Central Park." Translated by Lloyd Spencer. *New German Critique* 34 (Winter 1985): 32–58.

——. "Critique of Violence." In *Reflections: Essays, Aphorisms, Autobiographical Writings*. New York: Schocken, 1978.

——. "Eduard Fuchs, Collector and Historian." In Howard Eiland and Michael W. Jennings, eds *Walter Benjamin: Selected Writings, Vol. 3, 1935–1938.* Cambridge, Mass.: Belknap, 2002.

——. "On Some Motifs in Baudelaire." In *Illuminations: Essays and Reflections.* New York: Schocken, 1968.

——. *The Origin of German Tragic Drama (Ursprung des deutschen Trauerspiels).* London: NLB, 1977.

——. "Theological-Political Fragment." In Howard Eiland and Michael W. Jennings, eds., *Walter Benjamin: Selected Writings, Vol. 3, 1935–1938.* Cambridge, Mass.: Belknap, 2002.

——. "Theses on the Philosophy of History." In *Illuminations: Essays and Reflections.* New York: Schocken, 1968.

——. "The Work of Art in the Age of Mechanical Reproduction." In *Illuminations: Essays and Reflections.* New York: Schocken, 1968.

——. *The Writer of Modern Life: Essays on Charles Baudelaire.* Cambridge, Mass.: Belknap, 2006.

Berlin, Isaiah. "Two Concepts of Liberty." In *The Proper Study of Mankind: An Anthology of Essays.* New York: Farrar, Straus and Giroux, 1997.

Bernasconi, Robert. "Opening the Future: The Paradox of Promising in the Hobbesian Social Contract." *Philosophy Today* (Spring 1997): 77–86.

Bertman, Martin. "Hobbes and Performatives." *Critica* 10, no. 30 (December 1978): 41–52.

Botwinick. Aryeh. *Hobbes and Modernity: Five Exercises in Political Philosophical Exegesis.* Lanham, Md.: University Press of America, 1983.

——. *Skepticism, Belief, and the Modern: Maimonides to Nietzsche.* Ithaca: Cornell University Press, 1997.

Bowle, John. *Hobbes and His Critics: A Study in Seventeenth Century Constitutionalism.* London: Cape, 1951.

Brown, Wendy. "Learning to Love Again: An Interview with Wendy Brown." *Contretemps* 6 (January 2006): 25–42.

——. *Politics Out of History.* Princeton: Princeton University Press, 2001.

——. *Regulating Aversion: Tolerance in the Age of Identity and Empire.* Princeton: Princeton University Press, 2006.

Buck-Morss, Susan. *The Dialectics of Seeing: Walter Benjamin and the Arcades Project.* Cambridge: MIT Press, 1999.

Burgess, Stanley M. *The Holy Spirit: Medieval Roman Catholic and Reformation Traditions (Sixth-Sixteenth Centuries)*. Peabody, Mass.: Hendrickson, 1997.

Burke, Kenneth. *A Rhetoric of Motives*. Berkeley: University of California Press, 1969.

Butler, Judith. *Excitable Speech: A Politics of the Performative*. New York: Routledge, 1997.

———. *Precarious Life: Powers of Mourning and Violence*. New York: Verso, 2004.

Collinson, Patrick. *The Elizabethan Puritan Movement*. Oxford: Clarendon, 1967.

———. *The Reformation*. London: Weidenfeld and Nicolson, 2003.

Constant, Benjamin. *Principles of Politics Applicable to All Governments*. Indianapolis, Ind.: Liberty Fund, 2003.

Dean, Jodi. *Publicity's Secret: How Technoculture Capitalizes on Democracy*. Ithaca: Cornell University Press, 2002.

Debord, Guy. *The Society of the Spectacle*. New York: Zone Books, 1995.

De Jouvenel, Bertrand. *Sovereignty: An Inquiry into the Political Good*. Indianapolis, Ind.: Liberty Fund, 1997.

De Man, Paul. *Allegories of Reading: Figural Language in Rousseau, Nietzsche, Rilke, and Proust*. New Haven: Yale University Press, 1979.

———. *Romanticism and Contemporary Criticism: The Gauss Seminar and Other Papers*. Baltimore: Johns Hopkins University Press, 1993.

Derrida, Jacques. "Force of Law: The 'Mystical Foundation of Authority.'" In Drucilla Cornell, Michel Rosenfeld, and David Gray Carlson, eds., *Deconstruction and the Possibility of Justice*, pp. 2–67. New York: Routledge, 1992.

———. *The Gift of Death*. Chicago: University of Chicago Press, 1995.

———. *Politics of Friendship*. New York: Verso, 2000.

———. Spectres of Marx: The State of the Debt, the Work of Mourning, and the New International. Translated by Peggy Kamuf. New York: Routledge, 1994.

Descartes, René. Meditations and Other Metaphysical Writings. New York: Penguin, 1998.

Duffy, Eamon. *The Stripping of the Altars: Traditional Religion in England c. 1400–1580*. New Haven: Yale University Press, 1992.

Dunn, John. *Locke: A Very Short Introduction*. Oxford: Oxford University Press, 1984.

———. *The Political Thought of John Locke: A Historical Account of the Argument of the 'Two Treatises of Government.'* Cambridge, U.K.: Cambridge University Press, 1969.

Dworkin, Ronald. "The Model of Rules I" and "The Model of Rules II." In *Taking Rights Seriously*. Cambridge: Harvard University Press, 1977.

Eisenach, Eldon J. *Two Worlds of Liberalism: Religion and Politics in Hobbes, Locke, and Mill.* Chicago: University of Chicago Press, 1981.

Feldman, Karen S. *Binding Words: Conscience and Rhetoric in Hobbes, Hegel, and Heidegger.* Evanston, Ill.: Northwestern University Press, 2006.

Ferguson, Kennan. "Liberalism's Threat: Review of *Reflections of a Would-Be Anarchist.*" *Theory and Event* 2, no. 3 (1998).

Flathman, Richard. *Reflections of a Would-Be Anarchist: Ideals and Institutions of Liberalism,* Minneapolis: University of Minnesota Press, 1998.

——. *Thomas Hobbes: Skepticism, Individuality, and Chastened Politics.* Newbury Park, Calif.: Sage, 1993.

——. *Willful Liberalism: Voluntarism and Individuality in Political Theory and Practice.* Ithaca: Cornell University Press, 1992.

Foucault, Michel. *"Society Must Be Defended."* New York: Picador, 2003.

——. "Truth and Power." In *Power/Knowledge: Selected Interviews and Other Writings, 1972–1977.* New York: Pantheon, 1980.

Frost, Samantha. "Faking It: Hobbes's Thinking-Bodies and the Ethics of Dissimulation." *Political Theory* 29, no. 1 (February 2001): 30–57.

——. *Lessons from a Materialist Thinker: Hobbesian Reflections on Ethics and Politics.* Stanford: Stanford University Press, forthcoming.

Gauthier, David P. *The Logic of Leviathan.* Oxford: Oxford University Press, 1969.

Gitlin, Todd. "Blips, Bites, and Savvy Talk: Television's Impact on American Politics." *Dissent* (Winter 1990): 18–26.

Goodrich, Peter. "The Iconography of Nothing: Blank Spaces and the Representation of Law in Edward VI and the Pope." In Costas Douzinas and Lynda Nead, eds., *Law and the Image: The Authority of Art and the Aesthetics of Law,* pp. 89–114. Chicago: University of Chicago Press, 1999.

Habermas, Jürgen. *Theory and Practice.* Boston: Beacon, 1973.

Haller, William. *Liberty and Reformation in the Puritan Revolution.* New York: Columbia University Press, 1955.

——. *The Rise of Puritanism: Or: The way to the new Jerusalem as set forth in pulpit and press from Thomas Cartwright to John Lilburne and John Milton, 1570–1643.* Philadelphia: University of Pennsylvania Press, 1938.

Hampton, Jean. *Hobbes and the Social Contract Tradition.* Cambridge, U.K.: Cambridge University Press, 1986.

Hardt, Michael, and Antonio Negri. *Empire.* Cambridge: Harvard University Press, 2000.

Hart, H. L. A. *The Concept of Law.* London: Oxford University Press, 1961.

Heidegger, Martin. *The Basic Problems of Phenomenology.* Bloomington: Indiana University Press, 1988.

Hill, Christopher. *The Century of Revolution: 1603–1714.* Edinburgh: Thomas Nelson and Sons, 1961.

———. *Puritanism and Revolution: Studies in Interpretation of the English Revolution of the 17th Century.* London: Secker and Warburg, 1965.

Hinsley, F. H. *Sovereignty.* New York: Basic Books, 1966.

Hobbes, Thomas. *Behemoth: The History of the causes of the civil wars of England, and of the counsels and artifices by which they were carried on from the year 1640 to the year 1660.* New York: Burt Franklin, 1963.

———. *The Elements of Law: Natural and Politic.* Edited by Ferdinand Tönnies with New Introduction by M. M. Goldsmith. London: Frank Cass and Co., 1969.

———. *Hobbes's Thucydides.* Edited by Richard Schlatter. New Brunswick: Rutgers University Press, 1975.

———. *Leviathan.* Edited by Richard Tuck. New York: Cambridge University Press, 1996.

———. *Man and Citizen (De Homine and De Cive).* Edited by Bernard Gert. Indianapolis, Ind.: Hackett, 1991.

Honig, Bonnie. "Declarations of Independence: Arendt and Derrida on the Problem of Founding a Republic." *American Political Science Review* 85, no. 1 (March 1991): 97–113.

———. *Political Theory and the Displacement of Politics.* Ithaca: Cornell University Press, 1993.

Hood, F. C. *The Divine Politics of Thomas Hobbes: An Interpretation of Leviathan.* Oxford: Clarendon, 1964.

Johnson, Paul J. "Hobbes's Anglican Doctrine of Salvation." In Ralph Ross, Herbert W. Scheider, and Theodore Waldman, eds., *Thomas Hobbes in His Time,* pp. 102–25. Minneapolis: University of Minnesota Press, 1974.

Johnston, David. *The Rhetoric of Leviathan: Thomas Hobbes and the Politics of Cultural Transformation.* Princeton: Princeton University Press, 1986.

Kahn, Victoria. *Machiavellian Rhetoric: From the Counter-Reformation to Milton.* Princeton: Princeton University Press, 1994.

———. *Rhetoric, Prudence, and Skepticism in the Renaissance.* Ithaca, N.Y.: Cornell University Press, 1985.

Kavka, Gregory S. *Hobbesian Moral and Political Theory.* Princeton: Princeton University Press, 1986.

Kramer, Matthew H. *Hobbes and the Paradoxes of Political Origins.* New York: St. Martin's, 1997.

Krook, Dorothea. "Thomas Hobbes's Doctrine of Meaning and Truth." *Philosophy* 31 (1956): 3–22.

Ladenson, Robert. "In Defense of a Hobbesian Conception of Law." In Joseph Raz, ed., *Authority*, pp. 32–55. New York: New York University Press, 1990.

Levinas, Emmanuel. *Difficult Freedom: Essays on Judaism*. Baltimore: Johns Hopkins, 1990.

——. *Totality and Infinity: An Essay on Exteriority*. Pittsburgh: Duquesne University Press, 1961.

Machiavelli, Niccolò. *The Prince and The Discourses*. New York: Modern Library, 1950.

Martel, James. *Love Is a Sweet Chain: Desire, Autonomy, and Friendship in Liberal Political Theory*. New York: Routledge, 2001.

Martinich, A. P. *Hobbes: A Biography*. New York: Cambridge University Press, 1999.

——. *The Two Gods of Leviathan: Thomas Hobbes on Religion and Politics*. New York: Cambridge University Press, 1992.

Mathie, William. "Reason and Rhetoric in Hobbes's *Leviathan*." *Interpretation* 14 (May–September 1986): 281–98.

Mill, John Stuart. *On Liberty and Utilitarianism*. New York: Bantam, 1993.

Mintz, Samuel I. *The Hunting of Leviathan: Seventeenth-Century Reactions to the Materialism and Moral Philosophy of Thomas Hobbes*. Cambridge, U.K.: Cambridge University Press, 1962.

——. "Leviathan as Metaphor." *Hobbes Studies* 1 (1988): 3–9.

Missac, Pierre. *Walter Benjamin's Passages*. Translated by Shierry Weber Nicholsen. Cambridge: MIT Press, 1996.

New, John F. H. *Anglican and Puritan: The Basis of Their Opposition, 1558–1640*. Stanford, Calif.: Stanford University Press, 1964.

Nuttall, Geoffrey F. *The Holy Spirit in Puritan Faith and Experience*. Oxford: Basil Blackwell, 1947.

Oakeshott, Michael. *Hobbes on Civil Association*. Berkeley: University of California Press, 1975.

Parry, Geraint. "Performative Utterances and Obligation in Hobbes." *Philosophical Quarterly* 17 (1969): 246–52.

Phillips, John. *The Reformation of Images: Destruction of Art in England, 1535–1660*. Berkeley: University of California Press, 1973.

Pitkin, Hanna Fenichel. *The Attack of the Blob: Hannah Arendt's Concept of the Social*. Chicago: University of Chicago Press, 1998.

———. *The Concept of Representation.* Berkeley: University of California Press, 1967.

———. *Fortune Is a Woman: Gender and Politics in the Thought of Niccolò Machiavelli.* Berkeley: University of California Press, 1984.

Plamenatz, John. "Mr. Warrender's Hobbes." In K. C. Brown, ed., *Hobbes Studies,* pp. 73–87. Oxford: Basil Blackwell, 1965.

Pocock, J. G.. A. *Politics, Language and Time: Essays on Political Thought in History.* New York: Atheneum, 1973.

Polin, Raymond. *Hobbes, Dieu et les hommes.* Paris: Presses Universitaires de France, 1981.

Prokhovnik, Raia. *Rhetoric and Philosophy in Hobbes' Leviathan.* New York: Garland, 1991.

Pye, Christopher. "The Sovereign, the Theater, and the Kingdome of Darknesse: Hobbes and the Spectacle of Power." *Representations* 8 (Fall 1984): 85–106.

Rawls, John. *The Law of Peoples.* Cambridge: Harvard University Press, 1999.

Rayner, .Jeremy. "Hobbes and the Rhetoricians." *Hobbes Studies* 4 (1991): 76–95.

Raz, Joseph. "Authority and Justification." In Joseph Raz, ed., *Authority,* pp. 115–41. New York: New York University Press, 1990.

Reik, Miriam. *The Golden Lands of Thomas Hobbes.* Detroit: Wayne State University Press, 1977.

Ryan, Alan. "Hobbes, Toleration, and the Inner Life." In David Miller and Larry Siedentop, eds., *The Nature of Political Theory,* pp. 197–218. Oxford: Clarendon, 1983.

Schmitt, Carl. *Political Theology: Four Chapters on the Concept of Sovereignty.* Cambridge: MIT Press, 1985.

Schochet, Gordon J. "Intending (Political) Obligation: Hobbes and the Voluntary Basis of Society." In Mary Dietz, ed., *Thomas Hobbes and Political Theory,* pp. 55–73. Lawrence: University Press of Kansas, 1990.

Shulman, George. "Metaphor and Modernization in the Political Thought of Thomas Hobbes." *Political Theory* 17, no. 3 (August 1989): 392–416.

Sharpe, Kevin. "Archbishop Laud." In Margo Todd, ed., *Reformation to Revolution: Politics and Religion in Early Modern England,* pp. 71–77. New York: Routledge, 1995.

Sheehan, Thomas. *The First Coming: How the Kingdom of God Became Christianity.* New York: Random House, 1986.

Silver, Victoria. "Hobbes on Rhetoric." In Tom Sorell, ed., *The Cambridge Companion to Hobbes,* pp. 329–45. Cambridge, U.K.: Cambridge University Press, 1996.

——. "A Matter of Interpretation." *Critical Inquiry* 20 (Autumn 1993): 160–71.

Simpson, Alan. *Puritanism in Old and New England.* Chicago: University of Chicago Press, 1964.

Skinner, Quentin. *Reason and Rhetoric in the Philosophy of Hobbes.* New York: Cambridge University Press, 1996.

Slomp, Gabriella. *Thomas Hobbes and the Political Philosophy of Glory.* New York: St. Martin's, 2000.

Sorell, Tom. "Hobbes's Persuasive Civil Science." *Philosophical Quarterly* 40, no. 160 (1990): 342–51.

——. "Hobbes's UnAristotelian Political Rhetoric." *Philosophy and Rhetoric* 23 (1990): 96–109.

Spraggon, Julie. *Puritan Iconoclasm during the English Civil War.* London: Boydell, 2003.

Springborg, Patricia. "Hobbes on Religion." In Tom Sorell, ed., *The Cambridge Companion to Hobbes,* pp. 346–80. New York: Cambridge University Press, 1996.

——. "*Leviathan* and the Problem of Ecclesiastical Authority." *Political Theory* 3, no. 3 (1975): 289–303.

Stauffer, Jill. "This Weakness is Needed: An Intervention in Social Contract Theory." Ph.D. diss., University of California, Berkeley, 2003.

Steinberg, Michael P. "The Collector as Allegorist: Goods, Gods, and the Objects of History." In Michael P. Steinberg, ed., *Walter Benjamin and the Demands of History,* pp. 88–118. Ithaca: Cornell University Press, 1996.

Stevens, Jacqueline. "The Reasonableness of John Locke's Majority." *Political Theory* 24:3 (August 1996): 423–63.

Strauss, Leo. *The Political Philosophy of Hobbes: Its Basis and Its Genesis.* Translated by Elsa M. Sinclair. Chicago: University of Chicago Press, 1952.

Strong, Tracy. "How to Write Scripture: Words, Authority, and Politics in Thomas Hobbes." *Critical Inquiry* 20 (Autumn 1993): 128–59.

Taminiaux, Jacques. "Athens and Rome." In Dana Villa, ed., *The Cambridge Companion to Hannah Arendt,* pp. 165–77. New York: Cambridge University Press, 2000.

Tuck, Richard. *Hobbes,* Oxford: Oxford University Press, 1989.

——. "Hobbes and Descartes." In G.. A. J. Rogers and Alan Ryan, *Perspectives on Thomas Hobbes,* pp. 11-41. Oxford: Clarendon, 1988.

——. "Hobbes and Locke on Toleration." In Mary Dietz, ed., *Thomas Hobbes and Political Theory,* pp. 153–171. Lawrence: University Press of Kansas, 1990.

Tyacke, Nicholas. "Puritanism, Arminianism and Counter-Revolution." In Margo Todd, ed., *Reformation to Revolution: Politics and Religion in Early Modern England*, pp. 53–70. New York: Routledge, 1995.

Walzer, Michael. *The Revolution of the Saints: A Study in the Origins of Radical Politics.* Cambridge: Harvard University Press, 1965.

Warrender, Howard. *The Political Theory of Thomas Hobbes: His Theory of Obligation.* Oxford: Oxford University Press, 1957.

——. "A Reply to Mr. Plamenatz." In K. C. Brown, ed., *Hobbes Studies*, pp. 89–100. Oxford: Basil Blackwell, 1965.

Weber, Max. *The Protestant Ethic and the Spirit of Capitalism.* New York: Charles Scribner's Sons, 1958.

Wolin, Sheldon. *Hobbes and the Epic Tradition of Political Theory*, Los Angeles: William Andrews Clark Memorial Library, 1970.

——. *Politics and Vision: Continuity and Innovation in Western Political Thought.* Expanded edition. Princeton: Princeton University Press, 2004.

Woodhouse, A. S. P., ed. *Puritanism and Liberty: Being the Army Debates (1647–9) from the CLARKE MANUSCRIPTS with Supplementary Documents.* London: J. M. Dent & Sons, 1974.

Zarka, Yves-Charles. "First Philosophy and the Foundations of Knowledge." In Tom Sorell, ed., *The Cambridge Companion to Hobbes*, pp. 62–85. Cambridge, U.K.: Cambridge University Press, 1996.

Zizek, Slavoj. *The Ticklish Subject: The Absent Centre of Political Ontology.* New York: Verso, 1999.

Index